ONE
NEW
MAN

RECONCILING JEW AND GENTILE
IN ONE BODY OF CHRIST

By

ARIEL LAURENCE BLUMENTHAL

ONE NEW MAN

RECONCILING JEW AND GENTILE IN ONE BODY OF CHRIST

by

ARIEL LAWRENCE BLUMENTHAL

ENDORSEMENTS

Ariel Blumenthal is a dear friend and coworker who has an amazingly broad and deep understanding of God's purposes for Israel and the nations of the world. He is himself a Jewish believer in Yeshua, and serves in leadership with Ahavat Yeshua congregation in Jerusalem and the Revive Israel ministry team. Ariel combines a love of the works of the Spirit of God with an academic analysis of the texts of Scripture. Ariel is also a unique bridge between Israel and the Far East, having lived and served many years in Japan, Korea, and China. Ariel's views of Israel, the church, and the kingdom of God are profound and provocative.

—Asher Intrater
Founder, Revive Israel Ministries,
Ahavat Yeshua Congregation Jerusalem

On a regular basis, our ministry is flooded with questions about Sabbath observance, dietary laws, the role of Torah in the life of Christians, and the meaning of "one new man" according to Paul. These are hot-button issues that intersect with many other critical questions, including God's plan for Israel and the nations, law vs. grace, and many more. Here, in one masterful book, Ariel Blumenthal addresses these questions in meticulous and logical order, but also in a way that is accessible to all. This is essential reading for everyone in the Messianic Jewish movement, and for all Christians who love the God of Israel.

—Michael L. Brown, PhD
President, FIRE School of Ministry;
author, *Answering Jewish Objections to Jesus,*
Our Hands Are Stained with Blood,* and *The Real Kosher Jesus

Ariel Blumenthal has written a very important book on the "one new man." It provides us with a well-argued perspective on how God has raised up Gentiles in Jesus to a priestly status that is no less than Messianic Jews—Jews who are disciples of Jesus. It argues for a true biblical multi-culturalism—not a relativistic one as in today's postmodern culture, but one which demonstrates God's desire to preserve distinct ethnicities. *One New Man* preserves a distinct ethnic and national Israel in God's unfolding plan, while at the same time establishing a true unity of Jew and Gentile in the Messiah. To accomplish this, Ariel presents a bold, creative, and persuasive interpretation of the key verses (Eph. 2:14–15), especially concerning the phrase at the heart of the "enmity" between Jew and Gentile which Yeshua so forcefully abolished on the cross—*the commandments contained in ordinances.* These are nothing less than the commandments of Torah at the heart of Jewish identity—sabbaths, dietary laws, etc. Ariel shows how these Jewish markers of identity still find a significant place, but one that no longer defines holiness or the boundaries of the people of God; and nor do these markers have a universal claim on believers, as some mistakenly teach today. They therefore lose their effect in creating hostility, pride, and jealousy among Jew and Gentile. Full fellowship in the commonwealth of Israel is now God's order for Jew and Gentile, with no possibility of superiority of one toward the other.

In addition, Ariel shows how the "one new man" of Ephesians (and Colossians) fits together in God's prophetic plan for Israel and the nations, as outlined in Romans 9–11. Together, they are part of God's plan to bring about the fullness of all things and the second coming of Yeshua. Also, while Ariel did not set out to do so, his presentation, in my mind, resolves the issues dividing those scholars who argue for either the new perspective on Paul (pro-Torah) and the old perspective (anti-Torah). Ariel shows where both understandings have validity, but for different texts and in different contexts.

—**Daniel Juster, ThD**
Restoration from Zion, Tikkun International;
past president, Union of Messianic Jewish Congregations

One New Man: God's Plan to Reconcile Jew and Gentile
© 2018 by Ariel Laurence Blumenthal

Published by Deep River Books
Sisters, Oregon
www.deepriverbooks.com

Printed in the United States of America

ISBN – 13: 9781632695116

LOC: 2019937885

Printed in the USA
2019—First Edition
27 26 25 24 23 22 21 20 19   10 9 8 7 6 5 4 3 2 1

TABLE OF CONTENTS

DEDICATION

I've probably read more than a thousand books in my life, and I read most of them while I was still single. In all honesty, I could never really understand all those touchy-feely dedications from the authors to their wives. "Sure, she was there supporting you and taking care of the kids and the house, but didn't you write the book yourself during work hours?" Or so I thought. . . .

But now, I've been married going on eight years; we have three small children; and I'm publishing my first book. And boy oh boy do I want to dedicate it to my beloved, Vered!

Writing a book may be as close as a man can come to the experience of giving birth. For more than a year, the research, teaching, and writing of this material was all-consuming, sort of like carrying a baby. Much of *One New Man* was written while we were on study and ministry assignment in China in 2015–16. Without Vered's patience, sacrifice, and input, it couldn't have happened. We Jewish men bless our wives on Shabbat eve with the words from Proverbs 31:10–31: "An excellent wife, who can find?" With God's help I found you, Vered!

אשת חיל מי ימצא? מצאתי אתך ורד ,הפנינה שלי!

FOREWORD

Questions, controversy, and divisions about Israel have persisted in the church ever since her beginning on the day of Pentecost nearly two thousand years ago. I grew up in a church where enthusiastic support for the state of Israel was an essential doctrine, and my early travels to Israel and other nations in the Middle East did not shake that belief.

Then, in the 1990s, I walked through much of Lebanon, Syria, Israel, and the Palestinian Territories. I was presenting a message of apology for the atrocities of the Crusades—wars which were initiated by the recognized church, committed in the name of Jesus. During those years I visited the Holocaust Museum several times, worshipped in Messianic churches—and I spent hours listening to the tragic stories of Arabs who lost homes and loved ones in recurring conflict with Jews. I met deeply gracious and forgiving Arab believers who were fighting in Israeli courts, to retain land that had been in their families for centuries but was now occupied by Orthodox Jewish settlers. I also met other Arab Christians who were angry at Jews and who deeply resented Christians like me who support Israel.

I grappled with the issues for years. I read and re-read the relevant biblical passages. I especially tried to understand what Paul wrote to the Romans and then tried to view the realities of the Middle East today through that lens.

If Ariel Blumenthal had written this book twenty-five years ago, and it had been put in my hands, it would have been a much less tortuous process! I value Ariel as a friend and, having seen his sacrificial obedience to the leading of the Holy Spirit (with his wife and family), his words are clearly more than academic theories and, therefore, carry more weight.

Ariel has put the biblical goal of "one new man" at the heart of this book and that provides a framework for navigating through the many, often conflicting views on the subject of Jews and Gentiles, Israel, and the church. I highly recommend it.

Lynn Green
Former chairman,
Youth with a Mission (YWAM);
former director, YWAM Europe

INTRODUCTION

"**D**o you keep the Torah?" "Do you Messianic Jews keep Shabbat?" "I am a Christian who loves Israel, the Jewish people, and God's Torah . . . should I be keeping the biblical feasts? Are we allowed to eat pork?" "How are we grafted into Israel?" "What is the role of our ethnic identities in God's plan?" "If God is still faithful to the Jewish people, what does it mean that there is neither Jew nor Gentile in Christ?"

Increasingly, these are the kinds of questions that all kinds of believers, both Jews and Gentiles, are asking. Whether it be at our home in Jerusalem or at Messianic congregations and Christian churches around the world, questions about the place of Israel, the relationship between Jew and Gentile, and the Torah of Moses are everywhere.

And what does all of this have to do with *One New Man*? With reconciliation and unity between Jew and Gentile, Israel and the nations in the end times? For many Christians and churches who subscribe to a replacement theology[1] position, these problems were taken care of a long time ago: In terms of covenants and salvation, God finished with Israel and the Jewish people—and thus, our laws and customs from the five books of Moses—two thousand years ago. We live in a new age, and it is the laws and customs of the church that are relevant for us. Behold, the "one new man" of Ephesians 2, where there is "neither Jew nor Gentile," but only the church of Jesus Christ!

But this theology has taken its hits over the last few hundred years, as we have witnessed a restoration of the historic, premillennial faith of

---

[1] Replacement theology teaches that the church has wholly replaced physical, literal Israel (the Jewish people and nation) as the focus of His covenant blessings and promises.

the earliest church. Today there are literally millions of Christians (and more and more churches and denominations) who believe in the covenantal validity of the restoration of Israel and the Jewish people—of God's continuing faithfulness to His promises to the physical, literal seed of Abraham, Isaac, and Jacob. This has taken place in parallel with the miraculous restoration of the Jewish nation of Israel in the biblical Promised Land. At the same time, we have witnessed the rebirth of Jewish faith in Jesus (Yeshua), including the establishing of so-called "Messianic Jewish" congregations—wherein the observance of Jewish culture based on Torah customs and practices has become the norm. But there's more: There are also myriads of Gentiles (non-Jews) who by reason of participation in a Messianic congregation, or by reason of "Hebrew Roots" teaching, have also come to observe Old Testament customs such as the seventh-day Sabbath and other biblical feasts, as well as biblical dietary laws. Yet to some, all of this seems to be nothing more than a restoration of the "Judaizing" tendency that the apostle Paul dealt so forcefully with in the New Testament (NT), especially in the book of Galatians.

So here we are, as if back in the first century, dealing with some of the most vexing issues that occasioned much of the NT writings: What is the relationship between the Old and New Covenants? What is unity in the church—particularly between Jew and Gentile—supposed to look like? If God's covenants with Israel are still valid, what does this mean for the Christian church? What does it say about its identity? If God is still faithful to Israel, then mustn't this mean that Israel's Torah—the very heart and "constitution" of her relationship with God, is still valid? And is it valid only for Jews? What about Gentiles?

And at the center of all this controversy is still a man, a self-declared "bond-servant" of the Lord, whose life seemed like one great paradox: the most "orthodox," Pharisaically trained of all the apostolic NT writers, and at the same time the great pioneer of the "Torah-free" gospel to the Gentiles (nations).

What Paul had to say on these complex issues, even then, didn't lend itself to simple, black-and-white formulations (see 2 Pet. 3:16). Despite this, for centuries the church highlighted only one side of Paul's life and teaching: his mission to the Gentiles and his often sharp and critical commentary of Torah (and Judaism) under the new covenant. But over the last 150 years, a gradual reclamation of a less "antinomian" Paul has occurred—highlighting his positive statements about the Torah of Moses, his devotion to Israel, and his ongoing Jewish identity. As such, many efforts have been made to nuance Paul's seemingly negative critique of Torah under the new covenant.

The result? Today there are well-meaning, Jesus-loving, Bible-loving teachers—both those with a strong replacement position and those with a Torah-positive, Israel-centered view of the kingdom—who all claim Paul as their "patron saint." How can this be? Was the man schizophrenic? Perhaps there were two men: Saul of Tarsus, the great student of Gamaliel, the Torah-observant, Messianic Jewish apostle; and St. Paul, the anti-Torah founder of Gentile Christianity? Of course not.

But wait a minute, isn't this supposed to be a book about the one new man—the mystery of reconciliation between Jew and Gentile in the Messiah, according to Ephesians 2–3? Why so much talk about Paul and the Law?

Indeed, the first half of this book is dedicated to understanding Paul's view of Torah, and its place under the new covenant for both Jew and Gentile. Why? Because, when we approach the subject of the one new man, and the very verses in Ephesians 2 where the apostle Paul writes about it, we are immediately confronted with this thorny issue that dogged the apostle throughout his ministry. He writes that the new-covenant dynamic of Jew/Gentile unity is based on Yeshua having "broke down the barrier of the dividing wall, by abolishing in His flesh, the enmity, *which is the Law of commandments contained in ordinances*, that in Himself He might make the two into *one new man*, thus establishing peace" (Eph. 2:14–15, emphasis added).

The purpose of this book is to establish, as clearly as possible, the answers to the following questions which emerge from these verses in Ephesians (and parallel ones in Colossians):

- Why and how is this dividing wall described as "enmity" between Jew and Gentile?
- How did Yeshua "abolish in his flesh," on the cross, this enmity?
- What is the identity and content of that enmity that is here described as "the law of Commandments contained in *ordinances*"?
- If this enmity is, in some way, talking about the Torah of Moses, what does this mean for: a) Messianic Jewish identity—both in Israel and the Diaspora; b) Gentile identity in Christ, and c) our unity which Yeshua worked so hard to gain for us?
- How are we to understand spiritual warfare—the role of "principalities and powers" in resisting the one-new-man unity?
- How does all of this fit God's plan of salvation for us as Jew and Gentile—as peoples?
- How does the one new man function in the end times, in God's plan to bring "fullness" (Rom. 11), "the restoration of all things" (Acts 3:21), the second coming of Yeshua, and His millennial reign on Earth?

Finally, a word about the style, intended audience of this book, and its organization: It could be described as an academic book written in a popular style, or the opposite—a more popular book of general interest written with some academic elements. It is my conviction that all Christian believers will benefit from it, especially pastors and teachers in the body of Christ. I have an academic background (masters-level), and on some key issues of biblical interpretation I am aware of the scholarly dialogue. I try to include some references to this in my footnotes, and also in the appendices. Each chapter is not too long—usually about 2,500 words apiece. In the appendices, I deal with certain Scriptures and issues in much longer fashion, sometimes using more technical, theological terms.

It is my hope and prayer that *One New Man* will be a source of "wisdom and of revelation" to you, helping you to grow in the "hope of His calling," and to know more of "the riches of the glory of His inheritance in the saints" (Eph. 1:17–18). Enjoy!

1

BEFORE THE CROSS: THE STATE OF ENMITY BETWEEN JEW AND GENTILE

Therefore remember, that formerly you, the Gentiles in the flesh, who are called "Uncircumcision" by the so-called "Circumcision," which is performed in the flesh by human hands—remember that you were at that time separate from Christ, excluded from the commonwealth of Israel, and strangers to the covenants of promise, having no hope and without God in the world. (Eph. 2:11–12)

The one new man of Ephesians 2:15 builds on everything that Paul has written in the first chapter and a half of the book of Ephesians. Until chapter 2, verse 10, everything has been addressed to all believers in general, without making any distinctions between Jew and Gentile, male and female, etc.[2] But the key section of Scripture for the one-new-man teaching starts with verse 11, where the apostle makes it

---

[2] A few scholars would like to say that throughout, especially in his use of pronouns (we, you, etc.), the apostle distinguishes between Jew and Gentile, or Jerusalem church and Gentile church, throughout the epistle. I disagree.

clear that the Holy Spirit is now speaking to us not as individuals, but as peoples—as Jews and Gentiles. Right up through verse 22, the Greek verbs and pronouns are all in the plural: "we/us" and "you all."[3]

We must grasp this point well at the outset, or we will be in danger of totally misinterpreting the one-new-man Scriptures. As modern people, especially in the West, we are used to understanding human identity in primarily *individual* terms; indeed, most modern Christians are used to reading the Bible message as it speaks to them as individuals—discovering the universals in the Bible message that lead individual humans toward saving faith. Amen to that. But at this point in the book of Ephesians, the Scripture is speaking to us *not* at the level of our individual salvation and walk with God, but to the other side of our human identity—the "corporate" side. (For the English speaker/reader this can be easily missed, since our language does not distinguish between the second-person singular and plural pronouns—so our translations can only use the ambiguous "you.")

Let's do a short exercise to help get our minds in tune with the Scripture. If I ask you, "Who are you?" or, "Tell me about yourself," how would you answer? Maybe you'd respond something like this: "My name is John . . . I am an engineer, I am a Christian . . . I am British . . . I'm married and I have three children . . . I like to play tennis. . . ." Everyone answers this question in a way that reflects an important truth about human identity: Each of us is at the same time a unique individual (John, tennis), as well as a person who belongs to corporate, group realities that he shares in common with others (Christian, family, nationality). For me: "I am Jewish, I am American, I am Israeli; I am a Messianic Jew; I belong to congregation Ahavat Yeshua." All these things—and the accompanying culture that comes along with them—shape who I am over and against other people, and other peoples.

---

[3] Because of the lack of the second-person, plural pronoun in proper English, I will often use "you all" throughout this book.

Of course, how we answer this kind of question depends a lot on the context. Are you being interviewed for a job? Are you talking to a stranger whom you just met on the bus to work? Are you standing at Passport Control at an airport in a foreign country? Let's imagine this last scenario: You have just arrived at the airport after a long overseas flight, where the mass of people entering the country are split into different lines: nationals to one side, and all foreigners to another line. You are standing there, looking at the signs, and suddenly a uniformed officer approaches you and asks, "Who are you?" Most likely, the first thing you will think to say is not to give him your name, or tell him about your hobbies or educational background. No, you are far more likely to reach for your passport to show the officer who you are. In this case, he is not interested in you as an individual; he is interested in you as a citizen of some nation. If you are a local national, you get to go the "fast" lane, where there are usually shorter lines, more agents, and less waiting. Not so for the foreigners.

This can help us understand the picture that the apostle paints for us in verses 11–12: We Jews (the "Circumcision") are the "insiders"; we are the citizens of God's covenanted nation, Israel—possessing all the rights and privileges of citizenship, starting and finishing with a living faith and hope in the One True God of Abraham, Isaac, and Jacob. "You all" Gentiles have the wrong passport; you all are aliens (foreigners) from the commonwealth of Israel, strangers from the covenants of promise, without any clue concerning who or what the Messiah (Christ) is supposed to be; you have no hope, you're totally without God in the world. Sorry, you'd better get in the other line; you'd better go to the back of the bus; this is a Jewish story, about the Israeli nation—we are "in," and you are "out." We have God—and you don't!

If this declaration of the apostle Paul stood alone and was not simply an introduction to the good news of the one new man in the following verses, you can imagine how this might make Gentiles feel! Indeed, in this one verse the apostle summarizes the traditional "orthodox" Jewish attitude toward our own chosenness, and what this means for the nations. Like the psalmist's or Isaiah's commentary about Gentiles and their idols (Ps. 115; Isa. 40:18–26) it is, on the one hand, a bold statement of faith: Our God is the only true God, and thus our worship and religion are true, right, and pure. There is more than just a small "ring" of exclusivity and privilege in these statements! In many ways, this can be seen as a summary of the Old Testament (OT): the One True God, the Creator of heaven and Earth, uniquely chose the family of Abraham, Isaac, and Jacob; at Mt. Sinai He ratified and expanded this special covenant to include and form a new nation—the nation of the Hebrews, the nation of Israel (Jacob).

But of course, as we learn from the Torah itself, and especially from the Prophets who came later, this chosenness has implications for the other nations and peoples—especially those in the same Middle Eastern neighborhood. What kind of implications? This is where things begin to get messy. In a perfect, sinless world, the nations' attitude would be: "God chose one nation to reveal Himself and give His laws? Wonderful, let's go there and make friends and ask them to teach us!" But, because of human sin . . . pride, jealousy, resentment . . . this just isn't the case.

I am a student of East Asia (China, Japan, Korea)—its history, culture, and religions. What incredible history can be found there—the rise and fall of many great empires; amazing discoveries, cultures, religions, and philosophies can be found there! Zen Buddhism, Confucianism, Taoism, Shinto . . . a history of many amazing men and women, with amazing insights into life, death, and many other spiritual things. But along comes the Jew, announcing: "Ultimately, all of your spirituality is useless; you are pagans, you are idolaters, you worship what is not really God; you are far away from the true God and the true covenants, the true hope; all of your great ancestors, history, and empires cannot mediate the true God for you; only we, the people of Israel, are in the covenants; if you want to 'do business' with God, you have to come through us!"

"What?" replies the great Gentile nations. "You mean this tiny, otherwise insignificant nation, one which for most of its history has struggled to maintain a bare minimum of national sovereignty . . . the Jews? Until recently, we had never even heard of them! You mean to tell me that only their nation is truly chosen by God? Only their worship is the true worship of God?"

In Ephesians 2:14–15, the situation is described in more detail: It is not just that the Gentiles were "far off," as if it were only a matter of a great distance to be traversed by a diligent foreigner desiring to come near to Israel (like the three wise men in Yeshua's time); but as he nears his goal, he finds a "wall," a huge dividing structure, on which a sign hangs: "Israel, the Jewish nation—God's chosen . . . Gentiles not allowed."[4] Of course, Scripture is not talking about a physical wall made of brick and mortar; it is talking about something much deeper, and more difficult to grasp.[5] On the one hand, this wall of Israel's chosenness is of God Himself— He chose and sanctioned this exclusivity by divine covenant. On the other hand, because of human sin—Jewish selfishness and pride, and Gentile jealousy, resentment, and hatred—this wall is ultimately described as being the source of "enmity" between Jew and Gentile (v. 15).

The *Theological Dictionary of the New Testament* defines the Greek word *hexsthra* (enmity) as follows: "Hatred, hostility, as an inner disposition, as objective opposition and as actual conflict between nations, groups and individuals."[6] Hatred? Hostility? Conflict? What's the problem? One only has to study the Bible to discover that the world (Gentiles, which also means "nations") has never known quite how to relate to this chosen people; and this chosen people has had a similar

---

[4] Of course the OT has a few examples of lone Gentiles, like Ruth, who were able, by marriage, to enter the chosen people. But such were the exception, not the rule.

[5] There is much "temple language" in Ephesians 2 and 3 (especially 2:19–22); there really was an actual barrier in the temple, and Gentiles who went beyond it did so under threat of death. But 2:14–22 makes it clear that while a physical veil may have been rent at Yeshua's death (Matt. 27:51), it only symbolized a more abstract, spiritual separation between both God and man, and Jew and Gentile.

[6] G. Kittel, G. W. Bromiley and G. Friedrich, eds., *Vol. 2: Theological Dictionary of the New Testament* (Grand Rapids: Eerdmans, 1964), 815; electronic edition, Logos Bible Software.

problem in relating to the rest of the world—from our time in Egypt, where at first they loved and welcomed Joseph and his family but later turned to hatred, suspicion, and persecution; to the story of Balak and Balaam (should Israel be blessed or cursed?); to Haman and the book of Esther (why should we live with this people who have such different customs—kill them all!); to the NT problem of Judaizing (Acts 15; Galatians), this issue of Jewish-Gentile enmity has never been easy to resolve. Even today, one common thought to almost all Jews—be they Messianic, Orthodox, or secular—is, "Why does the world hate us so much? What did we do to deserve all this?"

This is the ultimate summary of the relationship between Jew and Gentile, Israel and the nations before the cross: Our chosenness was exclusive—that is the nature of chosenness. The moment one is chosen, this means that a multitude of others are not chosen. Because of human sin, this results in pride, a sense of privilege, even racism on the side of the chosen; and from the Gentiles a kind of admiration that can quickly morph into jealousy, rage, and genocidal hatred.

But there is hope! The one-new-man verses describe Yeshua as the one who breaks down this great wall of partition between Jew and Gentile, abolishing in his very flesh this "enmity," this opposition, even this hatred between Jew and Gentile. The one-new-man gospel is good news for Israel and good news for the nations—good news for us as peoples, as families. Thus, when the apostle prays at the close of this section of Scripture before moving on to his next subject, he begins with an address to Father God that is nowhere else used in the NT: "For this reason, I bow my knees before the Father, from whom *every family* in heaven and earth derives its name" (Eph. 3:14–15, emphasis added).

2

THE *DOGMA* BRICKS
OF THE WALL OF PARTITION

. . . by abolishing in His flesh the enmity, which is the Law
of commandments contained in **ordinances** *. . . (Eph. 2:15,*
emphasis added)

This brings us to the heart of the matter—and to what is the most difficult, and controversial aspect of the one-new-man teaching. I have heard teachings and read books ostensibly about the one new man which completely avoid this issue—even though it is central to the very verse of Scripture from which we get the term, Ephesians 2:15. It is a huge issue for us as believers, and one which stirs up some very strong passions and opinions, touching on vast issues of theology and history: What is the role of the Torah in the New Covenant? How much, or how little, continuity is there between Old and New Testaments? Is there a place for Jewish identity and/or practice in the new covenant? What about other religions and their practices? Other cultures? If so, on what basis? All of these issues are raised by this one verse (and several others from the pen of Paul).

As mentioned in the introduction, some may be surprised that a book on the one new man spends so much time on this question of Paul and the Law; but Ephesians 2:15 (and the parallel verse of Colossians 2:14) demand that we do so, because we find here some of the apostle's most extreme statements concerning the Torah. If we don't get this right at the foundation, we can miss the full blessing of the one new man, causing disunity and confusion in the body. So let's get to it!

We discovered in the first chapter of Ephesians that Paul characterizes the wall of partition between Jew and Gentile as representing (or causing) a relationship of enmity. We said that the sign on the inside of the wall essentially reads: "Jewish, Covenantal Chosen-ness," and on its outside, "No Gentiles Allowed."[7] In verse 15 he gives the key detail of what "bricks" make up this wall, the ones that Yeshua "abolished in His flesh" on the cross. He describes them as "the law of commandments in *ordinances.*" We might then expand this sign on the wall to read, "Jewish Chosenness, as expressed by the Law of Commandments in Ordinances—given only to Israel."

First, notice that he didn't just write "commandments" (*mitzvoth* in Hebrew)—if he had, Paul could be accused, as was often the case, of teaching a radical new "gospel of grace" which made all OT law obsolete and unnecessary. Instead, he seems to describe a subset of Torah commandments, those "contained in *ordinances*" (*dogma*, in Greek). Paul does not define these *dogma* commandments for us in Ephesians, but we don't have to look far to understand how he is using this word in context.[8] Colossians 2–3 are very much parallel to Ephesians 2–3: in both places Paul makes a specific address to Gentiles (the "uncircumcised" of Colossians 2:12–13). Ephesians focuses on reconciliation between Jew and Gentile, Colossians more on warnings of not returning to a kind of bondage that comes from the wrong kind of observance of

---

[7] Some kind of conversion or proselyte status was available at different times in history, but this was only for a few and meant a wholesale abandonment of the Gentile's native culture and lifestyle.

[8] This also suggests that his hearers/readers in Ephesians, having been previously taught by the apostle, would have some understanding of what Paul meant. This was therefore something he taught widely.

these *ordinances,* these *dogma* commandments. In Colossians 2, he uses the word *dogma* twice, translated in the NASB as "decrees" (emphases added): "having cancelled out the certificate of debt consisting of *decrees* which was hostile to us" (v. 14); and then "why, as if you were living in the world, do you submit yourself to *decrees,* such as, 'do not handle, do not taste, do not touch'" (v. 20–21).[9]

Verse 14 of Colossians 2 reads much like Ephesians 2:15: On the cross, Yeshua has *cancelled out the certificate of debt consisting of dogmas.* So which commandments is he referring to? Here, thankfully, the apostle immediately details the kind of commandments he is referring to, as he warns us of the danger of being judged and/or defrauded in regard to their observance—"food or drink . . . a festival or a new moon or a Sabbath day" (v. 16). In verses 20–21, he adds to this list those commandments which have to do with "taste" and/or "touch." He identifies all these *dogma*-decrees as dealing with "shadows" (not the true substance, source of light, who is Messiah-Christ), and as having something to do with the "elementary principles of the world" to which we have died in Christ (vv. 17, 20).

Now, we're getting closer to what the Lord is teaching us through the pen of Paul: There are a category of Torah commandments, called ordinances or decrees (*dogma* in Greek) that contain the following: food/dietary laws; Sabbaths, festivals, and new moons (all calendar-related); and "touch," i.e., other "priestly" laws of purity, uncleanness, etc. Not coincidentally, these are the very commands—along with circumcision—which have set us Jews apart from other peoples/nations for so many centuries. Some have even called them the "Jewish boundary marker" commands.[10] According to Ephesians, these Torah *dogma*

---

[9] Since the word is not used in the LXX, it is hard to fit *dogma* to one of the classic categories of חוקים, מצוות, משפתים laws, commands, judgments, etc. as in the Torah.

[10] In the rest of this book, I will continue to use the transliterated Greek word *dogma* rather than the clumsy "Jewish Boundary Marker Commands." Another reason is that from Colossians 2, we are not sure how exhaustive is the list of the Levitical, purity commands that the apostle has in mind.

commands somehow made up the very structure, like building blocks or bricks, of the dividing wall which caused enmity between Jew and Gentile. But now Yeshua has broken down this wall, abolishing these *dogmas* in his flesh on the cross, making peace between the two.

Pretty simple, yes? This more or less sounds like the traditional Christian understanding: Jesus came to die for our sins, cancel the Old Testament laws that made the Jewish people unique, and make one new man out of Jew and Gentile—a kind of new, Christian "third race" of humanity. We're not under law, but under grace; in Christ Jesus there is neither Jew nor Gentile, male nor female . . . Hallelujah! But wait a minute . . . is it really that simple?[11] Since about the third or fourth century, until fairly recently, the issue of the Torah in the new covenant was pretty well simplified: We got past the "Judaizing" problem of Paul's time, and developed our Christian doctrine on the premise of replacement theology—that God's abolishing of OT law was part of the dynamic by which the church replaced Israel as His new covenant people.[12] This seemed to make both theological and historical sense, in light of the destruction of the nation of Israel (Judea)—its temple, sacrifices, and priesthood; the scattering of the Jewish people, and the disappearance of any kind of Messianic Jewish remnant that was both "in Christ" and "Torah-observant."

---

[11] I am aware of the "new readings" of Paul which interpret the "commandments in ordinances" as Pharisaic, extrabiblical (oral law) additions to Torah, which made fellowship with pagans (Gentiles) even more unthinkable. I think this interpretation is impossible to support from the context of either Ephesians or Colossians, and is usually the eisogetical result of an imported agenda by those who are predisposed to believe that the apostle could never have actually meant to say anything negative about the Torah itself—only the addition to, or perversion thereof. I deal with this in depth in Appendix 3-1.

[12] Of course, there has also been a positive place for OT Law in some Christian theologies (see Calvin and Reformed theology especially); but such theologizing was almost always done in a context of a supercessionist assumption: God is finished with physical/literal Israel, and now this OT Law can be subsumed under the law of the church, or of Christendom. Such a reading causes one to entirely miss the cutting-edge message of Paul concerning the one new man and the mystery of God's ongoing election of Israel.

But now, over the last 150 years, we have witnessed the physical restoration of the nation of Israel to its biblical homeland—and, increasingly, the spiritual restoration of an Israel that believes in Yeshua. For we Messianic Jews, however, and those who sympathize with us, this teaching is one of the most difficult things for us to reconcile. Why? For most of my Gentile Christian readers, the message that Yeshua cancelled or abolished things like the Sabbath and the dietary laws (*kashrut*) is not particularly offensive or revolutionary: You didn't keep these things before, they were not part of your collective history or culture, and the idea that you don't have to be circumcised and keep the OT laws is mostly appealing. Plus, most of you have learned about this aspect of the Torah ("Law") and the new covenant in the context of Paul's discussion of works-righteousness versus grace as found in Galatians and Romans—all pertaining to the dynamics of your personal salvation and relationship with God. But what about for us Jews? Let me assure you— it is hard for you to hear, or to feel, the sharpness of Paul's teaching here—how radical and controversial it was in Paul's day, as in ours.

You see, for our people, these *dogma* commandments do not just represent some kind of internal, spiritual, works-based-salvation system; rather, *they define who we are* as the chosen people![13] The Torah is the Constitution, the Bill of Rights, the founding document of the Jewish nation. And it was given by God—the same God all Christians claim to believe in! How can the apostle so cavalierly speak of some of its commandments as "abolished"? "Cancelled"? He might as well have preached that Jesus came to do away with Jewish, covenantal identity itself! In fact, this is exactly what our people heard in his message two thousand years ago, and why Paul became "public enemy #1" in Israel (see Acts 21–22). Along with Stephen, the first believing martyr, Paul was accused of "speaking blasphemous words against Moses and against

---

[13] This is the problem of reading these passages only from the perspective of individual salvation, whereby observance of these Torah commandments only serves as a counterpoint to grace, in a grace vs. works/righteousness dichotomy.

God" (Acts 6:11; cf. Acts 21:21, 28), even though Paul professed and still maintained a Jewish pattern of life in Acts 21 and through the rest of Acts. What's more, in church history, this understanding of Paul's writings became a cornerstone of the uniquely Christian form of anti-Semitism: "The church has replaced Israel; God did away with Jewish, covenantal identity—so let's help Him finish the job!" We will see in a later chapter that, in fact, the same apostle has a clear place in his teaching and personal practice for continuing Jewish identity under the New Covenant—but according to a radically reworked definition of the Torah-*dogma* commandments under the one-new-man unity of Jew and Gentile in one body of Christ.

3

THE *STOICHEA* ELEMENTS—THE SAND AND MORTAR OF THE *DOGMA* BRICKS, PART 1—THE GENTILE SIDE OF THE WALL OF PARTITION

However at that time, when you did not know God, you were slaves to those which by nature are no gods. But now that you have come to know God, or rather to be known by God, how is it that you turn back again to the weak and worthless **elemental things***, to which you desire to be enslaved all over again? You observe days and months and seasons and years. (Galatians 4:8–10, emphasis added)*

In Chapter 2, we saw that the bricks which made up the wall of Jewish chosenness/exclusivity before Christ were the *dogma* commandments of Torah decreed by God through Moses—which, as observed by our people, became the very expression of our distinctiveness. (It is often said that it's not that the Jewish people have kept kosher, Sabbath, and circumcision—but that the dietary laws and the Sabbath have *kept* the Jewish people!) It is these same *dogma*-bricks which are declared to be have been violently dismantled on the cross. But this doctrine of the destruction of the dividing wall goes even deeper, and we will find that the Word of God, as a two-edged sword (Heb. 4:12), cuts both ways—demolishing the bricks *from both sides of the wall,* undercutting the potential of a sinful, ethnic, and/or national pride for *both* Jew and Gentile alike.

Expanding our view to some of Paul's other letters—especially Galatians—we come to the very substance, or material, of which the *dogma* bricks/commandments are comprised. This will first afford us a look at the *dogma* bricks from the outside of the wall: the Gentile side. Galatia appears to be Paul's most "Gentile" church; in his other congregations it is clear that there was a mixture of Jew and Gentile (1 Cor. 7:17–22), with many having some background in Judaism, the synagogue, biblical morality, the Messianic hope, etc. But in Galatia the congregation seems to be made up of Gentiles exclusively—in other words men and women who, before they came to Christ, were total pagans, idol worshippers, and the like. Paul describes their pre-Christian state: "However at that time, when you did not know God, you were slaves to those which by nature are no gods" (Gal. 4:8).

This sounds similar to his description of the pre-Christian, Gentile status that we studied in Ephesians 2:11–12; and here in Galatians a new dimension to this status is described: "slavery" or "bondage" to that "which by nature are not gods." Up to this point, most Jews throughout history would agree with the apostle: Gentiles are slaves to all kinds of polytheism, idols, superstitions, sorcery, divination, astrology, worship of ancestors, immorality, etc. (the list could go on forever!). But we Jews have "come out of Egypt," out of all this slavery and paganism, as we celebrate during Passover every year;[14] and we are free children of Abraham, as the Pharisees declared in their challenge to Yeshua in John 8:33.

---

[14] When drinking the four cups and eating the matzah, we lean on our left side to accentuate the fact that we are free people. In ancient times, only free people had the luxury of reclining while eating.

In Galatians, Paul is reminding the believers of another kind of deliverance and freedom: from sin, sickness, Satanic oppression, and even death—that is the believer's inheritance in Christ, giving birth to faith, hope, and love leading to eternal life. But now, something tragic has happened in Galatia in the apostle's absence: gifted, Messianic teachers[15] came to Galatia with a very subtle and powerful message, one which essentially says that the gospel of repentance, grace, and faith focused on the crucified and resurrected Son of God, and the life in the Holy Spirit—the gospel which they received and experienced through Paul—is not enough to maintain a position of righteousness before God (justification). Now, in order to be complete in their faith and practice, they need to observe Torah as the Jews do—its wisdom, its customs (dietary, circumcision), and especially, its calendar. In other words, they must observe the very *dogma* commandments—which Paul is teaching as having been somehow abolished—in order to be fully accepted members of the people of God. This has often been called the "Judaizing" tendency, or teaching.[16]

Next, Paul introduces a new concept, a deeper description of the nature of this Gentile bondage before Christ: "So also we, while we were children, were held in bondage under the *elemental things of the world*" (Gal. 4:3, emphasis added). What exactly are these "elemental things" (or "principles," "elements," or "spirits," depending on which English translation one uses), for the Greek *stoichea?*

---

[15] The assumption is always that they were Jewish teachers sent from Jacob-James in Jerusalem, based on Galatians 2:12.

[16] They did *not* come teaching, as some would oversimplify: "if you do these things you will not be *saved.*" Today, many evangelical and Messianic Torah teachers tend to take this approach: The Galatian, Judaizing error was preaching Torah observance and circumcision *for salvation*—not for *sanctification.* Therefore, many teach, there remains the possibility of a role for *dogma*-Torah observance in walking out/growing in our faith—as long as it is not confused with the preaching and doctrine of salvation. Ironically, the word or theme "salvation" never appears in Galatians. The main theme of the epistle is rather "justification," the maintaining of a standard of righteousness before God and in God's "house," that is, among His people, that is from the first to the last *by faith* in the Messiah, and *not* by Torah observance (Gal. 2:21–3:5).

There has been much scholarly debate about how exactly the believers in Galatia or Colossae would have understood Paul's use of this Greek term. The three main possibilities, in order of philological probability are: a) According to contemporary Greco-Roman philosophy and "science," the basic elements of the material universe/natural world from which everything is composed—earth, air, fire, and water. b) Rudimentary principles, the "abc's" of religious life by which means both Jew and Gentile, each in their own way, maintained their connection with the divine and with their ancestral past—and thus their unique identity as a people. This especially refers to calendrical observances—feasts, festivals, and sacrifices related to the movements of the sun, moon, planets, and stars. c) It refers to the spirits and gods which animate, or lie behind these elements and principles.

There is good reason why Greek NT scholars have found cause for all three understandings, and thus three different translations among major English Bibles: "elements," "principles," and/or "spirits."[17] For our purposes, we can understand the connection between all three definitions as being part of how the early Christians would have understood Paul, since in the ancient world, there was little separation between what we would today call "science" and "religion." In other words, the ancients—be it in Greece, Mesopotamia, or China—understood the elements of the material world as having spiritual sources, and thus the study of their relationship and movements was also a "religious" exercise performed by a cultural, literate elite—usually some kind of priesthood. Until modern times, almost all peoples understood the universe as being highly "animated" by spiritual forces. Further, this understanding was often founded on ancient wisdom or revelation from great, founding ancestors—usually kings, chiefs, or priests of the people group; and so the proper maintenance of ritual associated with this tradition comprised not just what we would call the "religion" of the people, but the

---

[17] Actually, the last one, "spirits/gods" is the most recent, based on the modern discovery of contemporary and later Greek texts.

foundations of their entire culture—as found in calendar, agriculture, language, music, literature, astronomy, medicine, etc. All of this made up their sense of identity and cohesion as a people or nation, as distinct from other peoples.[18]

Returning to the Ephesians "wall of partition," what Paul is teaching here can be summarized as follows: From the Jewish/Israel insider view, the bricks in the wall are the *dogma* commandments of Torah—especially those related to calendar, foods, and purity (clean/unclean); but looking from the outsider, Gentile side of the wall, we discover similar practices that were common to all ancient peoples—also connected to calendar, sacrifices, foods, and the like. Furthermore, the substantial elements (*stoichea*) of these bricks—the sand and mortar, if you will—has three aspects to it: the elements of the natural world from which all these things are formed; the basic principles of life and religion associated with these elements; and the service, worship, and propitiation of the gods/spirits believed to be associated with these elements.

In Galatians, Paul reminds the believers that they were once in bondage to this elemental, *stoichea* triad. Of course, they had been without the Jewish, biblical view of God and the universe as found in the first three chapters of Genesis: a) There is only one God who created everything; b) He is the source of anything truly holy and spiritual; and c) thus, there is a clear separation between nature and the Creator, and no need to look for "gods" or "spirits" behind everything in the material world. Therefore, what they once worshiped as "gods" of the natural world of elements are by nature not really "gods," and such worship was simply servitude and bondage. Now, in Christ, they have been "seated in heavenly places" far above all such principalities and powers (I realize this is a jump, but I will develop this in a later chapter); they are no longer "under" any such system, as they have direct access to the

---

[18] I write this from my desk in Xi'an, China where, even after several generations of Marxist, materialist, atheistic philosophy, the totems, quasi-animal demon-scaring statues, and dragons have everywhere reemerged as symbols of the Chinese civilization, identity, and culture—all dating from the ancient past.

Creator Himself through the cross of Yeshua, who took this wall—its bricks, sand, and mortar in their entirety—and nailed it to the cross, in his own flesh. Therefore, continues Paul, you Galatian Gentiles must now see yourself and your former identity as having been crucified with Christ (Gal. 2:20–21), so that you might know Him in the power of his resurrection, and live out a whole new identity in Christ—both as an individual, and as a culture-bearing member of a people group. This is the good news!

But what about the Jewish side of the wall and this teaching of the *stoichea*? What about the Torah? Shouldn't the culture of Torah—based on the commandments of God Himself, given to Moses—be in a totally different category than that of the pagans? Shouldn't it be *the* standard for true, correct practice of things like calendar, foods, sacrifices, etc.? How could it be said that these biblical, *dogma* commandment bricks in the wall are also made of the same substance as the pagan ones? The same *stoichea* elements? Before we probe the depths of this double-edged teaching on the *stoichea*, we need to understand a little bit more about Judaism—its self-understanding and how it views these *dogma* commandments.

THE *STOICHEA* ELEMENTS—THE SAND AND MORTAR OF THE *DOGMA* BRICKS, PART 2: THE JEWISH SIDE OF THE WALL OF PARTITION

However at that time, when you did not know God, you were slaves to those which by nature are no gods. But now that you have come to know God, or rather to be known by God, ***how is it that you turn back again to the weak and worthless elemental things, to which you desire to be enslaved all over again?*** *You observe days and months and seasons and years.* (Galatians 4:8–10, emphasis added)

This chapter begins with the same Scripture quote as the last chapter, from Galatians 4, because in just a few sentences we can see the two-edged sword of Scripture cutting in both directions. The equation is clear: You Gentiles were once in bondage to the gods and elements of pagan religion; you all have come to know the true God through Christ; and now, by submitting to the doctrine of the Torah teachers of circumcision, the biblical calendar, etc., you are essentially turning back to the same elements and their bondage all over again. Bondage under the *stoichea* of paganism equals bondage under the *stoichea* of Torah![19]

In this chapter, we are going to look at the *stoichea* teaching from the insider view of the wall—the Jewish/Israel/Torah side. It has often been said of our people: "It's not that the Jews have kept the Sabbath, but the Sabbath has kept the Jews." This saying sums up an important principle: Jewish identity has been inseparable from the observance of Torah, especially the kind of *dogma* commandments that we have been learning about: circumcision, dietary laws, and calendrical laws (Sabbaths, new moons, feasts). In "secular" terms, we could say that these practices have been the foundation of our particular *culture*—what makes us unique and different from other peoples of the world—since the time of Moses. But this is no ordinary culture! If we believe in the Bible, then we believe that these practices are nothing less than commandments from the Holy God of the universe to His unique, covenanted people. God chose us, and set us apart—not just in theory or in "spirit"—but in very real, down-to-earth customs and practices which guarantee that we remain a holy and unique people (e.g., Lev. 11:1–46).

Here are a few examples of traditional prayers from the Jewish prayer book, which illustrate this fact of our attitude toward the commandments, and their role in defining and keeping us as a chosen people.

> Blessed art thou, O Lord our God, King of the universe, *who hast sanctified us by thy commandments* and hast taken pleasure in us, and in love and favor hast given us thy holy Sabbath as an inheritance. . . . because you have chosen us and sanctified us from all the peoples, and have given us your holy sabbath in love. (Jewish Prayer Book, *Kiddush* for Sabbath, emphasis added)

---

[19] I'm aware of some recent efforts by today's Torah teachers to get around this by positing the existence of some kind of mixed, Torah astrology that was being practiced by the Galatians. For me, the evidence is totally unconvincing.

This well-known *kiddush* (sanctification) blessing/prayer is representative of many in Judaism that are prayed before the performance of Torah commandments from the five books of Moses—or even extrabiblical, rabbinic traditions like the lighting of Sabbath or Hanukah candles. It begins by blessing God who has "sanctified us by thy commandments." There are three key points to note here:

1. This is a blessing formula for the whole corpus of rabbinic "commands," which is viewed as a monolith. While some commandments are understood as "weightier" than others, even "lighter" ones are just as much "commands" as others. A faithful Jew, then and now, cannot pick and choose among the various commands which all carry divine imprimatur.[20]

2. It is these commandments (Sabbath, holidays, etc.) *and our observance of them* which *sanctify* us as a people (the word sanctify in Hebrew is based on the same root as "holy" and "holiness"). In other words, God gave us these commandments in order to make us a separate, unique, and "holy" people. It became a hallmark of Jewish self-understanding that such separation has moral implications—that what we eat or don't eat is more than just about defining the boundaries of Jewish culture; it is part of defining us as morally superior to "Gentile sinners" for whom idolatry and sexual immorality is tied up with the eating of blood, and the like (Acts 15; Rom. 2; Gal. 2:15).

3. Notice how many times the word "us" appears in this short prayer. In Hebrew, the emphasis is very strong: God sanctified *us;* God takes pleasure in *us;* God gave (literally, "caused us to inherit") *us* the Sabbath; God chose *us.* . . . What's the problem? Well, what about the rest of humanity? Why did God choose the

---

[20] This is why the apostle writes in Galatians 5:3 that anyone who comes under the sphere of rabbinic (Pharisaic) authority by submitting to the Judaizing teachers and being circumcised, is "indebted" to keep the whole of Torah.

Jewish people (or Abraham) in the first place? To make us a holy, separate people who keep Torah? Okay, but then what? What about being "a blessing to the whole earth"? What about, in this case, the Sabbath for the rest of the world? Inherent in almost all Jewish prayer and liturgy is this "spirit" of uniqueness for uniqueness' sake, if you will; that God chose *us* . . . which means he didn't choose *you*.

Let's take a look at a few other common prayers where this spirit is even more explicit.

Blessed are you Lord our God, King of the Universe—who has given my heart understanding to discern between day and night; and for not making me a Gentile . . . for not making me a slave; for not making me woman. (*Siddur*, Morning Blessings)

This list of "blessings" (really "thanksgivings") is one of the prayers with which an orthodox Jewish man starts his day each morning. I have only quoted four of the many blessings. Obviously, there is a big difference between praying on the one hand: "thank you God for making me a Jew, for making me a free person, a man or woman . . . for making me who I am" versus praying, "thank you God for *not making* me a Gentile or a woman." In the latter, there is an inherent comparison that takes place: As a Jew, I look at the pagan Gentiles, and I look at my own God-given, Torah-rooted identity, and I pray, "thank God that you didn't make me like them." This is reminiscent of Yeshua's parable of the prayers of the Pharisee and the tax collector from Luke 18:9–14: "The Pharisee stood and was praying this to himself, 'God, I thank Thee that I am not like other people: swindlers, unjust, adulterers, or even like this tax-gatherer'" (v. 11).

Perhaps you think I'm exaggerating, or nitpicking? Let's look at another of the most beautiful and common prayers, one of my personal favorites, the *Alenu,* which closes many a synagogue worship service:

> It is our duty to praise the Lord of all things, to ascribe greatness to him who formed the world in the beginning, since he has not made us like the nations of other lands, and has not placed us like other families of the earth, since he has not assigned unto us a portion as unto them, nor a lot as unto all their multitude.

Here, we see a declaration of something that is true and good—the unique chosenness of Israel. But, it comes with a sharp, "dividing knife" kind of comparison: We, as the chosen people, are uniquely called to praise and worship the Creator because he has made us to *not be* like the others; He has assigned us a different destiny than them. Or, we might paraphrase: The Jewish calling and election—this "portion" given by God—is for Jews only! We can and will do it alone! We certainly don't need help from any pagan Gentiles, who don't share in our privileged calling and destiny!

What's missing here should be obvious for us as new-covenant believers: What about the call to be a light to the nations? To bring the knowledge of God to the ends of the earth—to disciple the nations in the knowledge and ways of God? At the very least, we could have mentioned this aspect, that perhaps our chosenness is not just for us to celebrate—but in some way must serve to bless the nations, to fulfill Abraham's call to bless the families of the entire earth! But trust me, it's barely to be found in the standard, daily Jewish prayers—and there's no evidence that it was any different two thousand years ago. At the least we could have prayed: "Thank you God for separating us, making us holy by your commandments so that we could be an example of holiness to all the nations; and perhaps someday share with the world this wonderful inheritance that you have given us as the people of God."[21] But, instead,

---

[21] Some might argue that this prayer theme can be found in Judaism. Maybe yes, but in a very, very minor way. That is the problem.

because of our sinful nature, we fell into a trap that other peoples of the earth would have also fallen into if they had been specially chosen by God, that of pride, selfishness, and self-righteousness—exactly what Yeshua warned us of in Luke 18:9!

Yes, pride. And not just any pride—but the pride of being the chosen people, chosen by God Himself. And what does this pride cause among the Gentiles, among the nations? We have already dealt with this subject in Chapters 1 and 2; I think you get the idea. Can you also see that if these Torah-*dogma* commandments remain in effect under the new covenant, it would have to mean a wholesale Messianic Jewish conversion for all Gentiles? Can you see that it would spell the end of all other cultures, as more and more embrace the gospel? Can you also see that it would mean that Jews in the body of Christ would always have a special advantage, a special privilege—as the only truly "indigenous" ones of this very Jewish-looking kingdom?[22] That we would forever be in a position of teaching the world how to correctly observe this true, biblical inheritance of the holy culture? That there could therefore be no holy expression found in the cultural practices—in the language, literature, music, celebrations, etc.—of other cultures?

Let's close this chapter with one more quote from the *Siddur* (Prayer Book), the *Havdalah* prayer at the close of every Sabbath on Saturday evening:

> Blessed art thou, O Lord our God, King of the universe, who makes a distinction between holy and profane, between light and darkness, between Israel and other nations, between the seventh day and the six working days. Blessed are you, O Lord, who makes a distinction between holy and profane.

---

[22] Much like the English in the British Commonwealth, the Han Chinese in modern Greater China, or the Arabs in the wider Muslim world.

So this is the traditional Jewish view: Inside the wall of partition there is light, holiness, and sweet Sabbath rest; outside on the Gentile side of the wall—darkness, profanity, and bondage akin to the "sweat of your face" (Gen. 3:19) burden of work found on the other six days of the week. The great (and very controversial) revelation of the apostle was to see that in Christ, the "playing field" has been leveled—that the bondage to sin is equal on both sides of the wall. It may look different on the two sides, but insofar as one's source of personal or corporate holiness is based on the observance of the *stoichea*-based *dogma* commands, then the Jew is just as much a slave to sin as any Gentile—and being Abraham's physical seed is no help (John 8:31–47). Equally, for Jew and Gentile alike, the Messiah has become for us wisdom, righteousness, sanctification (holiness), and redemption; there is no place anymore for boasting in any identity that is based on the *stoichea*, material elements and principles of the universe—even those instructed to Israel through Moses (1 Cor. 1:29).

But how exactly did Yeshua accomplish this? How is it that in His death, "in His flesh," and in His resurrection He was able to abolish this wall of enmity, thus "making peace between the two?" This is what we will discuss next.

5

THE MYSTERY OF ONE NEW MAN—THE CRUCIFIED JEWISH MESSIAH, AND THE RESURRECTED BODY OF CHRIST

*. . . by abolishing **in His flesh** the enmity, which is the Law of commandments contained in ordinances, that **in Himself** He might make the two into one new man, thus establishing peace, and might reconcile them both **in one body** to God through the cross, by it having put to death the enmity.* (Eph. 2:15–16, emphasis added)

As Paul concludes the one-new-man teaching of Ephesians 2–3, he boasts of his unique insight into this "mystery of Christ" (3:4). There is a *mystery* here—a great and deep revelation of God's "manifold wisdom" (3:10)—the focal point of which is the crucifixion of our Lord Jesus Christ. (We will look more in depth at Ephesians 3:1–6 in Chapter 11.) In the foundational verses of the one new man quoted above, note the repetition in Paul's language: *in His flesh . . . in Himself . . . in one body.* This incredible reconciliation between Jew and Gentile, founded on the "abolishing" (Eph. 2:15) and "cancelling" (Col. 2:14) of the *dogma*-Torah commands, was somehow accomplished by the very real and agonizing death of Yeshua on the cross—*in His flesh*. In Colossians, the picture is one of a crucified legal document—a *certificate of debt* listing the *dogma* decrees—being nailed to the cross. But this is just a metaphor: there was no book of the law, or scroll, or any such list being nailed to the cross with the Savior—only the beaten, naked body of Yeshua, with a small sign overhead that read "King of the Jews."

In these verses, the apostle Paul is making a startling equation among the following elements: 1) the pre-Christian wall of hostility between Jew and Gentile; 2) the *dogma* commands, the holy boundary markers of Jewish identity, under the law of Moses, as distinct from the nations; 3) the body, the flesh of Yeshua, the Messiah and King of Israel; and 4) Israel—the people of God. It's like a mathematic formula:

> wall of enmity = *dogma*-Torah commands = the Body of Messiah Yeshua = Israel

In order to understand this mystery, we need to look at several Scriptures to understand the biblical Jewish thinking of the time that lay behind this uniquely Pauline revelation.

Yeshua, the Lawgiver and Living Torah

In Exodus 24:9–11, the Scripture teaches that seventy-four men went up Mount Sinai and "*saw* the God of Israel. And under His feet there appeared to be a pavement of sapphire as clear as the sky itself. Yet He did not stretch out His hand against the nobles of the sons of Israel; and they beheld God and they ate and drank" (v. 10–11, emphasis added). How to understand this in light of John 1:18: "No one has seen God at any time"? Or John 4:24: "God is spirit"? Whom did these men see on Mount Sinai? The description is brief, but leaves no room for guessing: The God whom they saw—the only God of Israel, Jehovah—has hands and feet![23] Who could this be? The rest of John 1:18 gives us the answer: "the only begotten Son, who is in the bosom of the Father, He has declared Him." God the Father is spirit; but God the Son is a man—with hands and feet and a face, mouth, digestive system, etc.

One of my mentors, Asher Intrater, has written a very important book called *Who Ate Lunch with Abraham?* The title is taken from the story in Genesis 18 of the three "men" who visit Abraham and Sarah at the oaks of Mamre. From verse 22 on, the Scripture makes it clear that this one who washes his feet, sits, reclines, and dines with Abraham also speaks in the first person for Jehovah (v. 17), and is thus none other than Jehovah Himself. Asher's book details the many OT appearances of this mysterious God-man, sometimes called Jehovah, sometimes "messenger/angel Jehovah" (מלאך יהוה). We understand this figure to be Yeshua, appearing to the people of Israel before his ultimate incarnation in Mary's womb. The one with whom the seventy-four "ate and drank" in Exodus 24 is none other than Yeshua, the preincarnate Son of God Himself.

Next, in verse 12 of Exodus 24, this same Jehovah commands Moses to come up the mountain again to receive "the stone tablets, with the Torah and the commandment which I have written for their instruction." Yeshua is Jehovah the lawgiver, the one who gave the Torah, and the one whose finger etched the Ten Commandments on stone tablets (Ex. 31:18). In Jewish thinking, the giving of the Torah is not to be imagined as some kind of "dry" transmission of information, whereby Jehovah the teacher simply gives instructions to his students. Mount Sinai is the ultimate revelation of God in the OT, when God Himself came down to the people of Israel to reveal Himself through His Torah—the expression of His very heart and mind, His authoritative *Word*. By the first century, this equation of Torah with God Himself had become a pillar of Judaism, and forms the background for the opening

---

[3] One could argue that "stretch out His hand" is not to be taken literally; but it is hard to argue similarly against "under his feet."

of John's gospel: "In the beginning was the Word, and the Word was with God, and the Word was God. He was in the beginning with God. All things came into being by Him" (John 1:1–3).[24] Now if we just substitute "Torah" for "Word" (*logos* in Greek) we can get the idea: Yeshua is the embodiment of Torah, the Word of God manifested in the flesh, the living Torah Himself.

What this means for us is two things: First, as the one who was present at Mount Sinai, as the Lawgiver himself, the Son of God has the authority to update, upgrade, and even change any aspect of the Torah that He chooses. This is why he can say, as he does several times in the Sermon on the Mount, "you have heard that it was said . . . but I tell you . . ." (Matt. 5:17–48). Second, if He is himself is the "Torah in the flesh," then obviously His death has implications for what Torah is! If the Living Word/Torah dies, is buried in a tomb, and then is resurrected to a new glorious, eternal life, what does this mean for everything we call Torah—and specifically, the *dogma*-Torah commands of Jewish distinctiveness that Paul focuses on in Ephesians and Colossians?

"Born of a woman, born under the law. . ."—Yeshua the Perfect, Complete Jew

The second element of the one-new-man mystery of the crucifixion of the *dogma* commands "in His flesh" is to see Him as the perfect Jew, the one who kept Torah perfectly. In Galatians 4:4, the apostle writes: "when the fullness of the time came, God sent forth His son, born of a woman, born under the law." Yeshua comes to fulfill every aspect of OT prophecy (Matt. 5:17–18), starting with the earliest promise of redemption—that the "seed of the woman" would crush the head of the enemy, the one who deceived us and stole our inheritance in the garden of Eden (Gen. 3:15). The Messiah also had to be Jewish—from the tribe of Judah—and specifically from the house of David; but he also was "born

---

[24] Much has been researched and written on this understanding of the living *logos* (Greek) *Mamre* (Aramaic), and Torah.

under the Torah," meaning that He had to be completely faithful to the Torah of Moses if He was to be qualified to redeem us from our sins.

For our purposes, this does not only mean that Jesus was the perfect, sinless, spotless "lamb of God"; He was a distinctively Jewish lamb, one who was totally obedient to the Torah of Moses. Many gospel stories illustrate this, but let's look at just one: the story of the Canaanite woman in Matthew 15:21–27. Yeshua travelled north with His disciples to Tyre and Sidon in present-day Lebanon—not known to be Jewish territory, not then and not now. A certain Canaanite (very Gentile!) woman followed them, shouting and begging the "Son of David" to have mercy on her demonized daughter. Yeshua famously refuses her entreaty, saying, "I was sent only to the lost sheep of the house of Israel.... It is not good to take the children's bread and throw it to the dogs" (vv. 24, 26). Her clever, faith-filled answer earns a miracle deliverance for her daughter. But what to make of Yeshua's rebuke? Did our Lord look down on Gentile "dogs" like so many Jews of His time (and ours!)?

This story teaches us very clearly that in Yeshua's life and ministry before the cross, He could not "legally" bring the good news to the Gentiles. It was necessary for Him, "born under the Torah," to be totally obedient to the existence of the *dogma*-Torah "wall of enmity" between the "house of Israel" and everyone else. (The story also poignantly describes the pathos on both sides of the wall of enmity—the longing, the jealousy, the pride. . . .) After all, as we just saw, it is He Himself who gave the holy commands to Moses on Mount Sinai, including those like the dietary laws, the calendar, and the purity laws—all the *dogma* commands which comprise the bricks of the cultural wall which separated Israel from the nations. Yeshua may have made a special exception for this Canaanite woman, but this didn't lead to a "revival" in Tyre or Sidon as it did in the city of the half-Jewish Samaritans in John 4:39. Before the one-new-man gospel of the cross, the Messianic hope and its message was only available, by divine covenant, to "the lost sheep of the house of Israel." As Paul wrote in Ephesians 2:12 of the Gentile state before and outside of the cross: "you were at that time separate from Christ."[25]

The "Servant Songs" of Isaiah 41–53: Messiah and Israel Are One

From chapters 41–53 of Isaiah there are five prophecies that some have called "servant songs": 41:8–16; 42:1–4; 49:1–6; 50:4–9; 52:13–53:12. Each one is a detailed picture of the work and character of the Redeemer of Israel, the servant Messiah. Mostly, the prophecies are of a singular man, a servant from among the people who will redeem Israel and the nations; and twice, in 41:8 and 49:3, the voice of Jehovah cries, "Israel, my servant. . . ." The Messiah is both one from *within* Israel and at the same time is wholly *identified as* Israel-Jacob. So for Paul, Yeshua is not just the Lawgiver, the living Torah, nor the perfect Jew who comes to fulfill Torah: He is also to be understood as Israel, as Israel-Jacob's greatest son, the promised seed in whom all of Israel's calling and destiny is embodied. We find the same identification in Matthew's quoting of Hosea 11:1 as he depicts the journey of Joseph, Mary, and Yeshua to Egypt: "Out of Egypt I called my son" (Matt. 2:15). In the context of the book of Hosea, this verse is simply a description of God's love and deliverance of the Jewish nation ("My son") from the bondage of slavery in Egypt, with seemingly no Messianic implications at all. But in Matthew, it becomes a foreshadowing of the infant Yeshua's escape to and return from Egypt. Just as the name "Israel" signifies both a singular person (Jacob) and the nation that would come from his loins (Israel), so is the identity of Israel's Messiah the full, covenantal DNA of everything God intended when he created and called "Israel."

---

[25] This can't mean, "before you were Christian you were without Christ, i.e., a non-Christian." That is too obvious, the same as saying "before you woke up you were sleeping!" It means that before the cross the Gentiles (nations) outside of Israel had no Messianic hope, no expectation of deliverance and salvation in the Jewish Messiah.

Summary

Now, with all of this scriptural background, we are better able to comprehend the one-new-man equation of the apostle from Ephesians 2 and Colossians 2: the wall of hostility/enmity = *dogma*-Torah commands = Yeshua = Israel. Let's try to picture this a little more.

Yeshua, in His Jewishness based on His perfect obedience to Torah, is Himself identified as the wall of hostility between Israel and the nations. The Jewishness of the Messiah—and the Messianic hope associated with Him—was like a giant wall in the midst of humanity. He was only recognizable—and legally/covenantally available—to those on the inside of the wall, the Jewish side. From the outside, no matter how hard they might pray, or try to peer in, or even scale the wall, the Gentile nations were shut out from the covenants of promise and any hope of being part of God's Israel—*as* Gentiles, as Egyptians, Moabites, Chinese, French, etc. The "way in" was carefully guarded by the holy, *dogma*-Torah commands at the heart of Jewishness; only by abandoning one's Gentile identity and "converting" into Israel, like Ruth, could one hope to enter.

Paul says it this way: "But before faith came, we were kept in custody under the law, being shut up to the faith which was later to be revealed" (Gal. 3:23). We're used to hearing this verse as it pertains to our *individual* bondage to "the Law," or to some kind of law-keeping that Christ came to liberate us from. But for Paul—especially in Ephesians and Colossians, and here in Galatians—he has much more in mind: This unique chosenness of Israel as expressed by the Torah-*dogma* commands tended to magnify sin at the collective level, the sin of racial and ethnic pride, of racism and discrimination based on tribal identifications, culture, and history. And just like sin at the personal level, it required a blood-atonement, a crucifixion—nothing less than the sacrificial death of the Jewish Messiah, in order to reconcile Israel and the nations in His flesh, in Himself—one new man, the body of Christ.

Before His incarnation, and especially before His death and resurrection, the Messianic hope was an exclusively Jewish hope. This exclusivity, this chosenness, contains a paradox: On the one hand, God had to make sure that there would be no mistaking the identity of His Son's incarnation in human flesh. In this world of priests, rabbis, gurus, kings, and all manner of false messiahs, there had to be only one, unmistakable, promised-by-covenant genealogy of the "Son of Man." He was to be the son of the woman (Eve), of Noah, of Shem; the son of Abraham, Isaac, and Jacob; and ultimately, the Son of David. By necessity, the unique, incarnate Son of God had to have a history, a family, an ethnicity, and a nation. His Jewish, Israelite identity was defined by and protected by the wall of the *dogma* commands. But on the other hand, this "fence" of His Jewishness represented a stumbling block to the rest of humanity—one which caused (and continues to cause) pride, jealousy, hatred, exclusivity, etc. God's love for, and choosing of Israel, meant that He couldn't choose another nation; you can only have one firstborn, eldest child! But God's heart longs for all the nations (Gentiles) whom He has made, for all of His children to know Him and praise Him (Ps. 117). It is His desire that all should "be saved and come to the knowledge of the truth" (1 Tim. 2:4).

So, what could the Father do to remedy this situation? In the "fullness of the time" God sent His Son into this world to redeem us—first to the Jew and then everyone else (Gal. 4:4; Rom. 1:16). He lived as Jew, under Torah, and He died as one as well. At his death on the cross, the long-promised hope of Israel (and thus of all humanity) was finished. The King of Israel was crucified—and with Him the whole nation, its Torah, its distinct identity, and everything it was supposed to stand for. Like a grain of wheat (or any other seed) falling into the ground, the body of Jesus began to disintegrate (John 12:24). He was really dead, and not just for an hour or two. Satan had seemingly triumphed over the Son of David.

But then after three days, on that incredible Sunday morning, the power of the Holy Spirit visited His dead flesh, raising Him from the dead into a totally new life. This grain of wheat experienced a total transformation—from seed, to death/disintegration into the earth, to a new kind of glorified body that the world had never seen (1 Cor. 15:35–49). But this body is still the same person, the same Jesus of Nazareth, the King of the Jews with the marks of crucifixion on His hands and side, and still (presumably) with the mark of Abrahamic covenant in His circumcised flesh (John 20:27). In His glorified state in the book of Revelation He is triumphantly described as the "Lion that is from the tribe of Judah, the Root of David" (Rev. 5:5). Just as the seed and the fully developed plant contain the exact same DNA, so in His resurrection He is still the same human being, the son of Mary, God, and Joseph!

Yeshua has become the first "one new man"—the representative of, and template for, an entirely new kind of humanity. Just as He is forever the "Root of David," there is forever a Jewish root to the gospel, and in this sense "salvation is from the Jews" (John 4:22). But the "downside" of His Jewishness—the wall of enmity as expressed by the *dogma* commands and their observance "in His flesh"—has also experienced a radical transformation through his death and resurrection. When Jesus the ultimate Jew and "living Torah" died, the wall of enmity between Jew and Gentile came crashing down in His dead Jewish flesh. When he rose from the dead, His body was transformed so that there is now a new wall in the midst of humanity—this one not composed of the *dogma* command-bricks, but something of a different order entirely: Is one *in Christ* or not? From the beginning, God ordained that His Son would be the defining standard for all humanity, but a standard that was not ultimately to be defined by His *dogma*-based Jewishness. Now anyone—from any tribe, tongue, or nation—can be an insider to God's Israel (Gal. 6:16) by faith in Him, by the circumcision of the heart, not the flesh.

The biblical commands related to dietary laws, calendar, and priestly purity still exist and function for the Jewish people, but in the glory of the resurrection body and in the light of the age to come, their observance no longer determines personal or corporate holiness. Now, the Jewish Messiah is free to be the covenantal mediator of every tribe, tongue, and nation—bringing them into the Abrahamic family, while honoring their distinct culture and identity. In His new body, Israel and the nations are reconciled in a way that allows for the "redemption," transformation, and celebration of their unique, God-given identities—establishing a relationship of mutual blessing that precludes any sense of superiority based on things like food, calendar, or any other *stoichea*-based customs. Now His body is a place of reconciliation, of love and blessed identity for Jew and Gentile, for those from every tribe, tongue, and nation who will worship and receive Him.

The one-new-man gospel of Paul teaches us, as Jews and Gentiles, to see the message of the cross as far more than just pertaining to our individual salvation and inheritance of eternal life. But how did Paul come to see this? How did he receive this revelation? It is the nature of all biblical theology and revelation that it emerges not primarily in a mystical, "channeled" sense straight from the Holy Spirit; rather, men obeyed the voice of God and saw His hand in their personal and corporate histories. Their testimonies, and what they learned about God from these events, became the content of biblical revelation. In the next chapter, we will see how Paul's life and ministry among Jew and Gentile brought him to these conclusions.

6

THE LIFE, MINISTRY, AND REVELATION OF PAUL

Then the LORD came down in the cloud and spoke to [Moses]; and He took of the Spirit who was upon him and placed Him upon the seventy elders. And it came about that when the Spirit rested upon them, they prophesied. But they did not do it again.

. . .

Then Joshua the son of Nun, the attendant of Moses from his youth, said, "Moses, my lord, restrain them." But Moses said to him, "Are you jealous for my sake? Would that all the LORD's people were prophets, that the LORD would put His Spirit upon them!" (Num. 11:25, 28–29)

You may think it strange to start off a chapter on the life and ministry of the apostle Paul with this quote from the book of Numbers, but this passage from the Torah can be seen as a precursor to what Paul saw throughout his ministry in the Jewish Diaspora. But instead of God's Spirit being shared with seventy circumcised Jewish elders, as in Moses' time, Paul was witnessing something far more dramatic and controversial: the Spirit of God being poured out, in all its fullness, on uncircumcised, "pork-eating," "non-Sabbath-keeping" pagan "sinners."

And it wasn't just a one-time experience as in Numbers 11, but an ongoing, everyday regular occurrence. The Spirit of God Himself was here to stay, making Himself a new dwelling place—not in a temple made by hands, and not even among exclusively "kosher," Jewish flesh.

How did these Gentiles get the Holy Spirit, by which they worshipped, prophesied, healed, and did miracles? By "hearing with faith" (Gal. 3:2): by a simple and sincere prayer of repentance upon believing in Paul's message of the crucified and resurrected Messiah—His atoning sacrifice for sin, His resurrection, His return to judge the world, eternal life—and then being baptized in His name (1 Cor. 2:2–5; Gal. 6:14). Clearly, there was something "newer" to this "new covenant" than even the prophet Jeremiah had envisioned (Jer. 31:31–34). More than anyone else in the New Testament, it fell on the apostle Paul to witness, preach, and explain this mystery.

This "new thing" didn't begin with Paul, but started with Peter's revelation that led him to the house of Cornelius (Acts 10). There, while he was explaining the gospel, the Holy Spirit fell powerfully on Cornelius and his whole household. As difficult as it was for Peter to even consider entering a Gentile's home to have food and fellowship, God was merciful to him: He sent Peter to the home of one who was called a "God-fearer" (Acts 10:2), a Gentile who was a kind of proselyte to Judaism—who most certainly observed the major Jewish customs related to the calendar and foods. So Peter was going to the home of a Gentile, but this was as "kosher" a Gentile as one could find in Israel in those days. It was no coincidence that the Lord used the whole metaphor of clean and unclean foods to get Peter ready to go to an "unclean" Gentile's home (Acts 10:9–16)—for this was where the "rubber hits the pavement," where fellowship at a Gentile's home becomes really problematic. Honor and hospitality demands the serving of food and drink—but could this Gentile, even though a proselyte, really know how to run a "clean" kosher kitchen? What would Peter do?

Fortunately, Peter followed the Holy Spirit's leading and went, and the rest is history. But there is evidence that it was difficult for Peter to go the next step, of coming to the full understanding of what Paul came to see (Gal. 2:11–21); namely that God was creating a totally new reality by calling a people from "every tribe, tongue, and nation" *just as they are, as Gentiles—Greeks, French, Chinese, etc.* And in order for this reality—let's call it the *international church*—to come into being and prosper, a very serious change in the dispensation of God's grace, salvation, and Torah was coming to pass.

Let's first think about this man Saul/Paul. He was different from the other apostles who were fishermen and tax collectors; he was a highly educated "rabbi," trained at the highest institutions of Jewish learning for his time (under Gamaliel; Acts 5:24, 22:3). At the same time, he was a "card-carrying" Roman citizen, one who had an understanding of Greco-Roman culture and literature (Acts 17:28). It took someone trained so deeply in Judaism and Torah to understand the ramifications of the new covenant for Torah—just as only a trained geologist can interpret and explain the depth of shaking and shifting that takes place below the earth's surface during an earthquake.

What did Paul begin to see, and *how* did he come to see it? Once he left Antioch to begin his mission among the Diaspora (Acts 13), it is easy to chart Paul's strategy. If he went to a city with a Jewish community, he would begin his preaching at the local synagogue—where they first welcomed him as a kind of rabbi, or dignitary from Jerusalem. Depending on his reception, Paul would continue there for several weeks or months. Most of the time, as described from Acts 13–28, the pattern was the same: a handful of the Jews and a small number of Gentile "seekers"[26] believed the message and formed their own *havurah* (fellowship) that either continued to meet at the synagogue, or in someone's home. As they continued to grow they almost always experienced a pattern of resistance, harassment, and ultimately, persecution against

---

[26] It appears that there were many kinds of Gentiles "hanging around" the Diaspora synagogues: Some, like Cornelius (or Luke himself) were full-fledged proselyte "God-fearers;" but there were also many others, from the mildly curious to more serious ones at different stages of "conversion."

them from the local Jewish authorities. Why? Shouldn't Jewish leaders be excited about a growing movement of people believing in the God of Israel? Yes and no. You see, Paul's gospel of equality and reconciliation between Jew and Gentile, of the "circumcision of the heart," was correctly perceived as a direct threat to the authority of the Jewish leaders over their community. Think about the message in Ephesians: You have been raised up in Christ, seated in the most holy, heavenly places with Him. You who formerly were far off have been brought near by the blood of Christ. So then you are no longer strangers and aliens, but full members of God's household and the commonwealth of Israel (Eph. 2:6, 13, 19).

From the book of Acts and his letters, it is easy to imagine the reaction of the Jewish leaders: "Who says? By what authority do you preach these things, Paul? And you're not even requiring the Gentiles to be circumcised or keep kosher—but you expect us to welcome them with open arms into 'Israel'? Into our community? You tell them that they are now full members of God's covenant people, Israel, without having to submit to any of the traditional standards of our community? Who do you think you are? Get out of town!"

But, Paul explained, his authority came from none other than the crucified and risen Lord, the King of Israel. God initiated a new era in the history of Israel, one which would not leave Israel or the nations (Gentiles) in the same relationship of enmity as before. This era would be characterized, as Jeremiah had prophesied, by a new kind of "spiritual" or "religious" authority—one which comes directly from knowing God in a personal and intimate way, through a spiritual new birth, a circumcision of the *heart*—and *not* by coming under the authority of a rabbi or priest, nor of an institution based in Jerusalem or anywhere else (Jer. 31:31–34; John 4:21–24). All of this would have profound ramifications for how the world, including Israel, would understand the Law of Moses and its traditions, what had become known by one word: "Torah."

This brings us to the next thing to which Paul witnesses, of which there is evidence in almost all of his letters: that a certain kind "Torah teaching" (the "Judaizing" tendency) among the new communities of believers always caused trouble. Whenever people came (especially from the Jewish side[27]) to preach feasts, foods, or circumcision—the power of the Holy Spirit, almost in direct proportion, decreased; in its place came confusion, disunity, and a turning away from a clear focus on the gospel of the crucified, resurrected, and soon-coming Messiah-King. The goal of the preaching of Paul's gospel was "love from a pure heart and a good conscience and a sincere faith"; the result of Torah-teaching and its observance was "fruitless discussion" about the details of things like kosher and Sabbath keeping (1 Tim. 1:5–6).[28] The transforming and sanctifying power of the Holy Spirit was obscured by a "religious" focus on *dogma*-Torah observances; and, Paul taught, "These are matters which have, to be sure, the appearance of wisdom in self-made religion and self-abasement and severe treatment of the body, but are of no value against fleshly indulgence" (Col. 2:23).[29]

In conclusion, in Paul's lifetime and ministry he was watching, first-hand, the redrawing of the very boundaries of what he had been trained to understand as "Israel." The lines of the thousand-year-old categories of what it meant to be called "Jew" or "Gentile" were exploding before his very eyes. It is hard for us to imagine how dramatic, surprising, and controversial these events were—especially for the rest of the

---

[27] Today the situation is very different: there are just as many, if not more, "Torah teachers" from among the Gentile Christian world as from the Messianic Jewish one.

[28] When Torah is taught in this way, as a key to righteousness (correct living), or sanctification (holy living), it inevitably opens up a "Pandora's box" of questions/discussions like how to keep the Sabbath, "What is 'work' in relation to the Sabbath day?" "When exactly does the Sabbath begin/end?" "Who has the authority to set the calendar?" "Who can sanction/teach exactly how kosher animals are to be slaughtered?", or what to do in the case of the accidental eating of unkosher foods, or blood. These, of course, are the questions with which Pharisaic-rabbinic Judaism has been engaged for the better part of the last 2,500 years; and so it is only natural that believers would tend to turn to Jewish authorities to be "properly" instructed in these matters. Yet, then as now, these are the same authorities who are dead-set against faith in Yeshua!

[29] Some of this language even goes beyond Torah to ascetic ways of life that Scripture never commanded.

unbelieving Jewish nation.[30] Imagine waking up one morning to find that the sun had risen not from the east, but from the west; and as you look out your window you see all kinds of strange animals—pink elephants, unicorns. You would think, "the world has been turned upside down . . . something in the basic order of the universe has changed." It was that dramatic.

For Paul, all of this was not just a theological abstraction or some kind of philosophy—it was an intensely personal walk of faith, which entailed a daily identification with the crucified and resurrected King:

> For through the Law I died to the Law, that I might live to God. I have been crucified with Christ; and it is no longer I who live, but Christ lives in me; and the life which I now live in the flesh I live by faith in the Son of God, who loved me, and delivered Himself up for me. I do not nullify the grace of God; for if righteousness comes through the Law, then Christ died needlessly. (Gal. 2:19–21)

I hope you can hear these words in a fresh way: that "dying to the law (Torah)" was not just about dying to a kind of personal, religious attitude—one which seeks to please God by "religious" observances and good works ("works of the law"). For a Pharisaic/rabbinic Jew, "dying to Torah" meant dying to one's God-given, God-chosen Jewishness. With Yeshua, the apostle went through the same "dying to Torah," thus dying to his Jewishness as expressed by the *dogma* commands, so that he could "live to God" in a new way. Like Abraham (and Yeshua himself), Paul was willing to place his hope in God's promises to Israel on the altar of the cross—believing that God could and would resurrect His promises to the children of Abraham, Isaac, and Jacob in His own way, in His own time (Gen. 22). For the sake of knowing Him and the power of

---

[30] One only has to read of the Jerusalem riot in Acts 21–22 to understand just how passionate the Jewish people were about Yeshua's assertion to Paul, "I will send you far away to the Gentiles" (Acts 22:21).

His resurrection more and more, the apostle was willing to count his past—including his Jewish, covenantal identity—as deficit, as "loss," even as "rubbish" (Phil. 3:4–16).

So this is how Saul the Jew became Paul the Christian . . . or is it? Did Paul actually abandon His Jewish identity? For the apostle, did the one-new-man gospel mean an end to Jewish calling and uniqueness among the nations? Was he just cancelling Torah in order to preach a universal, ethnically "neutered" Christ that the world could more easily receive? How did he actually live? This is where it gets really interesting—the stuff of paradox.

7

SO HOW THEN SHALL WE LIVE?
PART 1: TORAH IN ITS PROPER PLACE

[A]s the Lord has assigned to each one, as God has called each, in this manner let him walk. And so I direct in all the churches. Was any man called when he was already circumcised? He is not to become uncircumcised. Has anyone been called in uncircumcision? He is not to be circumcised. Circumcision is nothing, and uncircumcision is nothing, but what matters is the keeping of the commandments of God. . . . Brethren, each one is to remain with God in that condition in which he was called. (1 Cor. 7:17–20, 24)

In Acts 16:3, the apostle Paul circumcises Timothy, a teenager, by his own hand. This is the same man who taught so vehemently against circumcision for the Galatians (albeit that they were Gentiles) and declares here in 1 Corinthians that "circumcision is nothing, and uncircumcision is nothing." In Galatians and Colossians he writes, "there is no distinction between Greek and Jew, circumcised and uncircumcised" (Col. 3:11; cf. Gal. 3:28).

In Acts 21:21–26, in response to the apostle Jacob's (James') report about the rumors surrounding Paul—that he was "teaching all the Jews who are among the Gentiles to forsake Moses . . . not to circumcise their

63

children nor to walk according to the customs" (Acts 21:21)—the apostle submits to ritual purification and pays for the offering of a sacrifice at the temple for himself and for four other men also under a Nazirite vow. All of this was in accordance with Jewish, Torah-based law and tradition (see Num. 6:13–18). In Romans 7:12, Paul writes that "the Law [Torah] is holy, and the commandment is holy and righteous and good." Remember, this is the same apostle who wrote Ephesians, Colossians, and Galatians; who wrote so powerfully of the body of Christ as a new kind of spiritual temple (Eph. 2:21-22); and who wrote of the fulfilling of the sacrifices and the priesthood by Yeshua.

We mentioned in the Introduction that those with just about every view of the role of Torah in the believer's life somehow claim authority from Paul. Was he a kind of "two-faced" hypocrite, who preached one thing here, and practiced another thing there, according to convenience and expediency? Perhaps there were actually two men—Saul the "Torah Jew," and Paul the "founder" of Gentile Christianity? Of course not. But Paul's teaching has always been prone to misunderstanding, as well as proof-texting in order to prove one's pet theology.[31] But there is hope! It is possible to put it all together in a cohesive whole, and the major keys to understanding these questions are all found in the passage from 1 Corinthians 7 quoted at the beginning of this chapter. Let's look at it, and the principles developed there.

First, in verse 17, Paul prefaces this teaching by saying that this is something he directs in all the churches. He is going to say something about the continuing identities of Jew and Gentile (the "circumcised" and the "uncircumcised") in the midst of the congregations he planted in the Roman-Jewish Diaspora. It should be noted that Paul did not have some kind of obsession concerning circumcision, or the male "member." It is simply that at this time, and probably since the time of

---

[31] Second Peter 3:16 teaches that this was even so in their time, when they were much closer to the events, contexts, and language of the Scripture. Note that already by the time Peter is writing, he refers to Paul's writing in the same category as "other Scriptures."

the Maccabees almost two hundred years earlier, the Jews had been thus nicknamed in Greco-Roman society. It is just a "catch-all, cover-all" nickname for the Jewish people, as "uncircumcised" is for the Gentiles. He could have just as easily said "Sabbath-keepers" and "non-Sabbath-keepers." [32] Next, we can learn—as we do from the stories of Paul's ministry in these cities in Acts—that these churches were all mixed, Jew and Gentile, unlike the mother church in Jerusalem which was exclusively Jewish, or at least proselyte Jewish converts. [33] Lastly, this was something that was important enough for the apostle to point out as something he "directs" in "all the churches." [34] This was not just a passing cultural dictum related to the Corinthian church, like head-coverings for women (1 Cor 11:5–15).

In verse 17 we find the main teaching repeated again at the conclusion of the section in verse 24: Each person should remain in the same social, ethnic (and today, we might add gender?) position as he/she was in when he/she was "called," i.e., became a Christian. This seems pretty straightforward: as elsewhere, Paul was not a social radical teaching slaves to rebel against their masters or wives against their husbands, all in the name of a newly found Christian liberty. He is saying this: If you are a Jew, remain that way (this is why he circumcised Timothy—in order to strengthen what was a weak identity because of his Greek father); if you are a Gentile, remain that way; and by extension, if you are Chinese or French, stay that way. Paul does not explain here *why* it

---

[32] In medieval China, the Kaifeng Jewish community was known as the people of *Tiao jin jiao* (挑筋教), loosely, "the religion which removes the sinew," because of the unusual (to the Chinese) custom of the Jewish prohibition against eating the sciatic nerve (Gen. 32:32). In the same way, circumcision was equally strange—and thus stood out—in the Greco-Roman world.

[33] Interestingly, this is exactly the situation of all Messianic Jewish congregations today, both in the Diaspora and even in Israel: mixed Jew and Gentile! (Our congregation in downtown Jerusalem is about half and half.) That is why I always prick at the notion that the early Jerusalem church, in its zeal for Torah and the traditions should somehow be *the* model for Messianic Judaism today (Acts 21:20). Like it or not, the one new man is here to stay; and thus Paul's teachings are more relevant for us—not to mention that they comprise one third of the entire NT!

[34] I look more in depth at this subject of the "weight" of NT, Apostolic instructions in Appendix 3-2.

is so important to retain one's ethnic, national identity—we will have to learn that from other places in coming chapters—but suffice to say that this was important enough to the Holy Spirit to inspire the apostle to make this a clear teaching in all of the churches.

Next is a seemingly paradoxical statement at the heart of Paul's theology: "Circumcision is nothing, and uncircumcision is nothing, but what matters is the keeping of the commandments of God." If we can unpack this verse properly, we can learn a great deal about the place of Torah and commandments in a biblically consistent NT theology that is at the heart of the one new man. First, if the *dogma* commands of the Torah of Moses are still in effect under the new covenant—as commandments—then Paul has penned a logical impossibility, because circumcision is *the* foundational Torah *mitzvah*! It is the only *dogma*-commandment that was given to Abraham—then repeated for all Israel in Leviticus 12:3, becoming the most prominent, physical sign of the covenant between God and the Jewish people. If this commandment is still in effect, or carries the same force under the new covenant as it did under the old, then the apostle has said something akin to, "It's not whether you run a red light or not—what matters is obeying the traffic laws." Of course, this is a logical impossibility!

Here the apostle has succinctly summarized what he has been teaching everywhere (as we have been learning): that circumcision and other *dogma-stoichea* commands—through the cross, resurrection, and ascension of Yeshua—have undergone such a radical transformation that they can even be spoken of as having been "abolished." They are still there in the books of Moses as Holy Scripture, but the Word of God in them speaks very differently now. Under the new covenant, *they must no longer be thought of as commandments in the same way as they were under the old covenant.* We learned in Chapter 4 that in Pharisaic-rabbinic Judaism, then and now, the commandments are a kind of monolith—the observance of which sanctifies and defines the holy, communal boundaries of God's people. Simply put, Paul is saying this: These commands no longer have that kind of authority, and thus no longer deserve to be called "commandments of God." (In a later chapter, we will explore their continuing validity for Jewish identity.)

Does this mean, as he was often accused, that according to his gospel of grace there are no longer *any* commandments for God's people (Rom. 3:8; cf. Matt. 5:17–19)? Not at all! Here in verse 19, in keeping with Yeshua's statement in John 14:15 ("If you love Me, you will keep My commandments"), Paul writes that keeping the commandments of God is of the utmost importance. The great question is this: What are these commandments?

We could envision Paul and the other NT apostles explaining it like this: "God is holy and moral, and we are called to be like him. Under the new covenant, the full revelation of God's moral, universal commandments has been finally, and perfectly explained by the Lord Himself, in what he taught His disciples—especially on the mount in Galilee" (Matt. 5–7).[35] This "Torah of Messiah" (Gal. 6:2) awaited the Lord coming fully as a man to not just teach and instruct, but to ratify the new covenant by his death and resurrection, having become both the perfect sacrifice, the perfect mediator/high priest, and the perfect example. Now, as we enter into this dynamic of death and resurrection ourselves, being filled with the Holy Spirit and bearing its fruit in our behavior and lifestyle, we are empowered to keep these holy, moral commandments in a relationship of loving grace with our Lord. Neither circumcision means anything nor uncircumcision, what counts is a new creation (Gal. 6:15; cf. 2 Cor. 5:17). This new creation is available equally for everyone who believes—Jew and Gentile, male and female, slave or Greek, etc. But make no mistake, we are still obligated to keep very real commandments, and if we willfully disobey them, we are in

---

[35] We will study this more in depth in an appendix on Matthew 5:17–19, but notice what is missing in the Lord's lengthy discourse on Torah, otherwise known as the Sermon on the Mount: Not a single mention of any *dogma-stoichea*-commandments—not Sabbath, not *kashrut*, and not circumcision. In Judaism, it's impossible to imagine a great rabbi giving his authoritative teaching of Torah and leaving these things out.

danger of being cut off from the people of God, and we may not inherit the kingdom of God!" (1 Cor. 6:9–11; Gal. 5:19–21).

In conclusion, Paul is saying, as he did elsewhere: Being Jewish or Gentile is not the essential thing in the kingdom of God—what matters most is faith and holiness, defined by the "Torah" of Messiah Yeshua. This new covenant Torah has not come to cancel or replace the old— but it is a significant condensing, refining, and "upgrading" of the old. But, once we are "born from above" and begin to experience the transforming of our mind and character according to the template of Yeshua Himself, we also need to remember that our God-given earthly identity is not something to be tossed away. God still has a purpose and calling for us here "down below." This includes one's gender, nationality, and social standing.

It is important to notice the context of 1 Corinthians 7: In his discussion of marriage, singleness, and sexuality, the apostle is very careful to distinguish between what is his own opinion as an apostle, and what is "command" or "from the Lord" (vv. 6–10, 25). When he comes to verse 17, he uses yet another expression, which is not as clear as the previous ones, "as the Lord has assigned to each one . . . so I direct in all the churches."[36]

As we saw at the beginning of this chapter, Paul indeed practiced what he preached: Insofar as he was able, he would visit the synagogue on the Sabbath; he kept Jewish, Torah customs enough so as to not be an offense to the Jewish community on those grounds; he practiced circumcision for Messianic Jews; and when in Jerusalem he demonstrated fidelity to Jewish law and tradition. Indeed, he remained a Jew—just as he teaches other Jewish believers in these verses. But on what grounds? How can we reconcile his teaching on the Torah with his lifestyle? We could imagine the following dialogue between Paul and a Jewish believer from his time:

---

[36] I take up this issue of the various "weights" and "levels" of NT commands in Appendix 3-2.

"Okay Paul, I'm a Jew like you, and you're telling me that I'm supposed to stay that way; and I assume I'm supposed to raise my Jewish kids that way as well. So, how do we do it? How should we then live? We all know that since Moses' time what defines our people and keeps us 'Jewish' are those same *dogma* commandments that you just taught us yesterday have been abolished in order to make one-new-man reconciliation and unity with the Gentiles possible. So are you proposing some new kind of Jewish culture? Some kind of Jew-Gentile hybrid culture? A new 'church' culture for all of us?"

"No, I am not suggesting this," replies the apostle, "my teaching on the *dogma* commands has a context, that of them functioning as weighty commandments which define righteousness, holiness, and the only possible practice for God's people—as they functioned under the old covenant and continue to function in Messiah-less Judaism. As Moses said concerning the Sabbath and many other such commands, the one who violates them deserves the punishment of being 'cut off from the people.' In all of these senses, these commandments are no longer in effect, having been abolished *as commandments* by Yeshua, the Jew, being crucified with him along with the entire cosmos of *stoichea*-based religion and spirituality, both Jewish and Gentile.

"Yet, as you rightly point out and as you can see from my continuing Jewish lifestyle, these commandments still have a place in defining the *cultural*, even *covenantal*, boundaries of the Jewish people/nation—just as similar practices (foods, calendrical observances, etc.) function in defining the culture of all peoples.[37] *The one new man is not about abolishing distinctions in our human identities, but about transformed self-understandings and relationships.* Through the gospel of the crucified and risen Messiah, His authoritative teaching (much of it based on the previous revelations to the Patriarchs, Moses, and the Prophets), and the indwelling of the Holy Spirit, God has given us the discern-

---

[37] As previous noted, some scholars describe this use of these commands as "Jewish boundary markers."

ment to determine what is truly universal *commandment.* That is why we must remember that the kingdom of God is not eating and drinking, but righteousness, peace, and joy in the Holy Spirit—and that this is available to everyone, Jew and Gentile equally (Rom. 14:17). In Christ, we are seated in the heavenly places (Eph. 2:6), above the earthly distinctions of Jew and Gentile, male and female; and from this place we clearly see that for personal holiness and righteous living, circumcision is nothing and uncircumcision is nothing;[38] what matters is keeping the Torah (commandments) of Messiah."

"Okay, I think I'm getting it, Paul. . . . So the old *dogma* commandments of foods, Shabbat, feasts, new moon, etc., are still in effect simply as the culture of the Jewish people? Just like the foods and feasts of other peoples?"

"Yes, and no!" continues Paul. "All of the Scriptures, including these commands, are 'inspired by God and profitable for teaching, for reproof, for correction, [and] for training in righteousness' (2 Tim. 3:16). This means that the Torah, and all the old-covenant Scriptures, must be studied for moral instruction in light of new-covenant gospel teachings. In addition, the Lord taught that 'until heaven and earth pass away, not the smallest letter or stroke shall pass away from the [Torah] until all is accomplished' (Matt. 5:18).[39] This means that there are many things in the Torah with a prophetic dimension, and this is especially so concerning the feasts and the calendar. For example, the Lord's first coming was timed with the spring feasts of Passover (Unleavened Bread), Firstfruits, Omer, and Shavuot (Pentecost). In the same way, there is much to be learned concerning the timing and manner of his second coming from studying the fall feasts. Whether you actually keep these feasts during

---

[38] "What is gone with the crucifixion of the cosmos is not simply circumcision, but rather circumcision and uncircumcision, and thus the distinction of Jew from Gentile. Or, to take the matter to its root, what has suffered eclipse is not simply the Law, but rather the cosmos that had at its foundation both the Law and the not-Law" (Martyn, 402).

[39] We will look at these key verses in Matthew in Appendix 2-1.

their appointed season, as in Judaism, is not of importance[40]—what matters most is learning the deeper, prophetic, and typological truths and their fulfillment in the new covenant.

"Further, the Torah with its *dogma* commands represents the only culture that was clearly imparted, however imperfectly, by the one God to Moses; and when understood properly can be a great advantage for the Jew (Rom. 3:1–2, 9:4–5; Gal. 3:19–22).[41] But without an understanding of the temporary nature of many Torah commandments, the primacy of its Messianic promises over the observance of *dogma* commandments, its role in exposing sin (Gal. 3:15–29), and without faith in the Messiah and an understanding of the one-new-man gospel that I preach, this 'advantage' inevitably leads to religious and ethnic pride; a wrong relationship of bondage to the *dogma* commandments; and a Jewishly warped, parochial understanding of God (Rom. 3:27–31).

"Therefore, in Christ, this advantage comes to fulfill God's promise to Abraham to be a blessing to all the families of the earth, and a key to the 'restoration of all things about which God spoke by the mouth of His holy prophets' (Acts 3:21), end-times revival, fulfilling the Great Commission, the return of the Lord, and the establishing of His kingdom on earth (Rom. 11)."

---

[40] Indeed, for those living in the southern hemisphere the spring is fall, and fall is spring! What's more, no one keeps them as exactly as written by Moses, especially because we no longer offer the various sacrifices required on the feast days.

[41] In Romans 2 Paul uses different language to make the same point: Circumcision has value if you observe the law, but if you break the law, you have become as though you had not been circumcised (v. 25). He then goes on to emphasize the universal, moral commands and not the other specific *dogma*-commands that lie at the heart of Jewish identity. Again we see the same Pauline priorities and balancing: Circumcision has value, but its status is secondary to the universal standards which Gentiles can share in without circumcision. If those who are not circumcised keep the law's requirements, will they not be regarded as though they were circumcised (v. 26)?

8

SO HOW THEN SHALL WE LIVE?
PART 2: THE BIBLICAL INEVITABILITY
AND NECESSITY OF CULTURE

*He Himself gives to all life and breath and all things; and He
made from one, every nation of mankind to live on all the face
of the earth, having determined their appointed times, and the
boundaries of their habitation, that they should seek God, if perhaps they might grope for Him and find Him, though He is not
far from each one of us; for in Him we live and move and exist.*
(Acts 17:25–28)

I hope at this point that you can see that Paul was not confused or
double-minded. He was a man who had been set free—free from
any bondage to his own Jewish, Torah-based culture; but at the same
time free to engage, enjoy, and use his Jewish identity to witness of
Christ and to bless others (1 Cor. 9:19–23). Because of his focus on,
and constant identification with, the crucified and risen Messiah (Gal.
2:19–21), the man simply had his priorities straight. The first and highest truth is that there is "neither Jew nor Greek [Gentile] . . . male nor

female" in Christ (Gal. 3:28). Citizenship in the kingdom of God is equally available to every individual, without regard to race, gender, or social status. The next truth, the next reality, is that both before and after our conversions, we are still who we are—Jew and Gentile, male and female—and God has a purpose and calling for us in these identities as well.

While the church has a long history of confusion about whether the Jew can still exist as a Jew in Christ, it seems to not have been similarly confused concerning the next pair of "opposites" mentioned in Galatians 3:28. Since gender is biologically determined at birth and seemingly unchangeable,[42] it has always been patently obvious to Christians that "neither male nor female" doesn't mean that the male believer ceases to be a man; or that a woman should, in her desire to be more Christlike, become less feminine and more masculine! When I teach on this, I ask my students: "Does 'neither Jew nor Gentile . . . male nor female' mean that I can wear a pink dress to church, if that's what I feel like doing in the name of the freedom of being a totally new creation in Christ?" Of course not. True, unlike gender, the distinction between Jew and Gentile is something that comes much later, and there have always been those who are not biologically Jewish who have fully joined themselves to Israel. God promises Abraham, the Hebrew, that He will make a great *goy* of him and his seed; this word *goy* is the same as "Gentile" or "nation." There was a time when there were no "Jews" and "Gentiles" on this earth—not so for male and female.

Yet, Paul's apostolic instruction to all his churches in 1 Corinthians 7 (as we studied in the previous chapter) means that God intends for us to take our ethnic, national, and cultural identities very seriously. But why? This is the question we will explore in this chapter, and the next several. Biblically, I can see at least four important reasons.

---

[42] All this is changing today . . . transgender . . . or is it?

1. Personal and Social Integrity

In Acts 17, Paul had occasion to visit Athens and preach to a group of Greek intellectuals. He declared to them the "unknown God" worshipped at a certain Greek temple, and the verses quoted at the beginning of this chapter. Here the apostle agrees with what we learn from the earliest chapters of Genesis, and from modern archaeology and anthropology: Mankind progressed, probably about five thousand years, ago from being wandering herders and nomads ("hunter-gatherers" with some animal husbandry) to the beginning of what we know as "civilization" today, with its roots in settled agriculture and villages—what Paul calls the "boundaries of habitation" (Acts 17:26). Once mankind began to "settle down" in this way, it opened up the possibility of developing many things which we take for granted today: written language; a literate cultural elite; economic means based on something other than food production and trading of basic commodities; a specialized, religious priesthood; etc. In other words, Paul teaches that in order for humans to begin to develop some kind of organized religion, however vague and misguided the attempt may be to "grope for Him" and/or "find Him," we need to first settle down in communities that are self-perpetuating, able to transmit things like spiritual revelations, texts, prosperity, and empirical knowledge from one generation to the next. The most defining features of such civilization are a written language; and second is what the apostle refers to as "appointed times," i.e., calendar, feasts, and holidays—most often based on the agricultural cycles and seasons unique to every part of the earth.[43]

---

[43] This helps to explain why the apostle so vehemently opposed the wholesale Gentile adoption of the Jewish calendar. He knew that most of the biblical Jewish feasts are timed to, and have foundational meaning, in the unique climate and planting/harvest cycles of the eastern Mediterranean. Clearly, the apostle had a healthy respect for other cultures, believing that God was somehow present at the formation of their boundaries and times (feasts, etc.). This is the foundation for the gospel, which goes out to redeem and transform cultures, bringing out the deepest meaning of many ancient customs while filtering out their idolatrous, morally corrupt practices. All one has to do is think about the peoples in the Southern Hemisphere—their agricultural calendar is opposite to the biblical one! A wholesale adoption of the biblical feasts/ calendar would make no sense.

Imagine a person today who drops out of school at an early age, and is then forced to move several times between different countries, each time learning enough of the local spoken language to "get by." As an adult he is illiterate, and very uncertain about who he is—his sense of identity is very mixed-up. You could share the gospel of salvation with such a man, but it will be difficult to explain to him many biblical concepts. He can't read the Bible, and if he goes to church, he can barely understand what is being sung or taught. Without long training and education, such a person would likely be very unstable; and it is hard to imagine him/her becoming a successful and fruit-bearing disciple of Yeshua. Think of it: You are able to read and understand (hopefully!) the ideas set forth in this book in your native, educated language—but it took you how many years of education and enculturating to be able to do so? In our modern, literate societies we can easily take for granted what a great and precious gift this is.

So this is the first reason behind Paul's teaching in 1 Corinthians 7: There is an inevitable necessity to culture based on a corporate, "civilized" identity. We need it in order to feel grounded in this world; we need it in order to be able to successfully search for God, find Him, know Him in ever-deepening ways, and transmit this knowledge to future generations through written texts. In short, we need the integrity of a settled, ethnic/social identity in order to succeed in this age—and the next!

2. The Importance of Israel's Continuing, Irrevocable Call (Rom. 11:28–29)

As we will study more in depth later, Paul's one-new-man teaching of the transformation of significant parts of Israel's Torah in no way implies some kind of "replacement theology," by which Israel's call as a chosen nation is either cancelled or replaced by others. In other words, Paul's gospel of reconciliation was not about the crucifixion of Jewish identity for crucifixion's sake, but rather so that covenantal, Jewish identity could be resurrected, set free in order to serve the fullness of God's purposes—especially to be a light to the nations (Rom. 11:11–15). We might say that he taught a kind of *unity amidst continuing distinctions*—not a bland uniformity; he saw that if God's "gifts and calling" for Israel are "irrevocable" (Rom. 11:29), then it means that the integrity of Jewish identity—in Christ—must somehow be preserved.[44] That there is "no longer Jew or Gentile" in Christ is a statement at the highest level of personal, spiritual relationship with God; it is not a statement concerning the ongoing validity (or not) of Jewish—or any other—ethnic identity. Conversely, as Jesus also spoke in John's Revelation, Paul was not in favor of somehow diluting Jewish uniqueness by Gentile Christians taking on some kind of quasi-Jewish identity (Rev. 3:9).

3. Loving Witness

In writing to the Jews and Gentiles in the church at Rome, the apostle spoke of the need to never put a "stumbling block" in the way of a brother who may be of a "weaker" faith (Rom. 14:13–18). In this particular context, he was talking about foods and calendar issues among believers, but we can extend the meaning to all Christian witness: Morally "neutral" cultural practices must never be allowed to become a stumbling block to those of weak faith, or of no faith (those being witnessed to). Imagine (as many Torah teachers today are trying to reintroduce to believers) that Paul had not written what he did about Torah; imagine that the gospel "line" had followed the Judaizing teachers in Galatia. This would mean that everywhere that the faith spreads, the earliest believers from that nation or ethnicity would essentially convert to a kind of Messianic Judaism (or Jewish Christianity)—quickly abandoning key elements of their own culture. While this might attract a few at first, the vast majority—especially those with a strong sense of ethnic-national identification, like the leaders of society and the cultural

---

[44] This book is not primarily one on instructing Jewish believers in how to maintain Jewish identity by keeping a Messianic Torah. There are many good books out there on this subject—see *Jewish Roots* by Dan Juster, etc.

elite—would be deeply offended by this witness. "What?" they might say, "Believing in the one true Christian (and Jewish!) God means I have to stop being (Chinese, French, Japanese, etc.)?"

Paul's one-new-man gospel laid the foundation for what modern missiologists call the "contextualization" of the gospel—or the necessity of the essential gospel to adapt itself to the cultural norms and expressions of the local people while, of course, adhering to biblical standards (commands!) of morality, and the prohibition against any form of idol worship. This becomes hugely important when the gospel crosses ethnic or national boundaries that are permeated with enmity resulting from long histories of conflict, competition, racism, and the like.

For example, here in China (from where I currently write), for most of history the Christian faith was viewed as a foreign religion—most recently associated with the hostile, colonizing western powers of the nineteenth century. Ever since the first entry of Christianity to China in the sixth or seventh centuries, there have always been native backlashes against the missionaries and their Chinese converts. But today, after the huge revival of the last generation, there are 80–100 million Chinese Christians—few of them connected by organization or denomination with foreign churches. On any given day now in China, the non-Christian can encounter a Chinese Christian witness that is 100% indigenous. The gospel, which originated thousands of years ago from among the Jewish people, is now part of the context, the social landscape, of the Chinese nation. Yeshua, Jesus, 耶稣(Yesu) our collective "elder brother" (Rom. 8:29) can now be seen by millions of Chinese not as a westerner or a foreigner, but as one of them!

4. The Redemption/Transformation of an Entire Nation or People Group

This is the final rationale for Paul's emphasis on the importance of continuing ethnic/national identity in Christ—one which we will look at in more detail in later chapters. God's plan is for the "yeast" of the gospel of the kingdom of God (Matt. 13:33, 24:14) to permeate the culture of every tribe, tongue, and nation. Thus, it is required of the believers who represent each and every ethnic group to demonstrate the "manifold wisdom of God" (Eph. 3:10) in the real-time, down-to-earth contexts of their own social realities. Just as with loving witness, this requires an integrity of social and cultural identity. For the yeast of the kingdom to successfully transform a society, like Japan for example, it would require that Japanese Christians function and rise with integrity in every major sphere of their society. Imagine if they came under the teaching of the Judaizers in Galatia (or many a One Torah teacher today). These Japanese believers would literally cut themselves off from many family and corporate events simply because of the all the unkosher food that they would be almost forced to eat!

In conclusion, God is love and love always has a down-to-earth human context. Part of the message of the incarnation of the Son of God is that in order to redeem us, God had to come into our world—which by necessity means a particular place, people, tribe, and culture. Even though the message of salvation is one which transcends all such boundaries, at the same it respects those boundaries and even has a plan for our distinctions to be a blessing to one another—what has come to be known in some circles as an "economy of mutual blessing."

9

ONE NEW MAN—THE PATRIARCHAL COVENANT(S) AS THE PRIMARY FOUNDATION FOR JEWISH IDENTITY, PART 1

From these the coastlands of the nations were separated into their lands, every one according to his language, according to their families, into their nations. (Gen. 10:5)

When they came to the nations where they went, they profaned My holy name, because it was said of them, "These are the people of the LORD; yet they have come out of His land." (Ezek. 36:20)

In this chapter and the next, I bring this one-new-man teaching into our own day, applying it to present-day calling and identity issues for Jewish believers.

Introduction: Messianic Jewish Identity, Diaspora vs. Israel

On a recent visit to the US, I visited several Messianic Jewish congregations . . . and I was a little shocked. The experience was much like a traditional synagogue—far more so than ninety-nine percent of the

congregations in Israel; and during the very liturgical worship and message, I think I heard the word "Torah" twenty-eight times, and "Yeshua"
only seven times. (Yes, I actually started to count!) And, when "Yeshua"
was mentioned, it was often tagged on the end of a traditional, Jewish
prayer, "*b'shem* Yeshua—in Jesus' name." While the number of men-
tions is not necessarily an accurate barometer of theology, it nonetheless
reflects something that many have noticed: The Messianic congregations in the Diaspora—especially the US where they are most developed—seem to be far more oriented toward "Torah" and establishing a
clear identity as a Messianic *Judaism* than those in Israel.

I also am an American Jew, who spent five years in the Messianic
movement there before making *Aliyah* (emigrating) to Israel in 1998.
I was in involved as a leader in a UMJC congregation, and attended
many national conferences, seminars, and the like. I can testify to the
following: In the American movement, there is a great deal of time and
energy expended—both at the leadership level of theological training
and discussion, and at the level of the weekly service—to clearly establish Messianic *Jewish* identity. And not surprisingly, this identity finds
its primary expression in the same *dogma*-Torah commandments as in
traditional Judaism: Sabbath, calendar, *kashruth,* etc. Further, amidst
the context of the plurality of Judaisms in the US (orthodox, conservative, reform, reconstructionist), great (and worthy) efforts have been
made to express the faith in Yeshua as a kind of Judaism and not simply
a subset of Christianity, a religion that is viewed as foreign and "Gentile" by most Jews. In many cases, this has included the incorporation of
traditional Jewish liturgy—including some of the prayers we studied in
Chapter 4—into the Messianic worship service.[45]

All of this makes sense in the Diaspora context where, of course,
Jews are a tiny minority. In the modern West, and especially in the super-
melting-pot of the US, "assimilation" and "intermarriage" (marriage

---

[45] In some cases this is done "wholesale"; in others, the Jewish liturgy is tweaked to reflect new-
covenant teachings.

with a Gentile) are huge, oft-debated issues for the Jewish community. Maintaining a unique, Jewish, covenantal identity—in what is perhaps the most pluralistic society in the history of humankind—is no small challenge! It takes a great deal of teaching and intentionality—as many Jewish believers are from a more secular background, and less familiar with Jewish practice and liturgy. As difficult as this may be for the wider Jewish community, there is an additional challenge for the Messianic Jewish congregation—one which brings the issue of one new man into sharp focus: There are great numbers of American, non-Jewish believers in Jesus looking for "biblical" culture and a sense of daily rootedness in the midst of so much cultural uncertainty; and many such people have found what they're looking for at a "Messianic" congregation.

To the serious Bible-believing person, popular American culture seems to become more perverted, godless, and materialistic every day. This, when coupled with the strong critique of traditional church customs, traditions, and theology found in the wider Messianic movement,[46] adds up to the ironic situation that in a majority of "Messianic" congregations in the US, there is a minority of Jews! In fact, there are some congregations with not a single Jew—only Gentiles who believe that this Messianic-Torah-Hebrew roots faith and practice is either the only correct one, or the one that they feel most comfortable with![47] As such, at least one group, the Union of Messianic Jewish Congregations, felt the need some ten years ago to specifically define a member congregation as one whose primary identity is to be a "congregational home to the *Jewish* believer!" In other words, we shouldn't leave out the "Jewish" part in "Messianic Jewish"—and that means Jewish people![48]

---

[46] Dan Juster calls this Messianic "church bashing" (from many conversations with him).

[47] Is it possible to apply 1 Cor. 7:17-23 to these brothers and sisters: they are supposed to maintain their non-Jewish identity, but what identity?! An American melting pot one? Madonna, KFC, and Michael Jackson? Baseball, hot dogs, and apple pie?

[48] A colleague, once teaching (rebuking?) at a "Messianic" congregation in Japan—one without a single Jew in it—said, "you can't make chicken soup without chicken! And you can't have a Messianic congregation without Jews!"

In Israel, the situation is radically different. It is the Jewish State—eighty percent of the population are Jews. Our primary language is Hebrew, and Arabic for the other twenty percent of the population. The national holy days are based on the biblical calendar, and our weekly day off is the Saturday Sabbath, beginning Friday at sundown. Sunday is the first day of the week, a day of work and study. Our most popular national foods are based on the Mediterranean chickpea—hummus and falafel—not a cheeseburger, fries, and cola (you can find these in Israel—but they don't stand up to their American counterparts!). Jewish history and basic knowledge of the OT are part of the normal school curriculum, and national service mandatory for all eighteen-year-olds. In Israeli cities, the streets are named after famous events and personages in Jewish and Israeli history. What's more, there is no real plurality of Judaisms; traditional Orthodoxy, in its many varieties, is the official religion of the Jewish state, enjoying many privileges and great political power.

What all of this means for an Israeli, Messianic Jewish person or congregation is that our priorities are different from our brethren in the Diaspora. First and foremost, the defensive struggle to maintain a Jewish identity is much less pronounced. Without much effort, our society and culture provides us, from childhood, with a strong sense of "Israeli Jewishness," only partly based on Torah and Judaism (and sometimes not at all![49])—in other words, a strong ethnic-national identity, much like many other nations in the world. This means—and I hope my brothers in the US will forgive me for saying so—that in Israeli congregations we are much more free to focus our time and energy on the central, universal truths of the gospel and the kingdom of God, and less on Torah observance and identity issues.[50]

---

[49] Increasingly, there are many secular Israelis whose sense of identity has nothing to do with Torah or Judaism.

[50] Many have noticed that Messianic congregations in Israel tend to resemble those in other nations, just with everything conducted in Hebrew, and with some light Torah elements. For some, this is a negative; for others a positive (more on this later).

How does all this connect with what we've been studying? What does all of this mean for the one new man?

Genesis 10; the Table of Nations; and the Unchanging Sources of Biblical, National Identity

Genesis 10—the so-called "Table of Nations"—is really the beginning of the patriarchal period of biblical history, the world into which Abraham, Isaac, and Jacob were born. It records the establishing of the original "nations" (*goyim* in Hebrew, also later the plural "Gentiles") of the earth after the flood, all descended from Noah's three sons. At the end of each nation's genealogy is the same refrain: The nations are separated into their lands, every one "according to his language, according to their families, into their nations" (v. 5, 20, 31). Herein is contained a simple yet profound definition of the three elements which buttress the identity of ancient people groups as they came to form a "nation": land, language, and family/tribe. According to Genesis 10, every nation was founded on these three pillars: a people starting off as a family descended from a great, founding ancestor; an ancestral homeland; and a unique language. These elements then provide a stable foundation for future cultural developments. The land determines the climate, the seasons, the relationship to the astral elements, the timing of agricultural feasts, etc.; the language determines the literature, religious expression, government; and the stories of the ancestors, provide a sense of corporate rootedness in the past and hope for the future. In this way, tribes and/or nations preserve their historical and cultural memories, narratives, and celebrations—all of which cement an ongoing sense of their corporate identity.

Not surprisingly, this is exactly what we see when we study God's promises to Abraham and his descendants—to make them to be a great *goy* (singular of "Gentile") or "nation" (Gen. 12:2). First, God makes a unique covenant with Abraham, which is then repeated and ratified in the succeeding two generations. God, known to them as El Shaddai, becomes the "God of Israel"—of Abraham, Isaac, and

Jacob-Israel. These three become the patriarchs—the great, noble, founding ancestors of the Jewish nation. God's first, and oft-repeated, promise to Abraham is of many offspring—of a great nation that will come into being through them (Gen. 13:16; 15:5; 17:1–2, 4–7, 15–21; 22:17; 26:24; 27:28–29). The second element of the patriarchal promises—repeated almost as many times as the first—is that of the ancestral homeland, the land of Canaan, the future land of Israel (Gen. 12:7; 13:14–15; 15:18; 17:8; 26:3–5; 28:14–15).[51] Third, we know that by the time of the generation of his grandson Jacob, Abraham's descendants were speaking an increasingly unique language, Hebrew, which developed both from the ancient Aramaic of Abraham and his immediate family and from the local Canaanite language of Isaac and Jacob's generations.[52]

These elements from Genesis are the unalterable foundations of any nation; if you remove one of them, as when a people is totally exiled or removed from its land for several generations, it usually spells the end

---

[51] As a Messianic Jewish, "biblical Zionist," it's almost embarrassing to realize how central and numerous are the "land promises" in the Abrahamic covenant. There is great controversy in the body of Christ surrounding the issue of the present-day validity of these promises and their applicability to the modern-day Jewish state. Over the last decade or so, we have witnessed many conferences in Israel bringing together Christians who preach that these so-called "land promises" have all been fulfilled in the gospel of Christ—and are thus no longer valid to the Jewish people or nation, effectively denying the biblical validity of modern Zionism. Yet, I have yet to hear any discussion that takes seriously what I am presenting here: that according to Paul and the NT, the patriarchal promises are the very foundation for the gospel of grace and the one new man; so shouldn't this mean that the new covenant, while rarely mentioning the land issue, can be understood to actually be reinforcing the irrevocability of *all* the promises to the offspring of Abraham, Isaac, and Jacob? Or is the only valid patriarchal promise in the NT the one that pertains to personal, spiritual salvation for all individuals?

[52] I base this on modern linguistic research, and the covenant pillar between Laban (his uncle) and Jacob in Genesis 31:47 (also see Isaiah 19:18). Their grandfathers, Nahor and Abraham, were brothers, sons of Terah. Laban and his side of the family remained in Ur and never journeyed to Canaan. Laban gives the pillar an Aramaic name, and Jacob a Hebrew name. This is probably one of the reasons why God gives Jacob (and not Isaac) a new name, Israel, which becomes the eternal name of the covenant nation; He waited until there had been two full generations born and raised in "the land," developing their own language and culture, that of the "Hebrews."

of the existence of that people as a unique nation. Or, if one nation is conquered by another and slowly adapts the language and culture of its conquerors, eventually this will mean assimilation and the death of any uniqueness for that people group. Or, if a nation loses all sense of connection or respect for its past and its founding ancestors, this will usually spell decline for the nation in the same way.[53] (See Paul's commentary on the fifth commandment, to "honor your father and mother . . . so that it may be well with you and that you may live long on the earth [in the land]"; Eph. 6:1–3.)

Notice what is missing in all the patriarchal narratives: no mention of Sabbaths, calendar, foods, purity laws, etc.—all the things that came hundreds of years later with the giving of Torah at Mount Sinai.[54] There is only one ritualistic element that is given by God to the Abrahamic family—circumcision, as *the* sign of the covenant (Gen. 17).[55] What this means is simply that the ancient Hebrew nation, like every other in the ancient (and most of the modern) world, found its deepest sense of identity, rootedness, and cohesion in these three elements—family/tribe, land, and language—not in later *dogma-stoichea* customs and commandments, the form and practice of which can

---

[53] This is one way of understanding what is happening in the US today, or many European countries: a total disrespect for the faith and values of the founding ancestors—take homosexual marriage as an example. Even in a non-ethnic, non-tribal nation like the US, this is certainly a recipe for decline and judgment.

[54] Yes, I am aware of Genesis 26:5: "because Abraham obeyed Me and kept My charge, My commandments, My statutes and My laws." But in context, this can only mean that he (and his sons) kept the "Torah" which they were aware of, which more resembles the universal Torah of the Messiah of the NT than it does the *dogma*-Torah commandments of Moses' time. Exodus 6:3 confirms this understanding, as God declares to Moses that the Patriarchs did not know Him as YHVH, but only as El Shaddai. This is not just about divine nomenclature, but the accompanying revelation that comes with a new stage in salvation history, where God's name is also updated, i.e., El Shaddai > YHVH > Yeshua.

[55] It could be argued that Genesis 32:32 is a dietary law (not eating the tendon attached to the hip). But it is not something spoken by God as commandment, only treated as explaining a contemporary custom of Moses' time.

change drastically according to time, place, and influences from other cultures.[56]

This understanding, central to Paul's teaching on the place of Torah and the one new man, is in direct conflict with that of the rabbis. In rabbinic Judaism—in its prayers, theology, and practice—the foundation of Jewish identity is found at the foot and the peak of Mount Sinai. According to the rabbis, only here did the Jewish people actually become a cohesive people, the people of God. The giving of Torah at Mount Sinai, through Moshe (Moses), is celebrated as *the* central event of OT "salvation history"; and this Torah—with *all* of its commandments—becomes *the* holy standard for all other revelation and practice.

This helps explain why Paul's teaching was (and still is!) so controversial to the Jewish people: His doctrine of Torah under the new covenant effectively lowers the place of the Sinai revelation (the epicenter of Pharisaic-rabbinic Judaism), while exalting patriarchal covenant, faith, and practice. Under Paul, Mount Sinai gets a lot lower, if you will, a lot smaller—while Mount Moriah (Gen. 22) seems to grow higher and higher. But this seemingly puts a major dent in the sense of Jewish chosenness and uniqueness; in effect, Paul's doctrine of Torah puts Jewish, *dogma*-Torah based culture on a level playing field with that of the nations—effectively returning us to the equality and simplicity of national identity found in Genesis 10. Is Paul then saying that the Torah from Mount Sinai is essentially a bad thing for Jewish identity? No, as he says in Romans 7:12 (cf. 9:4), "the [Torah] is holy,

---

[56] While the basic elements of Jewish, Torah practice have stayed the same, there is a huge variation in custom among different groups—Ashkenazi, Sephardi, etc. There has always been much debate concerning the practical details of *kashrut*, Sabbath, etc. The Japanese are another classic example of this principle: their *dogma-stoichea* culture has gone through radical changes throughout history—from Korean to Chinese influence; then German and American in the modern period. Contemporary Japanese culture is perhaps the most syncretistic and adaptable in the world. But there have remained three unchangeables: land, language, and the sense of unique familyhood as being descended from, or related to the imperial family and its ancestors. And so the Japanese are still very much Japanese!

and the commandment is holy and righteous and good."[57] But from the one-new-man perspective of the gospel and the Abrahamic adoption going out to the nations, the major problem with Sinai is a simple one: Only the Jewish nation was there; the Gentile nations were not. In other words, it is the collective, Jewish national covenant—and therefore cannot function in that way for any other nation. It can't be repeated. This is why Judaism, despite its universal claims and a few converts, can never break the mold of only being the "tribal religion" of the Jewish nation.

This is the great insight of the gospel according to Paul: To the degree that the Sinai covenant is "exalted" by preaching *dogma*-Torah commands as universally valid standards of holiness or righteousness, it becomes a great stumbling block to God's plan to redeem the Gentile nations, fulfilling His promise to Abraham to make him the "father of many nations." Instead, the simplicity of Abrahamic faith—starting with one man (not an entire people)—is more fit to the worldwide spreading of the gospel and national transformation, which will happen one person at a time without the benefit of a collective, national, Mount-Sinai-style revelation from God.

---

[57] "Extrabiblical" or "extra-Torah" Jewish history includes important developments that add to historical memory: We are a people who have a particular history with God—from the Exodus, to the experience of Sinai, to the exile, return, exile, and then return again. This memory includes many "highs" but also many tragic "lows." Jewish celebrations and days of remembrance (some connected to the Torah, some not) maintain that fullness of historical memory and also point to the ultimate fulfillments of the last days and the age to come.

10

ONE NEW MAN—THE PATRIARCHAL COVENANT(S) AS THE PRIMARY FOUNDATION FOR JEWISH IDENTITY, PART 2

What I am saying is this: the Law, which came four hundred and thirty years later, does not invalidate a covenant previously ratified by God, so as to nullify the promise. For if the inheritance is based on law, it is no longer based on a promise; but God has granted it to Abraham by means of a promise. (Gal. 3:17–18)

Patriarchal Covenant vs. Mosaic Covenant Identity in Jewish History

Given this understanding from Genesis 10 in the previous chapter, it is not surprising that Jewish exile from the land of Israel brings on a profound "identity crisis" for the Jewish people. For example, hundreds of years after Mount Sinai, a great change took place in Israelite identity and culture because of God's judgment of the nation that resulted in the destruction of the first temple and the Babylonian exile. With the loss of land and temple, and somewhat of language (the Judeans were forced to adapt the Babylonian Aramaic as their daily, spoken language), we see the beginnings of synagogue- (not temple-) based, Pharisaic-led, Diaspora Judaism. This is why the central text of rabbinic Judaism until this day, the Babylonian Talmud, is written in Aramaic, not in Hebrew! Even after the partial restoration of Judea seventy years later, the glory of God did not visit the temple as when the first one was dedicated under Solomon (2 Chr. 5:14; Ezra 6:16–18).[58] Simply put, when the chosen people is forced to live outside of the Promised Land, it brings on a great crisis in our identity and calling as God's people.

Yet, whatever loss of national identity took place during and after the Babylonian exile, it pales in comparison to what happened over the last two thousand years. As with the first exile, this one began with the destruction of the nation and its capital—Jerusalem. But the Romans were more systematic than the Babylonians, especially after the Bar-Kochba Rebellion of 133–136, in removing practically every Jew from the land of Israel. We lost our land and language (not totally, but close)[59] for not just seventy years, but almost two thousand! This should have spelled the end of the Jewish people's existence as a unique people.

However, even while being dispersed among many nations, we somehow were able to maintain our tribal identity. I know of no other example in human history of a people being totally separated from its homeland for so long, yet maintaining its unique identity—including the hope of a national restoration—and then seeing it take place on the stage of world history!

How did we do this? The first, and by far most important, answer is: We didn't do it, God did! In Scriptures like Jeremiah 31:35–37, the Lord promises that as long as the sun and moon continue to rise and

---

[58] Haggai 2:6–9 promises a time when the "latter glory of this house will be greater than its former glory."

[59] Hebrew was preserved as the Bible was preserved and studied, but it was done so and discussed by using the other living (spoken) languages of Diaspora Jewish communities, e.g., Aramaic, Greek, Arabic, Ladino, and Yiddish.

set and function as they should, the descendants of Israel would not cease to be a nation before Him. Because of Israel's role as a covenantal testimony to the truth of God's Word, God made sure to keep us a unique people despite the humanly impossible circumstances. He did this for the glory of His great name (see also Ezekiel 36)! But if you were to ask most Jews (and Gentiles) how it is that we maintained a unique identity, a majority would say: "It's because of our Judaism, our keeping of the *mitzvoth* (commandments) of *kashruth,* Shabbat, circumcision, the holidays, etc." In other words, on the earthly plane of history and culture it was these *dogma*-Torah practices, as instructed by the rabbis, that helped to maintain our uniqueness, keeping us a recognizably separate people with a hope of a national, even "Messianic" restoration. This points to what we learned (in Chapters 6 and 7) as an important, continuing function of the *dogma*-Torah commands—namely, the preservation of Jewish identity, *especially* in the absence of two of the three patriarchal foundations for national identity: land and language.

But now, over the last one hundred years, the situation has changed dramatically. The Jewish people are back in the land—speaking Hebrew, and developing a society and a unique culture in our ancestral homeland. *The foundational, biblical, and patriarchal conditions for nationhood and identity are once again a reality!* In light of what we have learned about the ultimate abolishing (or at least, transforming) of the *dogma*-Torah commandments under the new covenant, we must see the preservation of our people by means of the same commandments as a temporary "accommodation" by God, who ultimately kept us by divine grace. That is, we must see that God's highest purpose for Jewish covenantal identity (as in the one-new-man dynamic of unity, reconciliation, and being a blessing to the nations) finds its "center of gravity" in a Jewishness rooted in the patriarchal elements of Genesis—while the later practices of the Torah are given a place that has to be applied according to new-covenant, one-new-man realities. The full inheritance is firstly based on patriarchal promises and realities, not on a *dogma*-Torah-based identity: we are a people/nation of the land before we are people of the Book (Torah)![60]

All of this is in keeping with Paul's teaching in Galatians 3:15-22: "What I am saying is this: the Law, which came four hundred and thirty years later, does not invalidate a covenant previously ratified by God, so as to nullify the promise. For if the inheritance is based on law, it is no longer based on a promise; but God has granted it to Abraham by means of a promise" (v. 17–18). In the Galatians context, of course, Paul is talking about salvation and covenantal inclusion of the Gentiles without observance of *dogma*-Torah commands, not about ultimate Jewish inheritance/possession of the land. But what prevents us from applying the logic of these verses (and Paul's theology, in general) in an inverse way back to our ultimate Jewish inheritance and identity in the land—as promised to the same patriarch, Abraham?[61] We can similarly conclude that the fullness of God's inheritance for us is first and foremost based on the patriarchal promises of land, language, and nation—not the temporal, conditional *dogma*-Torah commands which came four hundred years later!

As we learned from our study of 1 Corinthians 7:17–23 in Chapters 6 and 7, and from the lifestyle of the apostle himself, the *dogma*-Torah commands continue to play a positive role in defining Jewish culture and identity—but not with the same force of commandment as they once held. You might say that during the 1,900 years of exile, there was a special "grace" on these commandments to maintain Jewish identity in the Diaspora. But over the last one hundred years this

---

[60] Of course there is a paradox here: the *dogma*-Torah still function to maintain distinction—but no longer as *the* primary source of covenantal identity or spirituality; and in the land, there is a pattern of life and celebration that naturally fits the new covenant order which has its roots in the Torah.

[61] Nothing prevents it, of course, except an understanding of Christianity that focuses exclusively on personal salvation; or one which sees the church as wholly replacing Israel (supercessionism/replacement theology).

grace is quickly fading; and not surprisingly, the Diaspora Jewish communities are increasingly plagued by the issue of assimilation as at no other time in Jewish history.[62] Similarly, as already mentioned, the major *dogma*-commands of calendar, dietary laws, and circumcision now function as a foundational part of the national culture of the modern-day Jewish state of Israel. According to the full counsel of God as found in the Scriptures—old and new covenants alike—these later *dogma*-Torah commands find their fullest and most "natural" expression as the national culture of the Jewish people dwelling in our land, speaking our language. It is simply a question of the right order: Like a tree, the patriarchal covenantal elements of land, tribe, and language are the roots, the foundation; while the later *dogma*-Torah commands are like the branches, fruit, and flowers of Jewish life. If the two are in their proper place, there is a strong, healthy, and beautiful tree—one which can bear much fruit on behalf of the nations.[63] But if the *dogma*-Torah commands become the center, or the "root" of Jewish identity—as in the Diaspora—it is an unnatural, "unhealthy," and confusing situation.

This is why I quoted Ezekiel 36:20 at the beginning of the previous chapter, as this short verse contains a world of truth for us: Insofar as our people exist in the Diaspora—and not in the land of Israel—we *profane His holy name.* Why? Because heaven and Earth, principalities, powers, kings and all manner of sceptics can simultaneously look at our situation of exile (*galut*) and the promises of the Bible and say, "These are the people of YHVH, but they have left His land . . . there is a problem with God's Word; it cannot be trusted as written." But there's more to this verse than just the absence of our physical presence from the land

---

[62] In the US, by far the largest Diaspora Jewish population (six million), the intermarriage rate over the last generation is close to fifty percent! This is only one barometer of the fact that traditional Jewish practices are losing their power to keep Diaspora Jewish identity.

[63] Indeed, the *dogma*-Torah commands were given in part to preserve the full memory of our history with God—from Abraham forward—and to point us to our eschatological future and the future of the whole world (see Deut. 26:5ff). The pattern of Sabbath and feasts was especially oriented to the agricultural year of Israel and then added later, historical content.

of Israel: to the degree that we have existed, and become comfortable in the Diaspora, our Jewish identity is based by necessity on a Judaism whose core (because of the lack of land and language) is the *dogma*-Torah commandments of Moses—especially Sabbaths/calendar, dietary laws, and circumcision. This means that even as Jewish people have begun to return to Yeshua and new-covenant faith, the fullness of that identity and calling is incomplete (by two-thirds?), insofar as it is based on a Messianic Jewish identity rooted in the *dogma*-Torah commands. It also means, as we will see, that the power to properly express and display the one new man together with the believers from the Gentile nations is greatly compromised.

For almost two thousand years, there wasn't much we could do about this "profanity" of God's name and His promise—but for the last 120 years, and especially since 1948, things have changed dramatically. We have entered a season where the curtain has been lifted on a new "act" of end-times fulfillment, in which it is time to see the fullness of all things spoken of in the prophets concerning the restoration of Israel, and the fullness of the nations (Gentiles) (Luke 21:24; Acts 3:21; Rom. 11:25–26). During this time, the continuing Jewish presence in the Diaspora is a "profanity" and a source of confusion to the spiritual world and the body of Christ. One verse which beautifully captures the promise of Jewish return to the Land and its consequence for the nations is Isaiah 27:6: "In the days to come Jacob will take root, Israel will blossom and sprout; and they will fill the whole world with fruit." This should remind of us of the olive tree imagery from Romans 11: As the Jewish people are rooted in the patriarchal promises of land, language, and nation—and in the gospel of Messiah Yeshua!—this root is to become a great source of fruit, of blessing, of revival and fullness for all the nations (Gentiles), the so-called "wild branches" grafted into the same covenantal, gospel tree (Rom. 11:17).

This means that if we Jews really want to embrace the fullness of our identity, gift, and calling, then it is time to come home to Israel! Only in doing so can we become a source of blessing to the nations, helping to extend the fatherhood of Abraham to many nations as we mutually submit to one another in one-new-man relationship. Only when we are rooted in the patriarchal promises and sources of our Jewish culture and identity—tribe, tongue, land—can we have the confidence to go out to the nations without fear of losing that identity, or having it be over-whelmed by so many Gentiles (sometimes well-meaning, sometimes misguided) in their own search for covenantal identity.

Of course, we have to be empathetic in the present situation and support those Messianic Jews in the Diaspora who are being prevented from returning by the Israeli government due to their belief in Yeshua. And we also have to embrace the callings of Messianic Jews in the Dias-pora who have callings of evangelism that are successful in that setting. But we must embrace the reality that the general thrust of biblical truth, and the historical trajectory of the last 120 years, dictates that it is time for us to return to Israel if at all possible!

Therefore, the potential for us—the descendants of Abraham, Isaac, and Jacob—to *fully* enter into our gifts and calling is here (Rom. 11:28). It's as if history were waiting for this moment, when all the elements for *fullness,* both for Israel and the nations, is in place: the Jewish people in our land; a restored nation and language according to the patriarchal promises; faith in Yeshua; the baptism in the Holy Spirit; the link with remnants from every other nation . . . together the one new man! For the fullness of the nations, we must see fullness in Israel; fullness in Israel means fullness in our land according to the promise—no nation can be blessed in its land without blessing Israel in hers.

But there's more: The one new man of Paul continues to instruct us concerning a great mystery, namely that "that the Gentiles are fel-low heirs and fellow members of the body, and fellow partakers of the promise in Christ Jesus through the gospel" (Eph. 3:6). In Romans 11:11–28, the apostle describes the same mystery from another angle: The fullness of the Gentile nations, in Christ, brings about the fullness of the restoration of Israel and "all Israel will be saved" (Rom. 11:26). We will study these themes in greater depth in the last chapters of this book.

Brothers and sisters, we are living in a time of amazing fulfillment of these ancient, unconditional promises to our father Abraham—to make him to be the father of many nations, and to see his promised seed fully established in the land of promise.

11

ONE NEW MAN—THE PATRIARCHAL COVENANT(S) AS THE FOUNDATION FOR GENTILE IDENTITY

*And I will appoint You as a **covenant of the people**, as a light to the nations . . . to restore the land, to make them inherit the desolate heritages.* (Isa. 42:6; 49:8, emphasis added)

*As for Me, behold, My covenant with you, and you will be the father of a multitude of nations. No longer shall your name be called Abram, but your name shall be Abraham; **for I will make you the father of a multitude of nations.*** (Gen. 17:4–5, emphasis added)

In Ephesians 3:1–6 and Colossians 1:25–29 the apostle Paul proclaims God's special grace on his ministry to the Gentiles, and declares something extraordinary: that what God is doing among Jew and Gentile was something that "in other generations was not made known to the sons of men, as it has now been revealed to His holy apostles and prophets by the Spirit" (Eph. 3:5). This is to say that the OT prophets didn't quite see this coming—and this is extraordinary because it comes from the pen of a man who in all of his letters goes to such lengths to solidly establish his teaching on the OT Scriptures. By comparison, he never says such a thing about any other key biblical doctrine like justification by faith—he simply shows how this can be learned from the OT life of Abraham, and other prophecies like Habakkuk 2:4 ("the righteous will live by his faith"). But when it came to this issue of the one new man—of God pouring out His spirit of adoption on "pagan sinners," while a majority of Jews refused the gospel—Paul had to confess that this was something that a simple reading of OT Scripture simply didn't bear witness to. It is a special mystery, a surprising revelation, that is only "now" being revealed to His NT "holy apostles and prophets."

To better understand why this is such a deep mystery (or revelation), in this chapter we will first look at what exactly the OT prophets believed and saw concerning the end of days, Israel, and the Gentiles. We don't have space to do a survey of all the OT prophets, and so we will focus on the one who is, by far, the most quoted in the NT: Isaiah. And with good reason, since he had the loftiest and most detailed visions of a worldwide kingdom of God with its capital in Jerusalem. We can summarize his vision as follows:

1. The Jewish King Messiah will restore the united kingdom of his "father" David, with its throne and center in Jerusalem (Isa. 9:6–7, 2:1–3).

2. The Davidic Messiah will rule not just his own Jewish empire, but establish His reign of righteousness and peace over the entire world (Isa. 2:3–4, 11:1–10; Zech. 14:9)!

3. As a result of this "fullness" of the kingdom in Israel, the Gentiles will come to honor and worship the King of Israel and the God of Israel, including bringing up to Jerusalem their offerings (Isa. 52:8–9, 11:10). According to Isaiah (and others), the order of the coming of the Messianic kingdom to this earth is clear: First comes the "fullness" of the kingdom to Israel, symbolized by

the redemption of Jerusalem; and only then His salvation is seen unto the "ends of the earth" (Isa. 52:10).[64]

Thus, according to the most universal vision of Israel's prophets, there was a place for the Gentile nations in the kingdom—after all, the God of Abraham, Isaac, and Israel is the one, true Creator God of all peoples—so He must have some kind of plan to include them![65] But according to the OT prophets, the place of Gentiles in this plan was very much secondary to Israel: All the "action," all the focus of God's promises, seems to center on Israel; the surrounding nations are seen mostly in a negative light, as those who oppose God's kingdom plans in Israel. It is only when we see the full Messianic, Davidic restoration take place that the Gentiles come into play *positively*—as worshipers, supporters, servants but *never as full heirs or citizens of the kingdom of God*, like the Jews (e.g., Isa. 60:1–14). The Gentiles are there, but there is little said about their individual nations or histories; they are there, but they are definitely second-class citizens in an essentially Jewish, Israeli kingdom.

God's Plan for the Nations—Genesis 17:4–5

Yet, there are hints in OT Scriptures of a more glorious, divine plan for the nations. First is the Hebrew of Genesis 17:4–5, quoted and translated at the beginning of this chapter. This is a key verse, as God expands Abram's name to "Abraham," symbolizing the promise to make him a "father of many nations." You will notice that my translation is different than most of your Bibles—this is because of two challenges in the text:

---

[64] This dynamic is also reflected in the NT prophecies of Simeon and Anna over the baby Jesus (Luke 2:21–38), who is described as the "consolation of Israel" who will be a "light of revelation to the Gentiles, and the glory of Your people Israel" (v. 32). All of this is centered on His role as the one to redeem Jerusalem (v. 38).
[65] In Judaism, the righteous Gentile has a "place" in the world to come, like every Jew, but it has never been clear exactly what that "place" is. Practically speaking, it is not the same place as the Jew.

1) the unusual use of *hinei* ("behold")—which is never followed, as it is here, with a full pronoun like "I." Usually the first-person suffix would be added to form *hineni*, or "Behold me" or "Here I am"; and 2) the fact that the verb "to be" is not necessary in a simple, Hebrew, nominal sentence, like "*ani* Ariel" (I *am* Ariel). These grammatical points mean that it is not clear in the first half of the verse who or what is the subject of the phrase, and where one should insert the verb "to be"; nor is it clear what to do with the "behold," the first word of the phrase. All major English translations (and other languages I have checked) choose to do something like, "Behold, as for me, my covenant is with you." But this is not the literal reading of the Hebrew, because a more straightforward reading is a little complex: "Behold, *I* am my covenant with you." This seems strange to us only because we don't understand who is speaking!

In his book *Who Ate Lunch with Abraham?*, Asher Intrater shows how we can understand the personal revelation of YHVH, or the angel of YHVH, to OT "saints" as being the appearances of the preincarnate Yeshua. Thus, here in Genesis 17, we need to imagine the preincarnate Yeshua speaking to Abram, announcing that: a) He Himself will be the essence, the very content of God's covenant with Abraham ("I AM my covenant with you"); and b) the promise that YHVH-Yeshua Himself would enter into Abraham's family line—in other words, God-Yeshua announcing to Abram that he will not only have many, many offspring as in the previous versions of the promise, but that YHVH-Yeshua will be one of them! Furthermore, c) as Abram's seed, He Himself will see to it that father Abram will be a "father to/of many nations."[66]

So, you might wonder, what's the big deal? We all know that Jesus came to make us children of God, and spiritual sons and daughters of Abraham (Rom. 4:11–25; Gal. 3:7). What is different here, I hope to

---

[66] Another struggle in understanding these texts is that the biblical Hebrew *goyim* can be translated as "nations" or "Gentiles." Because of our bias toward reading everything in terms of personal salvation, we have understood this only as "Gentiles"—meaning a plural number of individual, non-Jews. But, as this book repeatedly points out, certain sections of the NT are speaking to Gentiles in corporate plurality—as distinct peoples, even nations.

show you, is that we are discovering that God's one-new-man plan for the Gentiles is more than just the blessing of individual salvations, or even the formation of "national churches." It has to do with the very *extending of the fatherhood of God and of Abraham to entire people groups/ nations.* It is thus no coincidence that God chooses this point in time to change—or rather, expand—Abram's name to *Abraham* by adding the one Hebrew letter ה ("hey"). There is a double play on words (or letters) here: First, the "hey" echoes the first letter of המון—the "many" of the "many nations." Second, "hey" symbolizes YHVH, since there are two "heys" in God's OT covenant name. The change from Abram to Abraham represents the dynamic and promise of the interaction here in Genesis 17: By this covenant Yeshua-YHVH and Abraham will become one family, and through this family they will adopt *hamon* (many) nations!

God's Plan for the Nations: Isaiah 42:6 and 49:6–13

The next OT verses which shed light on this mystery are the Messianic prophecies found in Isaiah 42:6 and 49:6–13. In 49:6, the prophet first declares: "It is too small a thing that You should be My Servant to raise up the tribes of Jacob, and to restore the preserved ones of Israel; I will also make You a light of the nations" (also 42:6; Luke 2:32). If it were just a matter of being "a light to the nations," we could neatly fit this into the standard OT reading of the Messianic kingdom—that when David's Greatest Son finally comes and establishes his Israel-centered kingdom, this will be a great light to the nations. But next, while repeating the promise to be a "light to the nations," the prophet announces something even more staggering: The Servant-Messiah will also be a *brit am,* or "covenant for/of/to a people" (Isa. 42:6, 49:8).[67] This Hebrew term is only found in these two Messianic prophecies in Isaiah.

---

[67] These two nouns, "covenant" and "people," are connected not by a preposition as in English, but just by word order in the Hebrew *smichut.* Depending on context, one could use any number of prepositions in translation to English, with the simple possessive "of" being the most common, e.g., "Children of Israel," "Angel of YHVH," "God of Abraham."

Isaiah then continues by declaring the awesome results of this Messianic "covenant for the people/nation" in 42:7–8: opening blind eyes, redeeming, liberating prisoners from bondage in prison, and demonstrating God's glory and victory over idolatry. And again in 49:8–10: to establish/raise up the land(s); causing the people to "inherit the desolate heritages [inheritances/places]"; to release captives; and lastly, many images of great prosperity and comfort. We can summarize all these *brit am* promises as describing the "redemption" of nations: Every nation, every tribe has a heritage, an inheritance from YHVH— but it has been corrupted, decimated, and made "desolate" by idolatry and immorality; the nations are like blind prisoners to their own history of idolatry; and they need the Rescuer-Redeemer, the strong and mighty Messiah of Israel to come and liberate them, make covenant with them, and extend to them the fatherhood and ancestor-ship of Abraham in order to raise up their nation, redeem their past, and permanently *transform* them.

According to the OT, Israel—the Jewish nation—is the only *covenanted* nation with God. This is because of God's promises to our patriarchs, the Sinaitic covenant, and the Davidic-kingdom covenant. But here in Isaiah, the prophet is declaring that the day will come when the light of Messiah will reach out to the nations, inviting them to enter into a *brit am*—a "national-people-covenant" with the God of Israel. And according to what we learned in Genesis 17, Yeshua-Son-of-Abraham is the very essence of this covenant which extends the fatherhood of Abraham to any and every nation that will accept him. The preincarnate Son of God is promising Abraham not just the offspring, not just the great nation based in the land of Canaan, not just ruling over the earth; He is promising the Gentiles (nations) nothing less than the same Jewish, covenantal fatherhood of Abraham—and thus the fatherhood of God.

The good news of the one new man in Messiah fills out the picture: All of this is taking place in such a way so as not to replace Israel's status as the "firstborn son" in this expanding family, but *extend* Israel's firstborn blessing to the nations in such a way that the fullness of each is totally dependent on the other (Ex. 4:22–23; Jer. 31:9; Eph. 3:6). Accordingly, both the elder brother and younger brother (Jew and Gentile) are kept in a place of humility, dependent on one another for the mediation of God's mercy to their peoples, unto the fullness of all things (Rom. 11:28–32).[68]

---

[68] This is what Paul calls the "Commonwealth of Israel" (Eph. 2:12), according to many English translations.

12

ONE NEW MAN—COHEIRS, ONE BODY, SAME PROMISE

*The mystery of Christ, which in other generations was not made known to the sons of men, as it has now been revealed to His holy apostles and prophets in the Spirit; to be specific, that the Gentiles are **fellow heirs and fellow members of the body, and fellow partakers of the promise in Christ Jesus** through the gospel.* (Eph. 3:4–6, emphasis added)

Paul concludes the one-new-man teaching in Ephesians 2:18–3:6. He first proclaims, in direct contrast to the pre-Christian state of enmity described in 2:11–12, that the Gentile believers are now "no longer strangers and aliens, but you are fellow citizens [of the commonwealth of Israel] with the saints, and are of God's household" (v. 19). Under Moses, the best a Gentile could hope for was to be a well-treated *ger* (stranger, sojourner, resident alien) among Israel (Ex. 22:20; Lev. 19:33–34). The classic biblical example is that of the Moabitess Ruth, who declares her intention to follow her mother-in-law Naomi back to Bethlehem, saying, "Your people shall be my people, and your God, my God" (Ruth 1:16). Being a *ger* meant a complete abandoning of one's native people and culture. Throughout the book of Ruth, she is called "Ruth the Moabitess"; but from Ruth 4:13 forward, when she is given in marriage to Boaz, she is simply called Ruth—as she is likewise remembered in Yeshua's genealogy in Matthew 1:5. Once she married into Israel, her Moabite past was finished. Under the Mosaic covenant, "one new man" (or woman) meant one new Jewish-Israelite woman!

This was more or less the state of things in the first century, before the advent of the gospel. The rabbis (Pharisees) had developed a system of proselytism (conversion) for Gentiles, which was not uniformly practiced and very controversial (see Matt. 23:15). The Torah warns Israel, "The stranger who resides with you shall be to you as the native among you, and you shall love him as yourself; for you were aliens in the land of Egypt" (Lev. 19:34). But as the story of Peter and Cornelius demonstrates, the reality was rarely so pretty.[69] Think of it: Cornelius, the Roman centurion, is described as "a devout man, and one who feared God with all his household, and gave many alms to the Jewish people, and prayed to God continually" (Acts 10:2). He was some kind of proselyte, or "God-fearer" as they were called—and a very, very sincere one (Acts 13:43; 17:4, 17). Given this description, Cornelius most certainly knew of the Jewish dietary laws, and probably would have been extra-careful if a Jew like Peter came to visit. Yet Peter—a devout, traditional Jew—except for the vision and leading from the Holy Spirit, was extremely reluctant to enter his house, even though Cornelius feared the God of the Jews and contributed money to Jewish people and causes![70] The reality was that for even the most righteous of *gerim* (plural of *ger*), being a convert to Judaism still meant being a kind of second-class citizen in Israel.

---

[69] Even today, in Judaism, the rule is that the convert must be treated 100% as a Jew; yet from the testimonies of several converts whom I know in Jerusalem, there is much discrimination against them in the Haredi community, especially when it comes to treating them (especially a recognizably "formerly" gentile woman, like an Asian) as a worthy marriage partner.

[70] This same attitude is probably reflected by another centurion, the one who entreats Jesus to heal his servant in Matthew 8:5-13. "Lord, I am not worthy for you to come under my roof..." (v.8)

But now, in Christ, as explained by Paul in Ephesians, the Gentile believer has become a full citizen and member of the household of God, no longer just an alien or stranger (*ger*) among Israel. This conversion comes without physical circumcision and the other *dogma* requirements of Torah, and thus without the demand to leave one's people and heritage. Now, for the first time in biblical history, the apostle can describe Israel as a "commonwealth" (v. 12)—a grouping of nations, each with its own unique identity, yet each with the full right of citizenship in the commonwealth as anyone from the "mother" (central, original) nation of the commonwealth—Israel.[71] Amazing!

But it goes even deeper than this. Notice that Paul wrote, "you are fellow citizens *with the saints*" (v. 19, emphasis added). In other words, this new citizenship for Gentiles, this new commonwealth of nations (let's call it the "church") does not replace Israel (or, in this case the believing remnant of Israel—here called "the saints"), but represents an *expansion* of Israel that requires a kind of partnership, or at least a recognition of *shared* citizenship along with the believing Jews.

Paul further expounds on this theme in the first six verses of Ephesians 3. He calls it a "mystery,"[72] and then "the mystery of Christ," which was uniquely committed, by God's grace, to Paul in his ministry among Jews and Gentiles. Interestingly, he even declares that this mystery is something that was not revealed (or at least not in the same way) to the OT prophets, but is now being revealed to/by the NT apostles and prophets. (We will look at this mystery and its relation to OT prophecy in the next chapters.) He concludes, "to be specific, that the Gentiles are fellow heirs and fellow members of the body, and fellow partakers

---

[71] The most instructional example in our time is that of the British Commonwealth/Great Britain: a grouping of independent nations with a shared, English heritage and some common rights; a recognition of the centrality of the homeland, England—without which the commonwealth would cease to exist; and a common royal family whose "rule" extends throughout the commonwealth.

[72] Here, "mystery" refers to something that is found in a kind of hidden, "kernel" form in the OT; but was difficult, if not impossible, to interpret until the full revelation of it in NT times, especially under Paul's ministry.

of the promise in Christ Jesus through the gospel" (Eph. 3:4–6). Here, the apostle uses three compound words in the Greek to describe the mystery:[73] *synkleroma, sysoma, synmetoka*—all starting with the prefix "syn," from which we get English words like "synchronize," "synthesize," and "synergy."[74] NT Greek scholars tell us that it is hard to capture the clout of these three words in other languages.[75]

First is *synkleroma*—"coheirs." This legal term suggests not just an equality of shared privilege, as in two business partners or family members sharing profits or an inheritance; not simply "joint heirs" like the two brothers in the story of the prodigal son—i.e., "we have a common father, I get my portion and you get yours"; instead, it is more like two "blood-brothers" who have utterly bound themselves together, *dependent on each other* for whatever inheritance, hope, and success they can expect to receive from their common father. In Messiah, we Jews won't get our ultimate inheritance from the father until the nations get theirs—and vice versa!

Second is *sysoma*—"co-body" people, "of one body." As in Romans 12:5 or 1 Corinthians 12:27, the apostle describes the *ecclesia* with an organic, biological term—we are a living body, and Christ is the head. Now, in the gospel of Messiah, Jew and Gentile have become one living organism, with the same spiritual blood of Christ joining us together; we have the same heavenly DNA; we are of the same family/household (John 1:13). Whatever happens to one part of the body affects the whole.

Last is *synmetoka*—"*partakers* of the same promise" in Christ Jesus. "Promise" is in the singular, not "promises." In keeping with the rest

---

[73] The first, *synkleronoma* (joint-heirs) occurs in 1 Peter 3:7 (husband and wife as joint-heirs of the grace of life); Romans 8:17 (believers as children of God, coheirs with Christ); and Hebrews 11:9 (Isaac and Jacob as coheirs with Abraham of the same promise).

[74] This follows a pattern already established in Ephesians 2:5–6: "alive together," "raised [together]," and "seated [together]."

[75] E.g., Walter L. Liefeld, "Commentary on Verse 3:6," *Ephesians* (Downers Grove: IVPress, 1997; electronic edition, Logos Bible Software).

of Paul's writings, we can understand him to be specifically referring to the prefigured gospel promise made to Abraham, as taught in Romans 4, 8:17, and Galatians 3:26–29. Romans 4:11–17 brings together these ideas from Ephesians 3:6, and other chapters in this book:

> That he might be the father of all who believe without being circumcised, that righteousness might be reckoned to them, and the father of circumcision to those who not only are of the circumcision, but who also follow in the steps of the faith of our father Abraham which he had while uncircumcised. For the promise to Abraham or to his descendants that he would be heir of the world was not through the Law, but through the righteousness of faith. For if those who are of the Law are heirs, faith is made void and the promise is nullified; for the Law brings about wrath, but where there is no law, neither is there violation. For this reason it is by faith, that it might be in accordance with grace, in order that the promise may be certain to all the descendants, not only to those who are of the Law, but also to those who are of the faith of Abraham, who is the father of us all, (as it is written, "A FATHER OF MANY NATIONS HAVE I MADE YOU").

Here we see that to Abraham was made a promise (singular), described in two ways: that he would be the "heir of the world" and that he would be "a father of many nations." The incredible mystery of the gospel is that together in Christ Jesus (the greatest son of Abraham!) Jew and Gentile are coheirs of the same Abrahamic promise; we are members of the same Messianic family (the body of Messiah); and all of this is based on the very same promise made to our now mutual father/ancestor, Abraham.

The Scripture goes much further than to simply assert that Jews and Gentiles are now equal in terms of personal salvation and blessing, as in Galatians and Colossians ("there is neither Jew nor [Gentile] . . . male nor female"; Gal. 3:28): The Gentile peoples/nations are now partakers of the same hope and promises that were given to Israel—*as unique peoples and as nations*. This means that the Father's promise/invitation to the Son in Psalm 2:8—"Ask of me, and I will surely give the nations as Your inheritance, the very ends of the earth as Your possession"—is more than just a promise of a Jewish king, a son of David, ruling a Jewish, worldwide kingdom from Jerusalem.

Before we come to the closing section of this book—where we will look at how the one-new-man dynamic of unity and reconciliation is to play out in the end times—we must stop to consider the incredible resistance to the one new man that comes from human sin and from Satan. Not coincidentally, the same one-new-man letters of Ephesians and Colossians contain some of Paul's most detailed and potent descriptions of this "spiritual warfare." This will be our subject of study in the next three chapters.

13

THE STRUGGLE AGAINST PRINCIPALITIES AND POWERS, PART 1: BIBLICAL FOUNDATIONS

For by Him all things were created, both in the heavens and on earth, visible and invisible, whether thrones or dominions or rulers or authorities—all things have been created by Him and for Him. (Col. 1:16)

For our struggle is not against flesh and blood, but against the rulers, against the powers, against the world forces of this darkness, against the spiritual forces of wickedness in the heavenly places. (Eph. 6:12)

Submit yourselves for the Lord's sake to every human institution, whether to a king as the one in authority, or to governors as sent by him for the punishment of evildoers and the praise of those who do right. (1 Pet. 2:13–14)

Both of our central one-new-man texts, Ephesians and Colossians, teach that there is yet another dimension to Yeshua's reconciling work on the cross of "abolishing in His flesh the enmity" between Jew and Gentile. The apostle introduces us to a cosmic, spiritual—and very personal—struggle between Yeshua, His people, and His angels on one side, versus unseen spiritual forces in the "heavenly places" and their minions on Earth—the kings, institutions, and governments of this world. These forces are variously called "principalities and powers," "authorities," "dominions," "angels," or "thrones."

Why is it that so much of the NT teaching on this subject is found in the same epistles, even chapters, as the one-new-man teaching? In this chapter we explore the subject of how and why the powers resist the one-new-man gospel of reconciliation and unity by first looking at the subject in the OT. But writing anything short and systematic on this subject of principalities and powers is no easy task, for three reasons:

a. The realm of angels and demons is not normally open to us; and when it is "open" it comes in the form of intuitions, visions, dreams, and the like. It is a supernatural world that doesn't function according to the logic of this world.

b. Scripture contains no systematic teaching on the subject; there is no treatment of this subject parallel, for example, to Paul's lengthy treatment of the subject of the resurrection of the dead in 1 Corinthians 15.

c. Instead, the texts are varied, presenting a sometimes positive picture of the powers, and sometimes a negative one.

Look at the Scriptures just quoted above: Why is it that when the apostle declares that everything has been created by and for the Messiah, he must make special mention that this also includes "thrones or dominions or rulers or authorities" (Col. 1:16)? And, note the essentially positive quality here: All these powers are created by, through, and for Yeshua. If He created them, then they are somehow under His authority, right? A wonderful, unified picture of a world under God's authority! But the reality of this world—even after His cross, resurrection, and ascension—plagued by so much evil and wickedness, paints a very different picture. Paul describes this in Ephesians 6:12 as a "struggle" against the very same powers, now described as forces of "darkness" and "wickedness" in the "heavenly places." Lastly, Peter, along with Paul in Romans 13:1–7 and Titus 3:1, instructs the early believers to submit to kings and human institutions, because of their role in punishing evil and rewarding good behavior. Yet, as history instructs at practically every turn, these same kings, kingdoms, governments, and institutions are never perfect in meting out social justice, and all too often can morph—even in a single generation—into full-fledged, corrupt agents of the wicked heavenly powers, persecuting the church, rewarding evil and greed, promoting ethnic pride, racism, and nationalism that leads to wars, famines, destruction, and a tremendous loss of human life.

Further, the OT and the apocryphal, apocalyptic texts tend to identify the principalities and powers as heavenly angels; whereas the NT tends to emphasize the aspect of their authority structures on Earth.[76] All of this explains why a survey of the study of these heavenly powers in church history reveals a tendency toward one of two extremes—either the hyper-personalization of these powers—personal, Satanic demons to be bound or otherwise contended with; or the demythologizing of the language of the powers for our modern age, resulting in an understanding of them only as symbolic of human authority structures and institutions. In our day, we can see both extremes: Many charismatics and Pentecostals find a demon behind everything that is "bad": a "religious" spirit here, the spirit of "poverty," the spirit of "cancer" of "depression," etc. Almost anything evil in the world can be thus spiritualized, personalized, and bound (according to a popular understanding of Matthew 16:19 and 18:18). On the other hand, are more liberal Christians who view the whole spiritual realm of the demonic as a vestige of a primitive biblical, prescientific, age—and we now supposedly know better. In the middle, it seems to me, are many conservative evangelicals who, in practice, don't know really what to do with the whole question.

---

[76] Ephesians 6:12ff is an obvious exception to this.

We can make great progress in understanding this subject by first noticing a simple fact: Some of the most pointed and potent statements about the powers in the NT are found in the very same one-new-man letters which we have been studying. Furthermore, they are found at the very heart of the one-new-man verses of Colossians 2:15 and at the conclusion of that section of Paul's teaching in Ephesians at 3:10–11. Many believers know about "spiritual warfare" from Ephesians 6:12–16; but here we see that already in 3:11, Paul introduces this theme—as the reconciled, one-new-man *ecclesia* described in 2:11–3:10 is itself a powerful demonstration of the "manifold wisdom of God" to these same powers. It is even clearer in Colossians: The language of 2:15 is of a bold, militaristic triumph—a public "disarming" and "public display" of the enemy "rulers and authorities"—as if bound and captured in the midst of cosmic warfare. And all of this is accomplished by a naked, bleeding, Jewish man dying on a cross two thousand years ago on a lonely hill outside Jerusalem. What could it all mean?

Clearly, the first thing to be learned from the placement of these Scriptures is that the primary role of the principalities and powers has to do with their control and influence over humanity—humanity understood not as a great sea of individuals, but rather as tribes, peoples, and nations. Or we can say that there is a direct relationship between this theme of reconciliation among Jew and Gentile (and between all peoples and nations) on the one hand; and this subject of the principalities and powers on the other hand.

In the rest of this chapter and the next two we will look at this connection, seeking to answer the questions: Which powers did Yeshua so aggressively "disarm" and make a "public display" of? And, to which powers does the one-new-man church so boldly "declare the manifold wisdom of God"?

OT Background

First, in order to get at the depth of what these NT letters are teaching here, we need to look at the roots of revelation of the heavenly powers from the OT. Daniel 10 is key to understanding the existence and role of the heavenly, angelic (and demonic) powers. Continuing his intercession for the restoration of Israel (Judea) that he had begun in chapter 9, Daniel fasted and humbled himself for three weeks. At the end of this period, one who looks very much like the preincarnate Yeshua (compare verses 5–6 with Revelation 1:12–16) appears to him with the following message/revelation:

> O Daniel, man of high esteem, understand the words that I am about to tell you and stand upright, for I have now been sent to you. . . . Do not be afraid, Daniel, for from the first day that you set your heart on understanding this and on humbling yourself before your God, your words were heard, and I have come in response to your words. *But the prince of the kingdom of Persia was withstanding me for twenty-one days; then behold, Michael, one of the chief princes, came to help me, for I had been left there with the kings of Persia.* (Dan. 10:11–13, emphasis added)

There are eight points that we can derive from this text, with some help from a few others:

1. According to Daniel, the NT, and much second-temple Jewish literature, God rules the world indirectly, through the "proxy" services of countless angels.
2. At the highest levels, there are ruling, principality/throne level, "prince" angels who have authority over entire nations or people groups (Michael for Israel and the "prince" for Persia).
3. These principality level angels exist and function in the "heavenly places"—unseen dimensions of reality that are not, in most cases, directly experienced by humankind. Though hidden, they function as a source of authority and power behind their corresponding earthly kings and governments. They can be so closely

identified with their earthly counterparts that it can be difficult to determine if some OT prophesies speak of the angelic/demonic force or the earthly king, or both (e.g., the King of Tyre in Ezekiel 28:11–19).

4. There is struggle, even warfare among these "princes"—which means that some are good (i.e., allies of Yeshua), while are others are evil (i.e., minions of Satan, fighting to protect Satan's domain as the "ruler of this world" and the "prince of the power of the air"—the spiritual realms closest to the earth). These do everything in their power to prevent Yeshua and His people from restoring godly reign to the earth (John 12:31, 16:11; 2 Cor. 4:4; Eph. 2:2; Rev. 12:7–9). This warfare is not at all isolated to the spiritual realm, but has very down-to-earth consequences in real-time, earthly relationships, diplomacy and conflicts between the corresponding kings, governments, rulers, etc.

5. Israel, as the chosen nation by God, is the only people for whom we know the proper names of their principal, angelic "princes"— Michael and Gabriel—and can thus trust that they are somehow always the "good guys" (Dan. 8:16, 9:21; Luke 1:19).

6. God, in His sovereignty, has "designed" the universe with the intention that mankind—uniquely made in His image—be its ultimate, delegated rulers (Gen. 1:26–28; 1 Cor. 6:3). We thus play a decisive role in this warfare; just as the preincarnate Yeshua comes, and the heavenly struggle seems to have been engaged, because of Daniel's decision to fast and pray for three weeks.

7. The preincarnate Jesus seems somewhat restrained in his power— the struggle takes three weeks (twenty-one days), and He is in need of help from Michael and others!

8. Jesus and His people and his angels are assured ultimate victory (Rev. 12ff.)!

If we were to stop with Daniel and the OT, the picture of the principalities and powers seems relatively simple: Michael and Gabriel, the archangels of Israel, and Yeshua the King/Messiah of Israel are on the good side; Persia and its princes are on the bad side; and the prayers of Daniel, the Jew, are pivotal in the struggle to bring about the fulfillment of prophecy—the end of seventy years of exile according to Jeremiah, by restoring the Jewish people to Jerusalem. But what does this say about Israel and Persia—about Jewish and Persian people, then and now? Is God only on the side of Israel and the Jews? Is it the case that on the Jewish side there are only Michaels, Gabriels, and Daniels—great, powerful angelic allies of Yeshua, and great men of God? And only "bad guys"—demonic, fallen angels, and evil kings on the Gentile, Persian side?

Well, we Jews would like to think this is the case—and it certainly would make for a simpler world, both in heaven and on Earth: Our nation is the only one chosen by God; we have the God-given Torah and its holy practices; we have a unique destiny among the peoples, and thus our angels are all . . . well, just that—angels! The pagans, the Gentiles are not chosen; and so while they may have a few angels and saints here and there, their lot is mostly demons (fallen angels) and despots!

But even under the old covenant, the biblical reality is not so simple. Even a superficial reading of biblical Israel's history, from Judges through the Prophets, reveals a majority of bad, even evil, leaders of the Jewish nation; of a people prone to rebellion, unfaithfulness to God, and idolatry—ultimately of a divided kingdom and an exiled people. In Daniel's day, it is eventually King Cyrus of Persia who conquers Babylon (where Daniel and many Jews lived in exile), and is called the "anointed one" (*Moshiach*—"Messiah" in Hebrew) by Isaiah; he then uses his great authority to encourage the restoration of Israel—the return of the Jews to Judea and Jerusalem (Isaiah 45:1–7)! Remember, in Daniel 10 it is the heavenly "Prince of Persia"—the ruling angelic/demonic principality over the Persian kingdom/nation—who is fighting *against* Michael and Yeshua. How could it be that the next Persian king—the primary earthly agent through whom this "evil" principality rules—was used in such a Messianic, pro-Israel, pro-kingdom-restoration way? Could it be that from the beginning, God's sovereign plan was to use Cyrus and Persia in a redemptive way, to restore Israel, and so there was great warfare surrounding this plan? Could it be that Daniel's governmental presence, coupled with his extended times of prayer and fasting had something to do with tipping the scales in favor of Cyrus and the Persians fulfilling a positive, "Messianic" destiny—however briefly—in God's kingdom plans? Yes and amen!

What's more, I read this as a prophetic, OT "type" or picture of something God intended to bring to fruition under the new covenant. Imagine if in Persia, there was a great "remnant" of believers, even in high government positions like Cyrus and Daniel—all little "messiahs" in the image of the Great Messiah, Jesus? What if they came to represent a significant percentage of the population of that nation? This nation could be radically transformed, becoming a "sheep" nation that God could use mightily in His kingdom plans, tipping the scales of angelic/demonic struggle in favor of godly rule and influence throughout the society—a transformation that would affect many generations.

This is exactly what Paul began to see in its infancy, even though in his time he did not live to see the dynamic come to fullness. Yet, within a few generations of his passing, whole nations, people groups, and empires had become "Christian." The gospel penetrated to such a deep level in Europe and Asia Minor that whole new institutions—religious, governmental, educational, etc.—were founded on the foundation of the one-new-man gospel proclaimed by the apostle Paul. Christ, His cross, and many other biblical themes "cross-pollinated" with native cultures to form whole new expressions of art and worship. Pagan feasts (i.e., Christmas, Easter) were "baptized" by the gospel to become celebrations of Yeshua's birth and resurrection, and in the process became the primary "holy days" for all of Western civilization.[77] Without the

---

[77] Obviously, the process was never perfect: sometimes old paganisms exercised more influence than biblical themes, e.g., Mary and saint worship in the Catholic and some Orthodox churches.

clarity of Paul's teaching in Ephesians, Colossians, Galatians, etc., none of this would have been possible. Instead of the Gospel going "out" to transform nations and cultures, it would have been drawing them in a more centripetal kind of way toward Jewishness. The apostle saw into this mystery like no other, and understood its significance. This is why the apostle fought so hard for it—and why he also understood, better than anyone else, the incredible spiritual warfare surrounding these issues.

14

THE STRUGGLE AGAINST PRINCIPALITIES AND POWERS, PART 2: PETER, FOOD, JEWISH PRIDE AND THE PARADOX OF JEWISH CHOSENNESS

Peter went up on the housetop about the sixth hour to pray. And he became hungry, and was desiring to eat; but while they were making preparations, he fell into a trance; and he beheld the sky opened up, and a certain object like a great sheet coming down, lowered by four corners to the ground, and there were in it all kinds of four-footed animals and crawling creatures of the earth and birds of the air. And a voice came to him, "Arise, Peter, kill and eat!" But Peter said, "By no means, Lord, for I have never eaten anything unholy and unclean." And again a voice came to him a second time, "What God has cleansed, no longer consider unholy." And this happened three times; and immediately the object was taken up into the sky. (Acts 10:9–16)

In the previous chapter, we learned—especially from the book of Daniel—how the spiritual dynamics of the heavenly realms are intimately connected with what takes place here on Earth. It was Yeshua's "real-time" death on the cross that affected this victory over spiritual principalities and powers; now it has become our task to pray and act so as to bring about His victory amidst our personal and national histories. Thus, I want to use a similarly down-to-earth biblical illustration to further explain the struggle with the powers and its relationship to the *dogma* commands of Torah—the story of Peter's dream on that rooftop in Jaffa, and how it led to the baptism by the Holy Spirit of Cornelius and his household. These events marked the beginning of the process of applying Yeshua's atoning sacrifice to breaking open the wall of hostility between Jew and Gentile; releasing the Abrahamic adoption and potential for transformation to entire nations; and advancing His victory and reclamation of the thrones and powers over entire nations.

First, let's state the obvious: Peter, as most Jews of his day (and still many today!) had a big problem with Gentiles. At the least, the average Jew viewed Gentiles with an air of superiority, looking down on them as, foreign, unclean, idolatrous "sinners" (see Gal. 2:15), much the same way as so-called, "civilized" peoples have viewed the "less fortunate"— e.g., the Roman view of the barbarians; the Egyptians toward the original Hebrews from Canaan (Gen. 43:32); or whites toward Africans in nineteenth-century America, etc. At worst, they hated the Gentiles— especially those who ruled over them and seemed to represent everything that was wrong with the world outside of God's chosen people, Israel. Think of it: Peter had never sat down to a meal with a Gentile; had never entered their homes, perhaps not even their villages in the Galilee— except perhaps to sell some of his fish. In modern terms, we would call this a kind of bias or discrimination; or, more harshly, "racism." I know it's a bit anachronistic, but let's use the word here. Peter, and most Jews like him were, simply put, racist—they believed that Jewish people were different, chosen, more holy, and altogether superior to other peoples.[78] This attitude is obviously part of the "enmity" that Yeshua came to abolish, as detailed in Ephesians 2:11–15.

---

[78] If you think I'm exaggerating, on more than one occasion, I've had Orthodox Jews explain to me the reason why Gentiles can eat pork and it doesn't defile them: because their soul is of a different (i.e., lesser) quality than that of the Jew!

But this Jewish attitude toward non-Jews is hardly unique in human history, which is littered with examples of one race of people, or nation, or religion elevating itself above others in order to justify its own need for significance, greatness and glory. This is how supposedly "civilized" peoples have justified the mass raping, enslaving, dehumanizing, domination, and even the genocidal murder of other peoples. We are not just animals aggressively hunting for food; rather, as moral, thinking beings we need to utilize some rationale or ideology in order to justify (mostly to ourselves!) our behavior. An entire people group does not just wake up one day and declare: "A-ha, we are better than you! Now, we can rape and kill you, take your land, rob you of your natural resources, enslave you, etc."

In general, the ideological justifications for these awful sins based on racism and ethnic pride only come in three categories:[79]

a. Power, or brute force: We are simply bigger, more numerous, more powerful than you. The fact that we are able dominate you seems to justify the fact of our domination. Perhaps God, or our gods, have just blessed us to be more numerous and more powerful than you. The Mongols who came to dominate most of Asia in the twelfth and thirteenth centuries are a great example of this. This is the most brute, lowest level of justification.

b. Racial superiority: By reason of mythology—or in more modern times, science (or pseudoscience)—one people comes to believe that it is biologically superior to another. In recent history, this was the case for both Nazi Germany and the Japanese before and during WWII.

c. Moral-cultural superiority: The morals of our civilization are more advanced; we are morally superior, more educated, more "civilized"—perhaps more "chosen," and closer to the "divine" ideal. And thus the expressions of our culture are superior—our literature, our language, our science, our music . . . our Torah.

---

[79] I suppose a fourth could be added: desperation—by reasons of famine, and/or poverty—but usually such a people is not very mighty.

In many cases, the justification for national or ethnic superiority is a combination of all three of these categories.

How about the Jewish people? With the exception of the reign of David and Solomon, throughout most of our history Israel and Judah were smallish kingdoms subject to the changing politics of much larger nations like Egypt, Assyria, Babylon, Persia, and Rome. By Jesus' and Peter's time, we were a colonized people, not having enjoyed independent rule since the time that the last of the Maccabee descendants (Hasmoneans) ruled independently (63 BC). So a sense of Jewish superiority by means of demographic domination or brute force over the Gentiles was ruled out.[80] Instead, the Jewish sense of superiority depended on b) and c)—most of which was based on the Torah of Moses—both its *dogma* and moral commandments. If you could have interviewed Peter (before Acts 8) and his Jewish contemporaries, asking them the question, "Do you believe that Jews are superior to Gentiles?" their answer would most likely *not* have been an unequivocal, "yes." Probably, they would have said something more nuanced, like, "Well, of course all people are made in God's image (Gen. 1); but since God chose Israel and gave us His Torah—His laws—we do not behave like the idolatrous, barbaric, and sexually perverted Gentiles; in addition, we are not defiled by all the unclean things that they eat and touch. What's more, our holy Torah calendar and Sabbaths keep us 'in step' with the Creator and His creation in a way that they cannot be. . . ."[81]

Let's return to the story of Peter and Cornelius. The first thing to notice is that God's *primary* concern in this story is with people, not food. The ultimate point of the whole experience was that Peter and the

---

[80] "Fortunately" for the Jewish people, we have been in this subjugated position for most of our history, not allowing our racism to "play out" in domination of another people. Of course, there are many today who level this charge at the modern state of Israel—"apartheid," etc. I don't think this is accurate either.

[81] This is exactly what we studied in the prayers of Judaism in Chapter 4: The 613 commandments of Torah have been uniquely given to the Jewish people, and this fact together with our performance of all the commandments is what *sanctifies* us as a people—i.e., what makes us holy over and against those who do not have or practice the Torah (the Gentiles).

other apostles could understand that in this new dispensation of gospel grace, the Gentiles are no longer to be considered "unclean," but worthy of God's love as expressed by the Savior (Acts 11:1–18, 15:6–11). But couldn't God have spoken to Peter another way about the Gentiles now being "clean" for the gospel? When the Holy Spirit directed Paul to bring the gospel to Macedonia, he received a "night vision" of a Macedonian man crying out for help (Acts 16:9–10). Why not something similar here: a vision of Cornelius praying, meeting the angel, crying out for mercy and enlightenment? Instead, God, in a very dramatic and emphatic (three times!) manner, went straight at the Torah-*dogma-stoichea* issue of dietary laws and food. God did not show Peter a beautifully garnished roast-suckling pig; or a colorful presentation of unkosher, Japanese sushi containing shrimp and octopus. This was no light therapy for Peter, not a question of taste or culinary temptation, but instead a very "primitive" challenge to all of Peter's sensibilities: "Rise, kill, eat . . . you get up, go and slaughter these animals for yourself and then eat them!" No mention of at least cooking them or adding a few spices to deaden the effect—just kill and eat!

From Peter's response, we can see how shocking and challenging it was for him.[82] So while the main message is about people, this is not just a "disposable" parable—as some would teach[83]—but a very deep revelation and challenge to Peter and to every Jew, one which goes straight to the heart of our sense of identity, chosenness, and pride. In a kind of preview to Paul's fully developed theology of the effects of the cross on the cosmos of all *stoichea*-based human culture, the Holy Spirit challenges Peter to "rise, kill, eat" unkosher animals. You see, for Peter, Jews being

---

[82] For Christians, imagine that you had a vision from God seemingly leading you to commit sexual immorality, or steal your neighbor's car—you would be shocked and repulsed, and likely think that the voice and vision were from a demon and not from God! This is what it was like for Peter!

[83] Many Messianic/Torah teachers have been quick to point this out—that the food issue here is a parable for human beings, and therefore the import of this story has nothing to do with the cancelling of the dietary laws.

"clean" and Gentiles being "unclean" (read: Jews are more holy, closer to God) found expression in the most common, everyday thing that all people everywhere, including Jews, do—eat and drink. God chose Israel; God gave us the Holy Torah through Moses; He told us what is clean and unclean to eat; as a result of our observance of the commandments, we are sanctified and clean and the Gentile pagans are not. This is an essential part of our exalted, God-given, holy identity and calling.[84] Only by shattering this Jewish, *dogma*-Torah taboo could Peter even think to enter the house of a Gentile—where he might be offered unkosher food or drink. God began to teach Peter exactly what Paul later develops: Only by the utter abolishing of the force of these Torah commandments as "holy" commandments could true, one-new-man unity be established—without the tendency toward Jewish, Torah-based uniformity and the resulting dominance of one culture over another. Yes, the primary message of Peter's dream was about people, but we mustn't minimize the means by which God so forcefully spoke to Peter, for herein is contained a message that receives ratification later in Paul's letters. It is a new dispensation; we cannot be "under the law" in this way anymore: "rise, kill, eat!" It's not what enters your mouth that defiles you, but what comes out of it (Matt. 15:11).

But wait a minute: If such things, like the dietary laws, are so inseparably tied to the traditional sense of Jewish identity, holiness, and pride, doesn't their being "abolished" also mean the abolishing of Jewish, covenantal identity—and of any continuing relevance for the Jewish nation under the new covenant? As we have learned, this has been the conclusion of most of Christendom for close to 1,800 years, one which was anticipated by the apostle when he wrote his letter to the Romans. If the *dogma*-Torah commandments—the "real-time" expression of Jewish chosenness—have been abolished as divine commands, what does this mean for Israel? In the next chapter, we will look at this question by studying Peter's struggle from a more "heavenly" perspective, from that of the principalities and powers.

---

[84] The apostle clearly has this in mind as he wrote Romans 2:17–29.

15

THE STRUGGLE AGAINST PRINCIPALITIES AND POWERS, PART 3: ONE NEW MAN— DISPLAYING THE MANIFOLD WISDOM OF GOD BEFORE HEAVEN AND EARTH

*[The mystery is] that the Gentiles are fellow heirs and fellow members of the body, and fellow partakers of the promise in Christ Jesus through the gospel . . . to bring to light what is the administration of the mystery which for ages has been hidden in God, who created all things; in order that **the manifold wisdom of God might now be made known through the church to the rulers and the authorities in the heavenly places.*** (Eph. 3:6, 9–10, emphasis added)

*. . . having canceled out the certificate of debt consisting of decrees against us and which was hostile to us; and He has taken it out of the way, having nailed it to the cross. **When He had disarmed the rulers and authorities, He made a public display of them, having triumphed over them through Him.*** (Col. 2:14–15, emphasis added)

I n this chapter, we continue to look at the story of Peter's (and Cornelius') vision, focusing on these questions: What principalities and powers did the dying, crucified Yeshua so aggressively "disarm" and make "a public display of"? Or, when the reconciled church of Jew and Gentile, properly aligned in one-new-man formation, makes its declaration of "God's manifold wisdom" to the principalities and powers, exactly who or what is being referred to?

As we learned in Chapter 13, thrones, dominions, rulers, and authorities are part of the created order (Col. 1:16). There is a "throne"—a seat of authority—in God's created order called "Israel: the nation of the family of Abraham, Isaac, and Jacob." This nation is a key part of His plan to reestablish His rule on Earth; God established our foundational boundaries and language in the patriarchal period, and other aspects of our culture through the later Mosaic Torah. Then, by means of His covenant with King David, God promised to establish His kingdom—His throne on earth—through the everlasting kingdom of David's offspring, in Jerusalem, the "city of the great king" (2 Sam. 7:11–16; Ps. 48:2). All of this is a gracious, irrevocable gift from God, who *called* us to be a unique people, special to Him (Ex. 19:5; Deut. 7:6; Rom. 11:28–29). Peter, like almost every Jew, very much believed in these things.

This gift-calling of Israel is obviously a great privilege and a source of blessed identity for the Jewish people; but it is ultimately for the purpose of fulfilling the promise to Abraham to bring the fatherhood blessing (adoption as sons) of God to every nation. Then, Israel and her scriptural history can serve as the biblical "template" for all nations, and our experience of how God has dealt with us can be extrapolated onto every nation and people group—each with its own uniqueness and redemptive gift-calling. Like most Orthodox Jews both then and now, Peter's typical, Jewish upbringing made him quite blind to these points, which he could not begin to see until he received the exceptional, "shock therapy" revelation in Acts 10.

God has assigned mighty archangels to guard this throne of Israel and the authority that is to radiate blessing from it—at the least, we know from Scripture of Michael and Gabriel. Let us assume that there are similar angels for other nations/people groups, working in one-new-man cooperation with Gabriel and Michael. But in the Garden of Eden, Satan succeeded in subverting the rule of God, through mankind, on this earth. Since that time, he has become the "god of this world." He and his minions (one-third of the original angelic force?; Rev. 12:4) exert their rule from the "heavenly places." To the degree that a nation/people group follows Satan—by idolatry, murder, sexual immorality, lying, worship of the dead, of ancestors, etc.—the demons come to control the "throne" or "principality" which lies behind the earthly authority structures, especially the religious, governmental, and educational ones. This can happen for so long and to such a degree that it can seem impossible to see the original, redemptive purpose for the original "throne"; and so it seems as if the only thing we can do is to *struggle against* this evil principality (Eph. 6:12). This is just as true for Israel, with the caveat that only Israel is promised *complete* salvation and victory in the end of days (Rom. 11:25-26).

Satan is aware of the Scripture and God's plan to bring salvation and blessing from one nation to another, starting out of Israel (e.g., Ps. 67; Rev. 7:9)—the biblical vision of a remnant from every tribe, tongue, and nation worshipping and giving thanks to God. God's design is for the distinctions and cultures to be a beautiful tapestry of mutual submission, honor, service, and love. Therefore, Satan seeks (and has been mostly successful) in doing the opposite—exploiting the distinctions and enticing the nations toward jealousy, competition, racism, war, rape, genocide—the story of Cain and Abel on a nationalized, global scale. The material "stuff" of these distinctions are the systems of *dogma*-commandment-culture, all built on the foundation of the *stoichea* elements; and because of our sinful nature, these cultural structures—even the God-given Torah—quickly become the "front-line" expression of the real-time conflicts on Earth, used to justify all kinds of notions of ethnic or national superiority. Yet, in God's plan, mankind was meant to rule with the Son of God, above every principality, power, and throne (Eph. 1:21, 2:6), that is, *over* the material *and* spiritual world of the *stoichea,* not *under the law*—i.e., not in bondage to the *stoichea*—but using them as cultural resources to serve one another in an "economy" of mutual blessing.

Thus it is only in Christ, in the new-covenant gospel—through repentance, prayer, righteousness, and reconciliation with other people groups—that we can liberate our national, throne gift-calling from demonic possession, releasing it to the power of archangels obedient to Yeshua. This brings about the possibility of incredible transformation of the nation and its capacity to be a blessing to other nations. Now, because of Yeshua's incarnation, crucifixion, resurrection, and ascension "all authority in heaven and earth" has been given to Him (Matt. 28:18). He sits at the right hand of the Father, "far above all rule and authority and power and dominion, and every name that is named, not only in this age, but also in the one to come" (Eph. 1:21). His hands are not "tied" as they seemingly were in the book of Daniel, where He waited for help from Michael. Under the new covenant, all of our worship and prayer is directed toward Him and His throne of mercy and authority; while we need to have some understanding of the heavenly, angelic dynamics, we need not be obsessed with the function of demons, angels, or try to figure out their names.[85] Our ultimate victory is assured by His blood, our testimony of who He is, and our total dedication to Him, even unto death (Rev. 19:8–9, 12:11).

Returning to Peter and Cornelius, we can see how they were positioned in the midst of this cosmic warfare. Peter, like most of his fellow Jews, believed in Israel's chosenness and distinction, and was likely aware of our calling to be a "light to the nations." But he, and with him the gospel of Messiah, was stuck behind the wall of enmity—the wall made up of *dogma* bricks like the dietary laws, themselves formed from the substance of the material elements and principles (*stoichea*) of the universe, e.g., "don't eat, don't touch." Even if he had some kind

---

[85] This was the situation in second temple Judaism, especially among the Pharisaic schools, wherein angelic activity and mediation was a major part of Jewish revelation and spirituality.

of revelation from Genesis and/or Isaiah of God's plan for the nations, he couldn't do much about it: Jewishly speaking, it was culturally and "legally" impossible for him to go and be a light to the nations (Gentiles)—in this case, the Roman Cornelius and his household.[86] I imagine that because of the angelic involvement in both visions, there was great, heavenly warfare around the events, as if heaven and Earth were "sitting on the edge of their seats" watching how Peter would respond: Would he indeed follow the shocking vision and the invitation to a Gentile's home, resulting in the sudden beginning of the Holy Spirit being poured out on the nations? Or would his traditional Jewish bias win the day? As he was obedient, a whole new, giant chapter of salvation history was inaugurated. (Unfortunately, we know from Galatians 2:11–14 that years later Peter took a step back from this prophetic threshold, causing division and confusion at the church in Antioch.)

So back to the question: Who or what did Yeshua "disarm" on the cross, and how is it so closely tied to the abolishing, or "taking away" of the *dogma-stoichea* commandments of Torah? Remember, Scripture doesn't say that He has *destroyed* the powers—because the original principality, power, or throne is part of God's sovereign design of the universe, created by and for Yeshua himself. It only says that he *disarmed* them and *triumphed over* them. This means that Yeshua did not come to destroy what he had first created and decreed—in this case, the chosenness of the Jewish nation, ratified by divine covenant with Abraham and his offspring, and given moral and cultural shape by the Torah of Moses.[87] Rather, He came to bind and disarm the demonic powers who had "hijacked" the originally redemptive throne or principality—causing

---

[86] We just entertained an Orthodox Jewish couple at our home in China; they're life here is very much on the "defensive," especially because of food issues. They cannot share the most basic fellowship around a Chinese dinner table; and the only way they could effectively be a "light to the nations" would be by Chinese adopting Jewish, Torah standards!

[87] In the same way, the "abolishing" of the *dogma* commands in his flesh on the cross doesn't mean that he *destroyed* the same commands; as we studied, the commandments are still there, but they have lost their power to define the holy, righteous boundaries of God's people; they have been exposed for what they really are, as they simply function as the boundary markers of one people.

it to become a source of prideful and jealous enmity, of curse and not blessing. He came, in the fullness of the timing of God's plan, to liberate the throne of Israel's chosenness in order that our nation might fulfill its ultimate purpose of being a light to the nations; to proclaim freedom to the captives and to restore to Israel and the nations the promise of ruling the world as God's faithful stewards.

How did he accomplish this? By abolishing in His own flesh (i.e., His own earthly, ethnic identity) the particularly divisive enmity between Jew and Gentile—as contained by and expressed in the *dogma*-Torah commandments—Yeshua forever disarmed the "legality" of using the culture founded on the practice of these commandments as a source of *holy* (read: superior) exclusivity. He canceled out the certificate of debt consisting of decrees (*dogma*) against us and which was hostile to us; and He has taken it out of the way, having nailed it to the cross (Col. 2:14). By dying on the cross—the "tree of cursing"—Yeshua redeemed us from the curse (enmity!) of Torah, that the blessing of Abraham might come to the Gentiles/nations (Gal. 3:13–14). Outside of the gospel of the cross of Yeshua, this Torah of *dogma* commands is *against us*—that is, against the beautiful equality amidst continuing distinctions that God intends for the unity of Jew and Gentile, Israel and the nations. He forever "defanged," if you will, this demonic stratagem for bias, racism, competition, jealousy, and ascendancy (one nation "Lording" it over the other—even benignly). All the demons whose assignment it is to pervert a nation's calling to be a blessing to other nations have lost, in Christ, any "legal" way of doing so. Now it is our job to apply these gospel truths and finish the war (Ps. 145:5–9; 2 Cor. 10:3–6; Eph 6:12ff.)![88]

---

[88] "The fact is that the gospel often expands within a community but does not normally 'jump' across cultural boundaries between peoples, especially those created by hate or prejudice. Believers can readily influence their 'near neighbors' whose language and culture they understand, but religion is often bound up with cultural identity. Therefore, religious beliefs do not easily transfer from one group to another." Ralph D. Winter and Bruce A. Koch, "Finishing the Task: The Unreached Peoples Challenge," https://s3.amazonaws.com/files.frontierventures.org/pdf/FinishingTheTask.pdf, accessed July 1, 2018.

As the King-Prince of Israel, in both heaven and Earth, He came in utter humility and submission. Although He had the most exalted identity of any human being in all the history of the universe, when the time came for His incarnation—for heaven to visit Earth in the most profound way imaginable—He did not regard this identity as "a thing to be grasped" (Phil. 2:6), that is, as something to be "held on to." He gave it up—for a time. When Yeshua walked this earth—despite the imagery of centuries of western art—He came with no glowing halo over His head, with no special privileges; according to Isaiah, people were not drawn to Him for His beauty or stature—He was a man just like us in this dirty, fallen world, "a man of sorrows and acquainted with grief" (Isa. 53:3).

When God finally and decisively came to the "other"—in this case, humankind—he did so as a servant, as one who did not arrogantly parade His divinity for all to see but humbly, as one of us. When he took upon Himself the fullness of Israel's destiny and calling, including our sin, he embodied the full expression of this most central "throne" in God's kingdom plan. The demonic powers around this throne thought that by successfully rousing both Jewish religious pride—led by the Sanhedrin and Gentile, Roman anti-Jewish authorities, represented by Herod and Pilate—that they had successfully snuffed out the promise of God's kingdom coming to Earth by crucifying the Son of David, the Son of God (1 Cor. 2:8). The King of Israel, the promised Deliverer, had seemingly failed to bring the kingdom; instead He died an ignominious death on the tree of cursing (Gal. 3:13). But because of His total obedience and willingness, like His father Abraham with Isaac before Him, to place the embodiment of all God's promises on the altar of sacrifice—namely, Himself on the cross—God raised Him from the dead, highly exalted Him, and has given Him the name above every other name (Gen. 22; Phil. 2:6–11).[89] When God raised Yeshua from the dead, He became the first glorified, resurrected human being,

---

[89] Paul understood this more than anyone else, as he wrote Galatians 2:19–21.

filled with the power of an eternal, indestructible life (1 Cor. 15:20; Heb. 7:16). Just as He abolished the enmity and status of the *dogma* commandments and defeated the enemy powers "in His flesh" through His perfect atoning sacrifice on the cross, so in His new, resurrected flesh He is one new man—the "apostle" and pioneer of a new kind of humanity (Heb. 3:1, 12:2).

Only on this side of these events is it possible for the good news of salvation and the Abrahamic adoption of nations to go out in such a way that its messengers will no longer be encumbered by any cultural, *stoichea*-based taboos, biases, national sins, linguistic barriers, foods, etc.[90] Now, we can stand together in Him, Jew and Gentile, Israel and the nations—recognizably so because of our continuing identities, but in a totally new relationship of love and service to one another, reconciled on the foundation of His cross and resurrection. As we "stand" in this way, a powerful demonstration of "the manifold wisdom of God" is made to the heavenly principalities and powers—a demonstration which has the power to reclaim every nation's "throne-calling" and destiny from the wicked powers (Eph. 3:10). In Him, we are "one new Jew" and "one new Gentile"—together one new man/humanity. This is not some kind of academic presentation to the principalities, but a powerful declaration of the Lamb of God's victory over sin and the rulers of this wicked age—thus enacting at the "corporate," social level of our human identities what He has already authorized by His death, resurrection, and ascension. He has made the redemptive promise to Israel—and its extension to all nations—to be utterly dependent on this new relationship, in Himself.

In the next chapters we will conclude the main section of this book by taking a look at the one new man from a different, but complementary perspective—that found in Romans 9–11. In Ephesians and Colossians, the emphasis is on the *relational qualities* of the one new man—the

---

[90] No other faith/religion can be so universal and still preserve and celebrate ethnic/cultural/national distinctions; compare Islam, wherein everyone must learn Arabic to read the Koran.

earthly (and heavenly) dynamics of the mystery of how Jew and Gentile are reconciled in the gospel. In Romans, the apostle explains the same mystery in a different way, focusing more on the *historical, prophetic* quality of the relationship between Israel and the nations, and how this will play out in the end times, ultimately leading to the second coming of Yeshua and the establishing of His kingdom on Earth.

16

THE MYSTERY OF ROMANS 9–11: PAUL'S UNCEASING GRIEF AND HIS SURPRISING FIDELITY TO ISRAEL

I am telling the truth in Christ, I am not lying, my conscience bearing me witness in the Holy Spirit, that I have great sorrow and unceasing grief in my heart. For I could wish that I myself were accursed, separated from Christ for the sake of my brethren, my kinsmen according to the flesh, who are Israelites, to whom belongs the adoption as sons and the glory and the covenants and the giving of the Law and the temple service and the promises, whose are the fathers, and from whom is the Christ according to the flesh, who is over all, God blessed forever. Amen. (Rom. 9:1–5)

"**B**ehold, how good and how pleasant it is for brethren to dwell in unity!" (Ps. 133:1). Jew and Gentile perfectly reconciled, with their continuing unique identities, serving one another from the full security of being children of God in Messiah! Together, demonstrating God's awesome love and wisdom to the heavenly powers! Affecting transformation and revival in the nations and in Israel!

All leading up to the glorious return of Yeshua to rule and reign on the earth! What a beautiful picture of the kingdom of God. Like heaven on Earth? Exactly.

The great battle of the ages, and all spiritual warfare, centers around one thing: the return of Yeshua to this earth to establish His kingdom. If every Christian were to "die and go to heaven," and the rest be raptured, Satan would still be secure as the "ruler of this world."[91] What he, and all the evil principalities, fear the most is the second coming of Christ, when he returns to wage all-out warfare on Satan and his minions, and permanently redeem this world as He establishes the throne of His father David in Jerusalem.

What we have studied about the one new man from Ephesians, Colossians, Galatians, Hebrews, and Philippians describes the *relational dynamics and values* of the mystery of the reconciled relationship of Jew and Gentile—and thus of every other people group on the earth—in Christ. It describes how the "throne" of each group can be recaptured and redeemed, transforming the society to become a blessing in the earth; how we are then to co-exist with one another in a humble attitude of love, forgiveness, and service; and how we can never allow culture—even so-called "biblical" or "Torah" culture—to impede the dynamic of reconciliation, or quench the flame of mutual love. As we saw in Ephesians 3:1–6, this unity amidst the diversity of continuing identities is a great mystery that only began to be deciphered in Paul's ministry among Jew and Gentile in the first century. But where is it all headed? Is there something more to the mystery, even a missiological dimension? An eschatological dimension? Yes, indeed!

And there's even more to the revelation of the apostle as found in Romans 9–11. The Ephesians/Colossians one new man is like a wedding contract between Jew and Gentile; Romans 9–11 is more like a business plan, which describes how Israel and the nations together will

---

[91] In fact he would be pretty happy with the situation, which should signal to us the origins of doctrines which lead Christians to think that their eternal destiny is "up there."

accomplish the goal of Yeshua's return and bringing His kingdom reign to Earth. As we dive into these meaty chapters, we need to first ponder the irony that the greatest and most specific revelation of the end-times restoration and salvation of Israel, world missions, and the second coming of Jesus had come to this prophet-apostle who had become "public enemy #1" in Israel.

Romans 9:1–6

Paul introduces his treatise on God's ultimate faithfulness of His promises to Israel in a strange way: "I am telling the truth in Christ, I am not lying, my conscience bearing me witness in the Holy Spirit, that I have great sorrow and unceasing grief in my heart. For I could wish that I myself were accursed, separated from Christ for the sake of my brethren, my kinsmen according to the flesh." What a profound expression of love and utter sacrifice, a willingness to die, to even be "cut off from Christ" (if it were possible) for the sake of his people![92] But why the solemn avowal that what he is about to say is "the truth, not a lie," even to the point—in seeming contradiction to Yeshua's teaching against swearing oaths by invoking God's name (Matt. 5:33–38)—of invoking the "witness" of the Holy Spirit? Why not just straight-out declare his "great sorrow and unceasing grief" for his unsaved countrymen?

The most logical answer to these questions is that Paul sensed that the Roman Christians, most of whom had never met him personally, were going to have a very hard time believing the integrity of this statement of his continuing devotion, grief, and love for the Jewish people. This fits with everything we have learned thus far: By this time, the apostle had become infamous as the supposedly anti-Torah, anti-Israel "Apostle to the Gentiles" whose gospel teaching seemed to have laid the axe to the root of Israel's unique calling and identity. This status, as "public enemy

---

[92] He can speak of this readiness to be "separated from Christ" because he has just finished explaining at the end of chapter 8 that there is nothing in the universe that can separate us from His love!

#1" in Israel; as the founder of a supposedly anti-Israel, supercessionist (the church has replaced Israel) Christianity has continued down to our present day.[93] Plus, everyone in Rome had heard of him, and of his suffering at the hands of the Jewish authorities. Humanly speaking, they must have thought: "The man has every reason to reject—and believe in God's final rejection of—the Jewish people and nation." Perhaps rumor, or a copy of the letter itself, had already spread to the capital of what Paul had written of "the Jews" to the Thessalonian church: "who both killed the Lord Jesus and the prophets, and drove us out. They are not pleasing to God, but hostile to all men, hindering us from speaking to the Gentiles that they might be saved; with the result that they always fill up the measure of their sins. But wrath has come upon them to the utmost" (1 Thess. 2:15–16).[94] Hardly words which sound like they come from one who retains in his heart "great sorrow and unceasing grief" for these very same Jews!

It's as if the apostle were pleading: "Look, you all know who I am and what I preach, and you know what the rest of the Jewish community accuses me of; you know how much I have suffered at their hands (2 Cor. 11:23–26); I could have every reason to believe, even desire, that God might be finished with Israel; so what I am about to say must be from God. . . . I'm telling you that this grief and my enduring love for my nation—and what I am about to explain to you about its call and its future—it must be from the Holy Spirit, not from my flesh; it's the truth, not a lie or some subterfuge to ingratiate myself to all of you—especially my Jewish readers."

Paul reminds me of the prophet Jeremiah, who also was a lone voice in his generation, declaring Judah's sin and announcing God's impending judgment—even the destruction of the religious, political, and symbolic heart of the nation, the Jerusalem temple. To say the least, it

---

[93] Especially among Jewish intellectuals over the last century, a "reclamation" of Yeshua as a "good Jew" has taken place. But not so for Paul, who is viewed as the founder of a gentile religion based on the "myth" of Yeshua's divinity.

[94] Most experts believe 1 and 2 Thessalonians to pre-date Romans by at least three or four years.

was an unpopular message, and he was suspected of being a traitor, a turncoat who was perhaps collaborating with the Babylonian enemy; he was hated, tortured, imprisoned, and thrown into a dungeon/pit by the Jewish authorities (Jer. 37–38). Yet ironically, it is the very same prophet who received some of the most powerful and beautiful prophecies of God's continuing love and comfort for Israel—and His ultimate plan to forgive and restore the nation. Today, at every Jewish wedding, we sing one of them: "'Yet again there shall be heard in the cities of Judah and in the streets of Jerusalem: the voice of joy and the voice of gladness, the voice of the bridegroom and the voice of the bride. . . . For I will restore the fortunes of the land as they were at first,' says the LORD" (Jer. 33:10–11).

But even more significantly, Jeremiah received the most detailed OT prophecy of new-covenant theology—including the very name itself, "new covenant"—in chapter 31, verses 31–34 of the book by his name. This prophecy, perhaps more than any other, prefigures Paul's NT gospel by declaring that the new covenant will be categorically different from the Mosaic one, with the universal, moral Torah of God written on the very tablets of the hearts of all men—to the Jew ("House of Israel/ Judah") first, and also to the Gentile (Rom. 1:16). Now, it is possible for every person, small or great, to know God directly in this way—and all of this based on the fact that God will "forgive their iniquity, and their sin . . . remember no more" (v. 34).[95]

Next, in Romans 9:4–5—in case anyone still doubts Paul's "ortho-doxy" with respect to his theology of God's continuing faithfulness to physical, literal Israel[96]—he declares a list of eight things that can still be spoken of as "belonging" to Israel, the Jewish nation, in the new covenant present tense: "the adoption as sons, and the glory and the

---

[95] Herein lies an important principle: If we want greater revelation about the end times and God's plan of salvation and restoration, we must be "radical" in our obedience to Him, no matter the cost.

[96] That is, Israel the nation "according to the flesh" and according to a plain, literal understanding of the Scriptures.

covenants and the giving of the Law and the temple service and the promises, whose are the fathers, and from whom is the Christ according to the flesh." What an amazing breakdown of the irrevocable gift—the calling of Israel (Rom. 11:28), and a strategic affirmation from the "apostle of controversy!" He is even careful to include the statement "the giving of the law/Torah," a traditionally Jewish phrase he purposely and polemically avoids in Galatians. One can almost hear the Jewish-Christians and the wider Jewish community of Rome breathe a sigh of relief: "*Baruch HaShem!*" "Praise God! It looks like everything we heard about this man and his teaching concerning Israel is not correct; he's not just passionate about Israel, but he clearly believes in the Scriptures as understood by our people for generations. He sounds like a good, faithful, patriotic Jew after all!"

Well, not so fast! In the next verse, Paul introduces a statement—really a kind of rhetorical question—that will frame the sometimes paradoxical teaching of chapters 9–11: "But it is not as though the word of God has failed" (Rom. 9:6a). Before we continue, we must seek to understand the transition here, and the use of this verse.[97] The list of eight things in verses 4–5 which the apostle affirms as still belonging to Israel are all based on God's Word in the OT. So what's the problem?

Put simply, and there were certainly many in Rome and elsewhere who were already beginning to think this way: "If all these wonderful promises belong to Israel, the Jewish nation, where is their fulfillment? Why is it that a majority of Israel, and her leadership in particular, have rejected the Messiah/King through whom all of these promises were predicted to find their fulfillment?" Furthermore, Paul wrote this letter sometime in the late 50s AD, more than a decade before the first Jewish rebellion which culminated with the destruction of Jerusalem

---

[97] The language echoes Isaiah 55:11: "So shall My word be which goes forth from My mouth; **it shall not return to Me empty**, without accomplishing what I desire, And without succeeding in the matter for which I sent it."

and the temple by Roman armies. Then, sixty-three years later (133–136 AD), the Jews rebelled again under Simon Bar Kochba, a Messianic figure, and this time the Romans not only squashed the rebellion but slaughtered a huge number of Jews, sent tens of thousands into slavery and exile, and systematically erased the memory of everything Jewish from the newly named Roman province of "Palestina."[98] In other words, in the two generations after Paul wrote this letter, history witnessed not the fulfillment of the literal promises of God to Israel, but something which looked to be its antithesis: instead of blessing and fulfillment—judgment, destruction, scattering, and apparent rejection.[99]

Writing by the inspiration of the Holy Spirit, the apostle prophetically anticipates this theological predicament—one which, if not explained properly, can expose God's Word to the charge of being false—or at least un-believe-able according to its original, literal meaning without resort to allegorical and otherwise spiritualized interpretations. In Paul's time the "supercessionist" accusation—that God's literal words of promise to Israel have been completely fulfilled in Christ and the church—had already begun; and over the coming generations historical events would fuel the flames of theological accusation. Perhaps the Christian church has "replaced" Israel in the meaning of God's promises, which can be understood in a universal, spiritual way as applying to all believers individually, and to the church of Christ corporately? Or perhaps, as one named Marcion taught, the source of these OT promises to Israel is something or someone other than our Lord Jesus Christ? (Therefore, Marcion's doctrine went, the Christian church no longer needs the OT, except for Genesis, the Psalms, and a few books of wisdom.)

---

[98] This is the root of calling the land "Palestine." One can often quickly determine the theology toward Israel (replacement? restorationist?) of a Christian text by how it speaks of the historic Promised Land, calling it by this "pagan," Roman name, or by its biblical name, "Israel."

[99] What the rabbis refer to as *hester panim,* or "hiding His face," from Israel (Deut. 32:20).

"No, may it never be!" protests the apostle. "Not to worry, God's Word has not failed—it will not *return to Him void!*" But there is a great mystery in how exactly the fulfillment of this Word of God to Israel is unfolding in history; one which has everything to do with the one-new-man *eclessia* and the mystery of the gospel and the adoption going out to the nations, while the promises to Israel remain 100% valid.

17

THE MYSTERY OF ROMANS 9–11: DIVINE ELECTION, THE REMNANT, THE END OF TORAH FOR RIGHTEOUSNESS, AND THE PREACHING OF THE GOSPEL

But it is not as though the word of God has failed. For they are not all Israel who are descended from Israel; neither are they all children because they are Abraham's descendants, but: "THROUGH ISAAC YOUR DESCENDANTS WILL BE NAMED." (Rom. 9:6–7, emphasis added)

For Christ is the end of the law for righteousness to everyone who believes. (Rom. 10:4)

By now, it shouldn't surprise us that the first place Paul turns to in explaining the mystery of the new covenant fulfillment of God's Word to Israel is to the patriarchal stories in Genesis. We have seen from his other letters, especially Galatians, how he finds the center—or foundation—of biblical promise not in the Torah commandments given to the whole nation from Mount Sinai, but rather in the pure voice of promise which spoke to Abraham, Isaac, and Jacob-Israel. Thus, Paul begins his grandest explanation of the theology of Israel, its promises, the Gentile nations, the last days, the "fullness," and the second coming of Yeshua with the simplest of lessons from the stories of the great ancestors of the nation: While to both Abraham and Isaac more than one son was born, the covenantal promises of God for this family, first given to Abraham, must be inherited and perpetuated by *one son only*. Which son it is to be is a matter of God's sovereign choice—first through Abraham's son Isaac (not Ishmael or any other), and next through Jacob (not his twin, Esau) (Rom. 9:6–23). Thus, while there were many children and offspring to Abraham's family—the nascent Israel—only the chosen ones can be counted as the "children of promise." Not all of Abraham's offspring are thus counted as part of Jacob. Israel, the nation of promise—not all of literal, physical Israel—can be counted as part of what he will soon label the chosen "remnant" of Israel.[100]

Paul's Introduction of "Remnant Theology"

Recall that this is the first phase in Paul's exposition of how God's Word to the Jewish nation has not failed, but continues to accomplish God's will and desire (Isa. 55:11). Yet, before he gets to the subject of "all Israel's" future salvation in chapter 11, he is careful to establish the present-day legitimacy of God's promise by introducing what we call "remnant theology." He does this first in Romans 9, as we have just studied, finally summarizing with a verse from Isaiah: "Though the number of the sons of Israel be like the sand by the sea, it is the remnant that will be saved" (9:27, quoting Isaiah 10:22). He then picks up this theme again at the beginning of chapter 11 by recalling the story of Elijah, who thought that he was the lone child of promise in his generation (Rom. 11:3). The voice of God rebukes and encourages the prophet by declaring that the Lord has sovereignly "reserved" for Himself seven thousand who

---

[100] It is interesting that it is only in the third patriarchal generation, that *all* of Jacob's offspring are included in the promised, covenanted nation; with the promise of Messianic salvation and government then moving to one tribe, that of Judah.

had not bowed the knee to Baal (1 Kings 19:18). So now, as in Isaiah 10:22, the promise is not just to an individual son in each generation, but there is a group—seven thousand—whom God can call "children of promise." No matter how harsh God's judgment of Israel's idolatry and unfaithfulness may be in any given generation, God has sworn to preserve a faithful remnant in that same generation, one which will carry the promise forward to its ultimate fulfillment. His Word of promise to Abraham—to his physical and literal descendants, the nation of Israel—will not return to Him void. But before its ultimate fulfillment in the Messianic kingdom, one may need to "dig around" by faith to find the real-time, historical children of promise who are the continuing repository of this covenant, because "they are not all Israel who are descended from Israel" (Rom. 9:6).

This theme of the remnant comes into play again in 11:16, as the apostle brings the teaching to bear on his present time: "And if the first piece of dough be holy, the lump is also; and if the root is holy, the branches are too." The first reference is most likely based on Numbers 15:17–21: After Israel was to enter the land, and begins to eat of the "bread of the land," we were to "raise up" to the Lord a kind of firstfruits offering from the threshing floor by consecrating a first piece of the dough to the Lord. Once this was done, the rest of the "lump" of dough, that which will actually be baked and made into bread, was sufficiently consecrated. The whole bread—and by extension, all the bread that will be eaten from the harvest of that barley or wheat—is now "holy" and fit for consumption.[101] For the second image, that of the holiness of the root, and thus the branches, it is harder to pin down an OT reference.[102] But, since the idea is parallel to the first image of dough and lump, the meaning is quite clear: If the root, which is the earliest part of a tree to emerge from the seed, is chosen

---

[101] The reference to the threshing floor implies that this didn't need to be done every time we baked bread, only during the time of the harvest, when the wheat or barley was threshed.

[102] Jeremiah 11:16 speaks of Israel as a beautiful, "green olive tree," whose branches are now worthless, ready for the fire.

and consecrated, i.e., "holy"—then the rest of the tree, even to the outermost branch which is somehow connected to the root, is holy. In sum, the consecration of the first, or earliest, part covers the whole with its holiness. In every generation since God made His covenant with Abraham, there is a chosen, consecrated remnant; and this remnant carries within itself the holiness of God's promise, preserving it for the day of ultimate fullness. In Paul's day, this referred to the early Jewish church, including the apostle himself—and explains the reason why he begins his refutation of the idea that God has somehow "abandoned" Israel in chapter 11 by boldly pointing to himself: "For I too am an Israelite, a descendant of Abraham, of the tribe of Benjamin. God has not rejected His people whom He foreknew" (Rom. 11:1–2).

The Significance of Remnant Theology and Romans 10

Before we move on to the second "phase" of Paul's teaching of the full-blown, *future* (from his time forward) fulfillment of God's Word to Israel, we need to contemplate the significance of this "remnant theology" and why it was so important to the apostle and to the Holy Spirit to so convincingly establish it at this juncture. After all, once he declared in Romans 9:6 that God's word has not failed, he could have just "jumped" to Romans 11:11 and the explanation of how the Gentiles will provoke Israel to jealousy; how their fullness will ultimately bring about the fulfillment of all of God's promises to Israel, as "all Israel will be saved" (11:26). In other words, the message of chapters 9–11 could have been greatly simplified, resembling that of many of the OT prophets: "Don't worry, all these covenantal blessings still belong to chosen, physical, literal Israel; and while we may see judgment, destruction, and scattering for a time, God promises the physical restoration of the nation (ingathering) and its ultimate spiritual salvation as well. It's just a matter of time." But this is not exactly what Paul has to say, and in the rest of this chapter we will contemplate the reasons why, focusing on two points: Why the focus on the remnant? And why Romans 10, which seems like a digression?

"Remnant theology" means that through all the ups and downs of almost four thousand years of Jewish history, God was watching over his Abrahamic and Messianic promise. Over the last two thousand years, it means that despite the sometimes genocidal, even "Christian" anti-Semitism from the one side; and the vehemently anti-Yeshua (and anti-Paul) doctrines from the side of the rabbis, there was always a believing Jewish remnant—probably numbering somewhere between one and seven thousand! It means that God's plan always has the quality of "organic continuity" to it—not jumping from one plan to another; and certainly not teaching that God's promise was active in Israel only before Christ, and then again after he returns—while another promise is active now among the Gentiles during a parenthetical "church age."[103] This issue of covenantal continuity is a foundational one in the kingdom of God.[104] It must be established clearly so that we don't miss the fullness of the fullness! If in our theology of the restoration of Israel, we are always only looking to the future fulfillment, we could miss out on what God is presently doing among the Jewish people, its significance for the nations, and how this will lead us to the ultimate fullness of the second coming. We must be wary of any theology of God's promise to Israel which "over-futurizes," usually resulting in a false doctrine which says that there is presently no priority on sharing the gospel with the Jewish people—thus effectively removing us from the evangelistic passion and strategy of the NT Apostles.[105]

Remnant theology can also help us understand the placement of chapter 10 (actually starting from 9:24). Most studies of "Israel" in

---

[103] For those who have "ears to hear," this is an unabashed shot at the classic dispensational understanding of salvation history, one which causes its adherents to totally miss, or to sorely misunderstand, the present-day restoration of Israel and the Messianic remnant. More on this shortly.

[104] Yeshua also teaches concerning this "organic" quality of the kingdom through his parables of the seeds and leaven in Matthew 13.

[105] In modern times, especially after the Holocaust, this has been called *Dual-Covenant Theology*: Israel has her covenant with God through Moses and the patriarchs; while the church has hers through Christ.

Romans 9–11 tend to gloss over this chapter, or not mention it at all. Why? Because it promotes two subjects that are usually of little interest to many an "Israel teacher:" a) the one-new-man definition of Israel as comprised of believing Jews and Gentiles; and b) the place of the preaching of the gospel of individual salvation to both Jew and Gentile. Let's look at these points in detail.

After declaring the certainty of God's promise to Israel in the chosen Jewish remnant from 9:6-23, the apostle "preaches" one of the things that got him into such hot water with the Jewish community: This "remnant calling" is *not from among Jews only, but also from among Gentiles* (9:24). To prove his point, Paul this time quotes not from Genesis, but from the prophet Hosea: that God always intended to take for Himself a people "who were not My people" and adopt them as sons of the living God (Hos. 2:23). Then, in verses 27–29, he quotes Isaiah to strengthen and summarize this idea: "It is the remnant that will be saved," and this remnant is made up of only those who are in Christ, both Jew and Gentile. Next, from 9:30 through 10:8a, Paul summarizes the gospel that he has so carefully explained in Romans 1–8 and in all his other letters: the gospel of salvation by grace alone—the impartation of righteousness to those who believe in Jesus—not to those who look for righteousness elsewhere, especially in the *dogma*-Torah commandments. The content of this "saving" faith is exactly the same for Jew and Gentile—the one new man. This all culminates in verse 4: "Christ is the end [goal] of the law for righteousness to everyone who believes."[106] Now, it seems, whatever sigh of relief may have been heard among the Jewish community in Rome when they started to read chapter 9 is replaced by: "Oh no,

---

[106] Concerning whether *telos* should be translated as "end" or "goal": I don't obsess about this as many others do. It is only a concern for those who are addicted to prooftexting out of context, as so many Torah teachers have done with Matthew 5:17. In the immediate, and greater context of all of Paul's teaching, the nuances of both "end" and "goal" can be made to fit: "Goal" emphasizes the promise/fulfillment dimensions of Torah/OT revelation; "end" emphasizes the abolishing/cancelling/crucifying of the *dogma*-Torah commands as functioning in any way for righteousness, holiness, sanctification, etc.

here he goes again. . . . It looks like what we heard about him must be true after all; he seems too obsessed with Gentile equality, warping the traditional boundaries of Israel, and with the 'end' of our holy Torah."

From this point forward until the end of chapter 10, Paul declares many things which are more likely to be found in the handbooks for evangelists and missions agencies than in a book about Israel and the end times: "if you confess with your mouth Jesus is Lord, and believe in your heart that God raised Him from the dead, you will be saved" (v. 9); or, "How then will they call upon Him in whom they have not believed? And how will they believe in Him whom they have not heard? And how will they hear without a preacher? And how will they preach unless they are sent? Just as it is written, 'HOW BEAUTIFUL ARE THE FEET OF THOSE WHO BRING GLAD TIDINGS OF GOOD THINGS!' (vv. 14–15). Why, in these chapters which are supposedly devoted to explaining how God's words of promise to Israel are true and faithful, does the apostle make this seeming digression into revival and 'word of faith' (v. 8) gospel preaching to both Jew and Gentile? What's the connection?"

If we can only understand the passion, unction, and experience of this man, it all fits together. Forgive the metaphor, but if Romans 9–11 can be thought of as a sandwich, then chapters 9 and 11 are the slices of bread; and chapter 10 is no digression, but it is actually the irreplaceable "meat" of the sandwich. You see, Paul was no "Torah teacher," and not even an "Israel teacher."[107] He was a true apostle, meaning that he represented and led a full-orbed "fivefold ministry" team of the apostolic, prophetic, evangelistic, pastoral, and teaching ministries (Eph. 4:11). He knew, and practiced, that once apostles and prophets get vision and strategy from God, the next "ministry" or "minister" in line is the evangelist—for if no one goes out to evangelize and win people into the kingdom, then there is no one to "pastor" or "teach" (the next two gifts/offices/ministries). This passion for evangelism, for seeing people

---

[107] I recently met a brother, a pastor of a small church in Asia, who describes himself as an "Israel teacher."

154   One New Man

"saved" was the irreplaceable "engine" of all of Paul's ministry and theology. This is how he can write the following self-description:

> For though I am free from all men, I have made myself a slave to all, that I might win the more. And to the Jews I became as a Jew, that I might win Jews; to those who are under the Law, as under the Law, though not being myself under the Law, that I might win those who are under the Law; to those who are without law, as without law, though not being without the law of God but under the law of Christ, that I might win those who are without law. To the weak I became weak, that I might win the weak; I have become all things to all men, that I may by all means save some. And I do all things for the sake of the gospel, that I may become a fellow partaker of it. (1 Cor. 9:19–23)

All of this is a warning of getting too focused on the future, on the fulfillment of prophecy.[108] Paul is saying: "I keep coming back to the pure, simple gospel—the remnant, the one-new-man equality of Jew and Gentile because I am 'Christ-centered' and not 'Israel-centered.'" Yes, Israel is important, and "my heart's desire and my prayer to God from them is for their (the Jewish people's) salvation" (Rom. 10:1). Yes, the dynamics of the fulfillment of prophecy in the future are important, but don't be deceived! The way that we are going to get there is by preaching the Christ-centered gospel of God's grace and imparted righteousness, by the power of the Holy Spirit. The apostle refuses to allow us to "jump" to the future destiny of Israel; He wants us not to jump, but to proceed step by step up the ladder of the kingdom by focusing on present realities: the remnant, the one new man, and especially the preaching of the gospel.

---

[108] Similar to what Yeshua taught in Acts 1:6-8, where the disciples were focused on the timing of the fulfilling of God's promises—*are you now going to restore the Kingdom to Israel?* Yeshua's answer moves their focus, and should move ours similarly, from the "when" to the "who" and the "how": *You all* will be filled with the Holy Spirit and you all will be my witnesses. . . .

18

THE MYSTERY OF ROMANS 9–11: THE FULLNESS FORMULA, AND THE "HOW MUCH MORE" OF GOD'S SNOWBALLING GRACE AND MERCY

Now if their transgression be riches for the world and their failure be riches for the Gentiles, how much more will their fulfillment be! (Rom. 11:12)

As we saw in the last two chapters, Paul's "remnant theology" provides the promissory link between Israel's past and present: Because of God's unconditional covenant with the patriarchs, He will be sure of its continuity in every generation, even when it looks impossible to human eyes. Because of the promise, there is always a remnant; because of the remnant, the promise is sure, well-preserved until the day of fullness. Even in the midst of Israel's judgment and scattering during Paul's generation and after, the apostle prophetically assures us that God will still be faithful to physical/literal Israel, just as He always has been—because of this remnant. But is the presence of this saved remnant—along with the addition of a remnant from every tribe, tongue, and nation—enough to satisfy the full intent of God's promises to

Israel? Put differently, are these things enough to silence the accusation of Romans 9:6, that somehow God's word has not performed its full function, returning to Him *even a little* void? Is the reality of a spiritual church made up of Jew and Gentile enough to satisfy the full vision of Isaiah, as witnessed by some of the verses we studied in chapter 10 (covenant for the nations, redemption of Jerusalem, etc.)? [109]

In short, Scripture's answer to these questions is a resounding "No!" According to Paul, the complete fulfillment of many OT prophecies requires the literal restoration of the kingdom to Israel, as hoped by the disciples back in Acts 1:6. This is what the apostle, by the Holy Spirit, now begins to prophesy of, calling it the "fullness," and from Romans 11:11 through the end of the chapter it becomes the central theme. This glorious fullness, ultimately leading to the second coming of Christ and the establishing of His kingdom on Earth, will not just appear out of nowhere but will come about as a result of the preaching of the gospel, and the dynamic of the one-new-man remnant bearing more and more fruit, both in Israel and in all the nations.

The "Fullness Formula" of Romans 11:11–15

Paul starts this section with essentially the same rhetorical question as in verse one: "I say then, they did not stumble so as to fall, did they?" In other words, is Israel's majority rejection of the Messiah, and thus God's judgment of the entire nation, permanent? Whenever I read this verse, it reminds me of a boxer who has been knocked down, and lies there while the referee begins his count to 10: 1, 2, 3 . . . will he get up? Or has he lost, and the fight is over? No matter how desperate, or

---

[109] This view represents a kind of "middle road" between supercessionism and our restorationist view; it is popular among those who know that the exegetical "ways around" the plain meaning of Romans 11 by the supercessionist camp are impossible to support, but are not willing to allow any biblical "Zionism" into their theology, i.e., "God is faithful to spiritually save a Jewish remnant in every generation, perhaps with a large-scale revival in the End of Days, but this will have nothing to do with Israel as a nation in the biblical Promised Land—since the land promises are all fulfilled in Christ."

unconscious, he looks, Paul's answer is clear: No! May it never be! Physical, literal Israel is not "out for the count." She is not finished. There will be more than just a remnant, the day of fullness is assured!!

Then in the next sentence, the Apostle introduces an astounding principle: "But by their transgression salvation has come to the Gentiles, to make them jealous" (Rom. 11:11). Paul has already touched on this theme in 10:19, as he quotes the so-called "Song of Moses" from Deuteronomy 32. This "song" has Moses recounting the history of God's dealing with Israel, and prophesying her future. He speaks of how God lovingly chose Israel, and greatly blessed her; but then Israel (Jeshurun) "grew fat . . . Then he forsook God who made him, and scorned the Rock of his salvation. They made Him jealous with strange gods; with abominations they provoked Him to anger" (Deut. 32:15–16). Israel fell into idolatry, provoking God, their "husband" and "maker" (Isa. 54:5) to jealousy. So God promises to judge them accordingly. How? By promising to do the very same back to them: provoking them to jealousy by "those who are not a people . . . a foolish nation" (Deut. 32:21; see also Ps. 18:25–26).

Now, in verse 12 of Romans 11, this prophecy has become the cornerstone, from the Torah, of how the apostle has come to understand the chapter of salvation history that has been unfolding during his decades of gospel ministry among Jew and Gentile. Because of God's sovereign choice, and His faithfulness to the irrevocable call of the patriarchal (and Davidic) covenants, even Israel's transgression (majority rejection of the Messiah) is playing right into His hands: Its result means nothing less than the "riches" of the gospel going out to the nations (v. 12)—the "reconciliation of the world!" (v. 15). Now, the spirit of adoption (Rom. 9:4, et al.) is coming to every Gentile nation—those who were "once not a people" of God—in order to extend the Abrahamic family blessing to them, making them full sons and citizens of the commonwealth of Israel. What's more, this gospel expansion does not just move in one direction out from Jerusalem; it is designed to "rebound" back to the center by "provoking Israel to jealousy."

The next part of this astounding principle, what I call the "fullness formula," is found in the parallel verses of 12 and 15: "Now if their transgression be riches for the world and their failure be riches for the Gentiles, how much more will their fulfillment be! . . . For if their rejection be the reconciliation of the world, what will their acceptance be but life from the dead?" The logic of these verses relies on what is called in Jewish thinking *qal v'homer*, or "from the light to the heavy." Simply put, it means that if something is true concerning "A," which is something light, small, insignificant (even "negative"), then it will be even more true concerning "B," where "B" is understood to be heavier, larger, more glorious, or otherwise greater than "A." This logic is used throughout the book of Hebrews (2:1–4; 4:14–16); and Romans, especially in verses 5:9–21, which compares the sin of the first Adam—and the resulting judgment that entered the world through him—to the salvation and glorious blessing that ensued as a result of the obedience of the Second Adam, Jesus the Christ. It is worth a closer look at this text to gain a deeper understanding of how this principle works in Romans 11.

The "How Much More" Principle in Romans 5 and 11

The simple message of Romans 5 is: Yeshua, as the "Second Adam" came to graciously redeem us from the curse that came upon the world as a result of the first Adam's disobedience to God's command. As God warned, this brought the reign of death into human existence—and to the entire cosmos (Gen. 2:16–17; Rom. 5:17–19, 8:19–23). Yeshua's perfect obedience, represented by His sacrificial blood through the death of the cross, brings salvation and justification. The obedience of the Second Adam "reverses" the consequences of the disobedience of the first Adam, restoring mankind to its original, rightful place as those created and called to rule and reign with God (Gen. 1:28). Mathematically speaking, this is like a simple linear equation: $-10 + 10 = 0$; God has reversed the negative, "tit for tat," "eye for an eye, tooth for a tooth." Simple enough. But the apostle doesn't stop there, not in Romans 5, nor in Romans 11.

"But the free gift is not like the transgression . . . where sin increased, grace abounded all the more" (Rom. 5:15, 20). There is something in the loving, gracious, father heart of God that cannot stop at a simple, "zero-sum" redemption—it's too small a thing for Him; it somehow doesn't befit His character. Instead, God is like the father in the story of the prodigal son: When his son finally returns after so much time and sin have elapsed, his heart is overwhelmed with affection and forgiveness for him; instead of simply restoring him to his previous estate, he lavishes upon him a celebration the likes of which had never been seen in their house (Luke 15:29). This principle is at the very heart of the gospel of grace, as taught by the apostle: The gift of God's forgiveness is on a totally different scale than that of our trespass and the resulting judgment.

Yes, God is a holy, righteous judge; but the mercy aspect of His character is so much greater: "Mercy triumphs over judgment" (Jas. 2:13), not just narrowly, not just by some last-minute heroism that ekes out a slim victory. No! His grace, His lovingkindness is overwhelming us by an incalculable margin! The equation of His redemption in Jesus is not $-10 + 10 = 0$, but $-10 + 10$ million = a huge, positive number! (Ps. 117). If sin is increasing at a rate of 10x, then grace is increasing by 1,000x! 1,000,000x! Sin and disobedience can never have power to compromise the ultimate outcome of God's gracious call and election—not even close. God's word of grace and promise will not return to Him void—it will accomplish everything that God intended for it—and much more!!

Let's go back to Romans 11:12–15 and the one-new-man dynamic between Israel and the Gentiles. Israel sinned, stumbled on the rock that is Christ, and fell into a long season of disobedience. Like the sin of Adam which resulted in exile from the Garden of Eden, so Israel's transgression (our national rejection of the King-Messiah) has resulted in the longest judgment and exile in our history (almost two thousand years). But just as God's gracious provision of clothing (animal skins) for Adam and Eve spoke a word of hope and redemption amidst the judgment in the garden, so it was for Israel—there was a faithful Messianic Jewish remnant through whom the gospel of grace has gone out to the nations. So even the majority transgression/rejection of the Jewish people could not restrain the triumph of His mercy! The result? Nothing less than the "riches" of grace coming to the Gentiles, affecting the "reconciliation of the world." Amazing!

Yet, in the same way as we studied from Romans 5, the "how much more" of God's grace demands more than just God now blessing the nations in a way that He once blessed Israel. No, the Gentiles are experiencing a dispensation of God's grace that is far greater than Israel ever knew.[110] But there is even more!

If the riches of grace and divine-human reconciliation have come to the nations as a result of the majority, Israeli "no" to Jesus—and this through only a small, faithful remnant in Israel—what will happen at the advent of our acceptance? Our fullness? This is mind-boggling! This time, the "how much more" of God's loving promise will result in nothing less than the ultimate expression of God's redemptive promise to humanity and the universe: the resurrection of the dead—or at least something like it![111] This is the "fullness formula" of Romans 11:11–15, which then finds its fuller, prophetic explanation of the end of days from verse 25 forward. This is what we will look at in the next chapter.

---

[110] Of course there is grace in the giving of Torah; but it can't compare to the grace of the new covenant.

[111] Verse 15 could mean simply that Israel's restoration and its effect on the nations will be like a resurrection from the dead; or it could mean that this will bring about the return of Yeshua and the actual resurrection from the dead. Given what is taught in the rest of the chapter, I think it is both! See my article, "The End Times Reconciliation of the World," Revive Israel Ministries, September 9, 2016, https://reviveisrael.org/archive/language/english/2016/09-09-End-Times-Reconciliation-of-the-World.html.

19

THE MYSTERY OF ROMANS 9-11: THE FULLNESS FORMULA, WHAT IS NOT THE MYSTERY, AND THE MODERN-DAY RESTORATION OF ISRAEL

For I do not want you, brethren, to be uninformed of this mystery, lest you be wise in your own estimation, that a partial hardening has happened to Israel until the fullness of the Gentiles has come in; and thus all Israel will be saved; just as it is written. (Rom. 11:25–26)

A fter a discussion of the olive tree (verses 16–24),[112] the apostle returns to the fullness formula in verses 25–26. These verses are a recapitulation of what we studied from verses 11–15, and just as in Ephesians 3:1–6, the apostle describes it as a "mystery."[113] The partial hardening of Israel as a result of our majority rejection of Yeshua

---

[112] The olive tree is another metaphor for the historical, one-new-man-like dynamic of Jewish and Gentile together as the people of God.

[113] Just as in Ephesians, "mystery" means something that is in the plan and heart of God, that was only partially revealed and/or predicted in the OT. In the present NT tense, the mystery is being revealed.

in the first century—the stumbling, transgression, failure, and rejection in verses 11–15—is temporary. Our "fullness" is dependent upon, and waiting for something he now introduces as the "fullness of the Gentiles." Fullness of/for the nations equals fullness and salvation for Israel: "and thus all Israel will be saved" (v. 26). Then, in the next verses Paul describes, from Isaiah, what happens next—the second coming of Yeshua!

First: A Look at What Is *Not* the Mystery

Before we go on to see how this mystery is unfolding in our generation, we need to talk about a certain misunderstanding of this Romans 11 "mystery"—one which pervades the church among those who do not subscribe to the supercessionist, replacement position of historic Christianity.[114] Starting around two hundred years ago, a renewal began of the premillenial way of reading Scripture of the earliest, apostolic church, one which emphasizes the literal interpretation of OT (and NT) prophecy. In the middle of the nineteenth century, one stream of this emphasis (what came to be called "dispensationalism") began to teach that the promises of kingdom restoration to physical, literal Israel are still in effect, awaiting fulfillment at the end of the present period, called the "church age."

While it is a bit of an oversimplification, the classic dispensational way of reading Scripture goes like this: God has an eternal, unconditional plan for Israel based on the unconditional patriarchal covenant(s)—let's call it "Plan A"; but because of Israel's rejection of Messiah, God began a second, different plan for the Gentiles (and a few lucky Jews), called the "church"—this is "Plan B." According to Romans 11, God will return to "Plan A" once the last Gentile has been saved and the church is raptured

---

[114] Of course, for those who subscribe to a supercessionist theology, the "mystery" is solved by reading "Israel" as the church, and then one ends up with the apostle taking such great pains to explain how the already-saved (the church) get saved again—or get *fully* saved—"All Israel will be saved."

to heaven; then there will begin the end-times tribulation that will focus on Israel and ultimately lead to "all Israel being saved," the return of Christ, and the establishment of His millennial reign on Earth. For those who have been influenced by this way of reading Scripture, the "mystery" of Romans 11:25–26 seems to fit the view of a pretribulation rapture of the church leading to the restoration of the kingdom to Israel (Plan B back to Plan A). This causes one to read/translate verses 25–26 as: "a partial hardening has happened to Israel until the *full number* of Gentiles has come in, *and then* (after that) all Israel will be saved." This fits nicely with the dispensational emphasis on careful calculations of prophetic timing—and thus the mystery primarily becomes one about the timing of the end of the "church age" (when the last Gentile gets saved), the pretribulation rapture, and about God's ultimate faithfulness to His literal word of Davidic, kingdom restoration to Israel (three-and-a-half years, seven years, rapture).

Concerning dispensationalism, as a Messianic Jew there is much that I am thankful for—especially its emphasis on seeking to restore some of the literal meaning of OT (and NT) prophecies and the premillennial view of the early church. In addition, many of the most avid friends and supporters of Israel and Messianic Jews are from a dispensational background. Amen and many thanks! However, our understanding of Romans 11, and of end-times events, is quite different,[115] as it sees the Romans 11 "mystery" focusing more on the *how* of end-times fulfillment, not so much the precise calculation of *when*. Nor do we see the mystery as somehow pertaining to God's unfailing love for the Jewish people, His promise to restore the nation, and/or to establish Davidic, millennial Kingdom reign from Jerusalem. While all these things are true, they were not much of a "mystery" to the first-century apostolic Jewish writers of the NT; indeed, as witnessed by the disciples' question after forty days of teaching about the kingdom of God from

---

[115] I don't speak for all Messianic Jews, but I would say that for the majority who are not strict dispensationalists.

the resurrected Lord (and His answer), these things were basic to first-century eschatology and biblical, Jewish messianism (Acts 1:3–8). But after the influence of some 1,700 years of supercessionism and Christian anti-Semitism, the restoration of these truths to millions of Christians *seems* like the revelation of some great, hidden, "mystery." However, as we will see shortly, in the first-century context of the book of Romans and the ministry of Paul, he and the Holy Spirit had something else in mind when they penned verses 25 and 26 of chapter 11—something which has everything to do with the one-new-man dynamic between Jew and Gentile, Israel and the nations.

This understanding of the mystery is also why most English translations of Romans 11:25 read: "the fullness of the Gentiles, and *so/thus/ in this way* all Israel will be saved."[116] This reading is in keeping with what the apostle has already explained since Romans 9:1, and especially 11:11–15: Remnant theology means that this process of fullness is just that—a process, a historical dynamic that will see its fulfillment in stages as we draw closer and closer to its total fulfillment at the second coming. This is opposed to the "Plan A, then Plan B, and then back to Plan A" view, which seems to keep Israel and the church on eternally separate prophetic tracks—instead of the one-new-man mystery of their increasing unity under an economy of "mutual blessing." Our view is more holistic: God has one plan for Israel and the nations which is Christ-centered, Gospel-centered, Israel-centered, and "body of Christ"-centered. The plan contains a "back and forth" aspect, but it is the back and forth of the renewing work of the Holy Spirit among Jew and Gentile, Israel and the nations—*mutually and simultaneously.*[117]

---

[116] There is almost no precedent for translating *pleroma* as "full number," as it is translated "fullness" everywhere else in the NT (e.g., Col. 1:19, 2:9; Eph. 1.23) Paul meant fulfilled as in "complete, the state of being full." In its verb form *pleroma* means "to be full, or filled up"; thus "the fullness of the Gentiles has come in" refers to the yielding of Gentile believers to God's will. The result of this will be the salvation of Israel.

[117] For further study, see Appendix 3-3, "Why We Don't Believe in a Pretribulation Rapture." Also see *Israel, the Church, and the Last Days* by Daniel Juster and Asher Intrater (Shippensburg, PA: Destiny Image, 2003).

Instruction from the Life of Paul, and from Our Own Time

We can approach this more accurate reading of Romans 11 by observing the life and testimony of the man who wrote it—the apostle Paul. Toward the end of the letter, the apostle explains one of the key reasons for writing at such length to the church in Rome: He plans to come there on his way to Spain, a place at the outer limits of the Roman Empire that has yet to hear the gospel, and he is in need of financial support from the Roman church to accomplish this mission. But first, he is on his way to Jerusalem to minister to the saints (Rom. 15:24–25). The gospel going to the nations in order to "provoke Israel to jealousy" (salvation) was not just an ethereal, futuristic vision for the apostle. Paul was a practical man, and he knew that if he were to bring back material blessings from the Diaspora, mostly Gentile churches to the Messianic church in Jerusalem (the saints), this would not go unnoticed by the wider Jewish community (Rom. 11:12, 15:26–27). "What, the hated Gentiles are sending offerings and support to Jerusalem? To the Messianic Jews? What could this mean?" This is why, in the midst of explaining the fullness formula, the apostle can write: "Inasmuch then as I am an apostle of Gentiles, I magnify my ministry, if somehow I might move to jealousy my fellow countrymen and save some of them" (Rom. 11:13–14). This is not just inflated, apostolic boasting: Paul understood that the fulfillment of his passionate desire for Israel's salvation (Rom. 9:1–3; 10:1) depended on the proper administration of his personal ministry, or priesthood, to the nations (Rom. 15:16). The two are forever interlocked in Paul's mind—at least until Jesus returns.

Now, if Paul were a classic dispensationalist, his ministry strategy wouldn't make sense! He should have no interest in, or hope for, Israel's present salvation—or even seeing some of his fellow countrymen saved; if, since the apostolic generation, we are in the "church age" (Plan B) then this is not the time to preach the gospel to the Jews or hope to provoke them to jealousy and salvation! Paul should not be wasting his time (or the believers' money!) by bringing these offerings back to Jerusalem;

166 One New Man

nor should he so consistently maintain a gospel "to the Jew first" strategy in all of the Diaspora cities (Rom. 1:16; cf. Acts). Instead he should be *exclusively* focused on getting the gospel to Spain and everywhere else where it has not been proclaimed. Then, once the Great Commission of preaching the gospel to every nation is fulfilled, and the "full number of Gentiles" has come in, it would be time for the end-times scenario culminating in Israel's revival, salvation, and the millennial kingdom—*but not now!*

The next important reason which mitigates against this classical dispensational view (and in favor of our view) is the testimony of what has taken place among the Jewish people over the last 120 years, and especially the last fifty. First is the obvious: After almost two thousand years of exile and wandering, the nation of Israel is once again on the map—with Jerusalem as its capital. Watching news of terrorism and other problems in the Holy Land can numb us to the amazing fact of the physical restoration (and prospering) of this tiny nation. Never before in the history of human civilization has a people been so totally separated from its ancestral homeland for so long, and then restored to it! This is what God promised (e.g., Jer. 31:35–37), and what we are privileged to witness in our generation.

This process of restoration and return began with the birth of the Zionist movement in Europe in the 1880s, and gained momentum through the two World Wars. In 1948, the nation was officially recognized by the United Nations, and has been under attack by its Arab-Muslim neighbors ever since. This rebirth of the nation and the return of millions of Jews to the land promised to Abraham, Isaac, and Jacob is a major fulfillment of end-times, Messianic prophecies. In 1967, as a result of the Six-Day War, Israel conquered the Old City of Jerusalem, bringing biblical Jerusalem under (mostly!)[118] independent Jewish

---

[118] In order to keep peace in the Old City, Israel decided on a policy which maintains the status quo of the Muslim *waqf,* based in Jordan, governing sections of the Old City, especially the temple mount area.

control for the first time since the Maccabees 180 years before Christ. We understand this to be a fulfillment of another important prophecy, Luke 21:24: "and they will fall by the edge of the sword, and will be led captive into all the nations; and Jerusalem will be trampled underfoot by the Gentiles until the times of the Gentiles be fulfilled." Here again we can see the restoration of Israel (impossible without Jerusalem as its capital) connected with language of the "fullness" of the Gentile nations!

But this is not all: According to the Scriptures, the restoration and fullness of Israel (and the one new man!) is ultimately "in Christ," through the gospel. Over the last several generations we are witnessing the largest revival among the Jewish people since the first century—and this has been accelerating since 1967. Today, there are probably 150,000 Jewish believers in North America, another 10–15,000 in Israel, and another 50,000 in the former Soviet Union.[119] One hundred years ago, these numbers together probably did not reach one thousand—fifty years ago, probably not five thousand. This is an amazing, exponential increase in just two generations.

In addition, the beginnings of this revival can also be traced to the late 1800s, when a handful of Jewish "converts" to Christianity began to explore what it would mean to continue to live as Jews while following Jesus. Since 1967 we have witnessed the restoration of Messianic Jewish congregations both in the Diaspora and in Israel, which provide a home for Jewish believers to continue to identify as Jews and live out our faith in the Messiah. What this means is that the restoration and end-times "fullness" of Israel—the Jewish people/nation—is *already* underway. According to missiologists, more Jewish people have come to faith in Yeshua since 1967 than in all of the previous 1,900 years (since the early church) combined!

---

[119] More than twenty years ago Jews for Jesus did a survey in North America, which found that 10,000 Jewish believers associated with MJ congregations, and another 100,000 in traditional churches.

All of these facts simply do not fit with the classical dispensational understanding of end-times events: If Romans 11:25–26 means that Israel's salvation does not begin until the very end of the church age, after the last Gentile has "come in," then the present-day revival among the Jewish people is an aberration, like an infant born prematurely. Clearly, there is still much work left to do in world missions, and thousands of Gentiles are still turning to the Lord every day. This is not just a matter of splitting theological "hairs" about end-times prophecies; this misunderstanding of the mystery has caused, and continues to cause, a huge number of sincere, Israel-loving Christians to miss out on the revelation and blessings of the one new man and the fullness formula, as we will continue to see.

20

THE MYSTERY OF ROMANS 9–11: THE FULLNESS FORMULA AND REVIVAL AMONG THE NATIONS

For I do not want you, brethren, to be uninformed of this mystery—so that you will not be wise in your own estimation—that a partial hardening has happened to Israel until the fullness of the Gentiles has come in; and so all Israel will be saved; just as it is written. (Rom. 11:25–26)

The Fullness Formula and Parallel Revival among the Nations— Bible Translations

In the last chapter, we discovered that since the 1880s the physical restoration of the Jewish nation, as well as the promised spiritual revival, have been accelerating. The fullness is not full yet, but it has begun! According to the one new man and the fullness formula, we should be witnessing something parallel amidst the nations. This is the subject we will look at in this chapter.

In Matthew 24:14, Yeshua prophesied the following: "This gospel of the kingdom shall be preached in the whole world for a witness to all the nations, and then the end shall come." This is another way of speaking about the fullness of the Gentile nations in the gospel. It's interesting that Yeshua spoke of "this gospel of the kingdom"—not just the gospel of personal salvation. The "personal" gospel of repentance, forgiveness, and eternal life is the gate into the kingdom of God; but once inside, we find that there is much more to the kingdom than we may have first thought, including the healing of our bodies and souls; the transformation of our families, our values, even our nations; and the clear proclamation and hope of Yeshua's return to establish His kingdom over all the earth.

As we discovered earlier in this book, God has a plan to extend the blessings of Abrahamic adoption to every people group. I understand that Yeshua's prophecy here in Matthew 24 means that before the end (and thus His return), every *ethne* (people group) will have had the opportunity to not just hear the gospel of personal salvation on a mass scale—but to see the gospel penetrate the society to the degree that amazing transformation is possible. All of this together amounts to the condition of the "fullness of the Gentiles" which Paul described in Romans 11:25—a condition for all Israel being saved, and the return of Yeshua.

What about the fulfilling of this condition in our time? First, if the gospel of the kingdom is to seriously penetrate any society, that people group must have the Bible translated into its own language. If it were only a matter of personal salvation, of getting people to pray a basic prayer of repentance to accept Jesus as their Savior, this could be accomplished by a few short, verbal messages. But in order to see deeper discipleship, evangelism, and the beginnings of societal transformation, the full Bible must be available in the native language. Since the Christian message is so dependent on the biblical message, Bible translation has been in process from the time of the earliest churches. But until the 1800s the Bible had still only been translated into a handful of major languages—mostly in Europe and the Americas—for a total of about seventy, including partial translations (NT only). At the beginning of the nineteenth century, not only were there a small number of translations, but Christians were mostly unaware of just how great the task was to bring the Word of God into the language of every people group.

But the 1800s witnessed a great increase in world missions initiatives, including Bible societies and missions organizations sending workers deep into Africa, Asia and the islands of the Pacific. Increasingly, churches and missionaries began to focus on Bible translation as a central part of any cross-cultural mission activity. By 1930, the number of translations, whole or partial, had risen to nine hundred. This is an amazing increase—but according to the specialists, the actual number of spoken languages around the world today is close to seven thousand! Here are the statistics from 2014, according to Wycliffe Bible Translators, the largest of some 140 organizations involved in Bible translation:

- More than 1,300 people groups have access to the New Testament and some other portions of Scripture in their language.
- The Bible has been completely translated into more than five hundred languages. Almost seven thousand languages are known to be in use today.
- About 180 million people need Bible translation to begin in their language.
- More than 2,300 people groups across 131 countries have active translation and linguistic development work happening right now in their language.
- More than 1,800 languages still need a Bible translation project to begin.[120]

What all of this means is that for most of the last 1,800 years, this condition for the fulfilling of Matthew 24:14 and Romans 11:25 was like an impossible dream—a dream that most of the church didn't even

---

[120] Wycliffe, "Why Bible Translation?" https://www.wycliffe.org/about/why, accessed July 1, 2018.

know to dream! But over the last two hundred years, at an exponential rate, this process has been accelerating wildly—so much so that the end, the fulfillment is actually in sight: In 1999, Wycliffe Bible Translators announced Vision 2025—a project that intends to commence Bible translation in every remaining language community by 2025. They currently estimate that around 209 million people, representing 2.95 percent of the world's population, speak those 1,967 languages where translation work still needs to begin.[121] For the first time in church history, we have the knowledge, resources, and manpower to at least dream and strategize about completing this otherwise daunting task.

The Fullness Formula: World Missions and the Holy Spirit

Not surprisingly, we can see similar trends in the statistics related to world missions. Here are some to think about: It took eighteen centuries for practicing Christians to grow from 0% of the world's population to 2.5 percent in 1900, but only seventy years to grow from 2.5 percent to 5 percent in 1970, and just forty years to grow from 5 percent to 12 percent by the year 2010. Today, there is one practicing Christian for every seven people worldwide who are either nominal or non-Christian.[122] In the year 100 AD the ratio of local church congregations to unreached people groups was 1:12; in the year 1000, 1:5; in 1500, 1:1; 1900, 10:1; 1950, 33:1; 1980, 162:1; 1990, 416:1; 2000, 650:1; 2010, 1000:1.[123] According to these numbers, it took 1,800 years to see a net twenty-two times increase in this ratio of churches to unreached people groups; but from 1900 to the present that ratio has increased at least one hundredfold. That is amazing, exponential growth over the last 120 years and testifies to the incredible acceleration of world missions and the increase in worldwide Christian population which began around

[121] Stan Guthrie, "Wycliffe in Overdrive," *Christianity Today,* http://www.christianitytoday.com/ct/2005/february/28.74.html, accessed July 1, 2018.
[122] Ralph Winter, "Finishing the Task," https://s3.amazonaws.com/files.frontierventures.org/pdf/FinishingTheTask.pdf, accessed July 1, 2018.
[123] Ibid.

1900. I have written most of this book in China. In 1949 there were an estimated one million or less Christians in this huge country. Today, the number is close to 100 million!

Finally, just as with Bible translation, the "end" of which Yeshua prophesied in Matthew 24:14 is potentially in sight: "We can confidently speak of closure to this unreached peoples mission. There were an estimated 17,000 unreached peoples in 1976. Today there are only an estimated 8,000 unreached (unimax) peoples, and a dynamic global movement is now in full swing that is committed to seeing Christ worshipped and obeyed within every one of them."[124]

The last, accompanying "sign of the times" concerns the work, the power, and the baptism of the Holy Spirit. Not surprisingly, the great historical change occurred right around the same time that we are studying in reference to the restoration of Israel, world missions, and Bible translations. Until the 1800s the experience and doctrine concerning the *charismata*[125] of 99.9 percent of churches—Protestant, Catholic, and Orthodox—was *cessationism*: the belief that the miraculous "power" gifts (healing, prophetic utterances, words of knowledge, etc.) that we read of in the NT had *ceased* to be a part of normal Christianity. According to various doctrines, this cessation began sometime shortly after the apostolic age and/or the canonization of the NT. But starting in the mid-1800s, some Christians began to question this doctrine, both because of experience with the gifts and their own Bible study. And then, around the turn of the century, "Pentecostal" revivals broke out in several places, with manifestations of the power gifts, resulting in the formation of many Pentecostal denominations.[126] Later, in mid-century, a similar "charismatic

---

[124] Ibid.
[125] This is the Greek word for the "gifts" spoken of in many places of the NT. But the ones in question here concern the more miraculous "power" gifts associated with the baptism in the Holy Spirit in the NT—especially tongues, healing, prophecy, words of knowledge, dreams, visions, etc.
[126] The most famous of these revivals is the one at Azusa Street in Los Angeles, which lasted from 1906–1909.

renewal" touched many of the traditional denominations. Many of these charismatic groups eventually formed their own churches, especially as the traditional denominations became more "progressive" in their embrace of more liberal doctrines concerning Scripture and sexuality.

As of 2011, Pentecostals and charismatic Christians numbered more than 584 million, or a quarter of the world's two billion Christians. It is by far the fastest growing segment of Christianity, especially in the so-called "third world"—Africa,[127] Latin America,[128] Asia, etc. This makes us the second largest family of Christians, the largest being the Roman Catholic Church.[129] Some even refer to this phenomenon as a "third epoch" in church history: first the Catholic and Orthodox churches from the earliest centuries until the 1500s; then the Protestant Reformation; and now, in the last 150 years or so, the Pentecostal/charismatic "epoch."

Parallel Restoration in the Fullness Formula

If we were to chart the physical and spiritual restoration of Israel since the first century on a graph, it would go something like this: The x-axis represents time, and the y-axis the fulfillment of God's promise to the Jewish nation. After a surge in the first century, this restoration (or "fullness") decreased and was mostly dormant until the mid-nineteenth century. Since that time, we have witnessed the restoration of Israel on an ever-increasing, even exponential scale—both of the nation and of Jewish faith in Jesus. This is the beginning of the process of Israel's fullness, which will ultimately lead to "all Israel" being saved. Amazingly, if we

---

[127] In 1900 there were an estimated 10 million Christians in Africa; today the number is at least 500 million! Pew Research Center, "Global Christianity – A Report on the Size and Distribution of the World's Christian Population," Dec. 19, 2011, http://www.pewforum.org/2011/12/19/global-christianity-exec, accessed July 2, 2018.

[128] In 1900 there were about 50 thousand Evangelicals in South America; today the number is well over 60 million, the majority being Charismatic-Pentecostal. Ibid.

[129] Ibid. See also Stanley M. Burgess, "Part II Global Statistics: A Massive Worldwide Phenomenon," *The New International Dictionary* (Grand Rapids, MI: Zondervan, 2002), 67.

look at church growth and world missions over the same period, we see an almost perfectly parallel, exponential curve or restoration and revival since the late 1800s. Could this be coincidence? Perhaps, but according to Paul's revelation of the twin mysteries of the Ephesians one new man (shared inheritance), and the Romans fullness formula (simultaneous, complementary blessing in the end times), this is exactly what we might predict!

21

THE MYSTERY OF ROMANS 9–11: THE FULLNESS FORMULA, THE "HOW MUCH MORE" RESTORATION OF ALL THINGS, AND HIS SECOND COMING

Therefore repent and return, that your sins may be wiped away, in order that times of refreshing may come from the presence of the Lord; and that He may send Jesus, the Christ appointed for you, whom heaven must receive until the period of restoration of all things about which God spoke by the mouth of His holy prophets from ancient time. (Acts 3:19–21)

In this earliest preaching of the gospel, Peter gives a foundational synopsis of the gospel: repentance, receiving of the forgiveness of sins, the refreshing and power of the Holy Spirit ("presence of the Lord"), and the eager expectation of Jesus' return to this earth from His temporary dwelling in heaven. He declared that this great event, described by Paul as the "blessed hope" of our faith in Titus 2:13, will occur when we reach "the period of the restoration of all thing about which God spoke by the mouth of His holy prophets from ancient time" (Acts 3:20).[130] This is "restorationism," and we have studied it so far in this book from two primary perspectives—the one new man of Ephesians/Colossians, and the fullness formula of Romans 9–11.[131] The one new man gives us a clear picture of the restoration of the nations through the gospel, in reconciled partnership and unity with a restored Jewish nation in Messiah; it provides us with a sound, Christlike understanding of the meaning of our corporate, human identities in service to one another. Together, the two are one body of Christ, and co-inheritors of the same promise in the Messiah, son of Abraham. The Romans fullness formula describes the working out of this alliance—this linkage of Israel and the nations in the gospel—in historical, eschatological terms—predicting an age of incredible mutual blessing for Israel and the nations. In the last few chapters we have seen how this has been taking place over the last 150 years, an accelerating revelation of the "mystery" that is leading to the most exciting finish imaginable—or unimaginable!

One more word about our vision of the "restoration of all things:" many a revival movement throughout church history has looked to the book of Acts—to the power, miracles, holiness, and unity of the early church as a model. Amen. But the dynamic between the one new man and the fullness formula promises something even better for the end times—greater power, greater evangelism, more miracles, etc. This is why we are so optimistic and excited about the end times, even though we know there will also be great difficulties and tribulation. Yes, we can continue to look to the "heroes of faith" in the Scriptures, as outlined in Hebrews 11; but at the same time we know that "all these, having

---

[130] Literally, "*until* the period of restoration." This is a tantalizing phrase: Does it mean that all will be restored *before* Yeshua returns? Or *at* the advent of His return? It is left ambiguous, I believe, for a good reason: the Lord wants us to believe and work for as much "kingdom now" restoration as possible—while at the same time knowing that it will never be 100% complete until He returns. This is the paradox of the "already/not yet" of the kingdom of God.

[131] This is also the foundational verse for the movement I belong to, called "Tikkun" (repair, restoration) which was started thirty-five years ago by Dan Juster, Asher Intrater, and Eitan Shiskoff. Since that time, they have believed in the *dual restoration of both Israel and the church.*

gained approval through their faith, did not receive what was promised, because God had provided something better for us, so that apart from us they should not be made perfect" (Heb. 11:39–40). God is forever the God of the "how much more"; His grace, love, and power are inexhaustible, always increasing from generation to generation.

All Israel is Saved, and the Lord's Second Coming

The mystery comes to its climax in Romans 11:25–27: the fullness of the Gentile nations and the salvation of all Israel—and the return of Yeshua. We see this as a historical process of a continuing, accelerating, mutual restoration (fullness) for the nations, and for Israel—all in the gospel. I have called it the fullness *formula* because it has similarities with a scientific formula: God has established in the supernatural realm, in the *salvific* order of things, that Jew and Gentile, Israel and the nations are inextricably, "chemically" linked together in a relationship of mutual, "how much more" blessing. At a certain point, the acceleration and momentum of the "how much more" will come to its *full* fullness," like a critical mass—the extent necessary to produce an explosive reaction. This is nothing less than the universal, atmospheric transformation that will take place as the heavens are opened and Yeshua comes riding on the clouds on a great, white horse surrounded by a myriad of warring angels and resurrected saints (Zech. 14:1–5; Acts 1:11; 1 Thess. 4:13-18; Rev. 1:7, 19:11–19). He will come to war against a military coalition of "every nation" that has come up against Israel, all the way to Jerusalem. It will look as if Israel and the Jewish people are doomed, until Yeshua intervenes. This intervention is described in great detail from the earthly side in Zechariah chapters 12–14, and from the heavenly, spiritual side in Revelation 19. At this time God will pour out a spirit of grace and supplication on all Israel (or, more accurately, all Jerusalem and Judah) and "they will look on Me whom they have pierced; and mourn for Him, as one mourns for an only son" (Zech. 12:10). And so "all Israel will be saved"—literally, physically, and spiritually!

But in Romans 11:25–27, Paul doesn't go into great detail concerning the particular events at Yeshua's coming. (In a way, he doesn't need to, since they are taught so clearly elsewhere in Scripture.) Instead he just hints, by creatively quoting from at least three OT verses to describe this ultimate fullness: "The Deliverer will come from Zion; He will remove godlessness from Jacob. This is My covenant with them, when I take away their sins" (Rom. 11:25–26). We can learn a great deal by looking at these verses phrase by phrase, especially in parallel with their OT sources.

1. The Deliverer Will Come *from* Zion

Paul's OT citations start from Isaiah 59:20, which in the Hebrew original (and thus in our OT translations) reads: "And a deliverer will come *to* Zion." In the NT, there are many cases where a quotation from the OT reads slightly different from what we have in our Hebrew text and all its many translations today. Sometimes this is because of textual source issues, especially that in the Greek NT the writers were often quoting from the first, Greek translation of the Hebrew Scriptures called the Septuagint, which dates from the second or third century BC—while our oldest existing Hebrew OT (Masoretic text) dates from the Middle Ages. This is not the case here in Romans 11:26. Sometimes, under the inspiration of the same Holy Spirit who inspired the OT prophet, the NT writer uses the basic wording or theme of the OT text, but makes small changes in order to bring clarity to his new covenant teaching or application. This is what Paul does here.[132] So, "*from* Zion" or "*to* Zion"—and what's the difference?

We learned in Chapter 10, especially from Isaiah 52:8–10, that the vision of the OT prophets was highly "Israel-centric." At the event of the redemption of Jerusalem (which equals the salvation of all Israel), the Gentiles are at best innocent bystanders, or perhaps helping the Jews humanitarianly; at worst they are tools of Satan and the Antichrist.

---

[132] He also could be quoting from Psalm 14:7.

But as we have learned in this book, a mystery has been revealed in the new covenant which gives the Gentile nations—or at least the believing remnant within each nation—a glorious inheritance with Israel. We believe that at the peak of the fullness formula, as the hour of "spiritual critical mass" nears, a united church of all the nations—the bride of Christ—will be worshipping and interceding for besieged Israel-Jerusalem, and calling for Jesus to return (Rev. 22:17). At the same time, a great Messianic remnant will be doing the same in Jerusalem (Matt. 23:37–39). And so the Deliverer will come *from* Zion. If He comes *from* Zion, that means He was already there! So instead of just the Israel-centric OT view of the coming of Messiah—where He comes to Jerusalem and then the Gentiles finally see the salvation of our God, and that's more or less the end of the story—we see Him doing something more. After "wiping up" the enemy in Jerusalem, He will go out to do the same on behalf of His remnant bride in every nation. John saw the same thing as he expanded Zechariah's prophecy (12:10) to include "every eye" and "all the tribes of the earth": "BEHOLD, HE IS COMING WITH THE CLOUDS, and every eye will see Him, even those who pierced Him; and all the tribes of the earth will mourn over Him" (Rev. 1:7). Amazingly, God preserves the order of Isaiah 52—*all Israel* is saved at the redemption of Jerusalem *first*—and then He *goes out* to deliver His beloved in every nation, sealing their redemption as well.

2. He Will Remove Godlessness from Jacob

"He will remove godlessness from Jacob. This is my covenant with them, when I take away their sins." According to the continuation of the Hebrew text of Isaiah 59:20, the Deliverer comes to Zion—*to those in Jacob who turn away from transgression/godlessness.* This sounds like a smallish remnant among Jacob—the faithful, holy ones who are await-ing His coming. But this can't work for Paul in Romans 11:25–27, because at this point He is describing the full salvation of Israel, not just the remnant; what's more, he knows that it is only God who can undo the hardening (v. 25), rejection (v. 15), and unbelief (v. 23) of

Israel. Just as we were assured from God's Word of the seven-thousand-person remnant in Elijah's time, so we are here assured that God will save *all Israel* at the ultimate time of fullness, at Yeshua's return.[133] Isaiah and Paul continue: "This is my covenant with them, when I take away their sins." This is the full consummation of the new covenant that God promised to "cut" with "the house of Israel and with the house of Judah" (Jer. 31:31). The "how much more" gospel chemistry between Israel and the nations guarantees that the critical mass will be reached. But once it is reached, just as in a nuclear fissure reaction, the end is determined—the "nuclear explosion" of the open heavens at Yeshua's return, and the full restoration everything that God spoke of through the OT prophets (Acts 3:21). Hallelujah!

Well, there is much more that could be written about these things, but that will have to wait for another book! Finally, I want to quote the apostle as he closes his letter to the Romans with quotes from the Torah, the Prophets, and the Writings—the three traditional divisions of the Hebrew Bible:

> For I say that Christ has become a servant to the circumcision on behalf of the truth of God to confirm the promises given to the fathers, and for the Gentiles to glorify God for His mercy; as it is written,
>
> "THEREFORE I WILL GIVE PRAISE TO YOU AMONG THE GEN-TILES, AND I WILL SING TO YOUR NAME."

---

[133] "Commentators are agreed that 'all Israel' means Israel 'as a whole,' as a historical people who have a unique and particular identity, not necessarily including every individual Israelite. Support for this way of understanding the phrase 'all Israel' comes from a rabbinic tract (Sanhedrin X, 1), where the statement 'all Israelites have a share in the world to come' is immediately qualified by a list of exceptions, such as the Sadducees, heretics, magicians and so on. The salvation of Israel is comprehensive, but not all-inclusive. In this text, just as 'the fullness of the Gentiles' does not mean that each individual Gentile will believe in his heart and confess with his lips (Rom 10:10), so the 'fullness of Israel' cannot mean every individual Jew." Walter J. Kaiser, Jr., et al., "Romans 11:26," *Hard Sayings of the Bible* (Downers Grove, IL: InterVarsity Press, 1996); electronic edition, Logos Bible Software.

And again he says,

"REJOICE, O GENTILES, WITH HIS PEOPLE."

And again,

"PRAISE THE LORD ALL YOU GENTILES,
AND LET ALL THE PEOPLES PRAISE HIM."

Again Isaiah says,

"THERE SHALL COME THE ROOT OF JESSE,
AND HE WHO ARISES TO RULE OVER THE GENTILES,
IN HIM SHALL THE GENTILES HOPE." (Rom. 15:8–12)

And, with this prayer:

Now may the God of hope fill you with all joy and peace in believing, that you may abound in hope by the power of the Holy Spirit. (Rom. 15:13)

APPENDICES

APPENDIX 1-1

To Eat or Not to Eat? The Kosher Question

For everything [food] created by God is good, and nothing is to be rejected if it is received with gratitude; for it is sanctified by means of the word of God and prayer. (1 Tim. 4:4–5)

Beloved, I pray that in all respects you may prosper and be in good health, just as your soul prospers. (3 John 2)

"**C**an we eat pork?"

"Doesn't the Bible say that we shouldn't eat unkosher foods?"

"A kosher, 'biblical' diet must be more healthy than other diets, right? After all, these are the foods that God Himself commanded us to eat, or not eat!?"

This is a short list of some of the most common Torah-related question I am asked. There are many versions to this question—all revolving around this issue of the Bible, our faith, and food. Not surprisingly, this issue is close to the hearts—or stomachs—of just about everybody! Eating and drinking—and doing so several times a day—is a universal necessity for people, in every place and at all times. According to the Bible, God's first command to our ancestors Adam and Eve revolved around food and eating. And of the two "sacraments" commanded to us by the NT, one involves some kind of meal whereby we symbolically partake of the Lord's body and blood (the other is water baptism). What's more, after language, food tends to be a key defining factor for determining culture—when we think about visiting, or learning about, another nation or people group, one of the first things we consider is their unique cuisine . . . or am I the only one who thinks this way?

After reading this book, it should be clear that I'm no proponent of teaching the dietary laws as any kind of continuing commandment of God under the new covenant—neither for Jew nor Gentile, even though keeping kosher in some way[134] is still valid in terms of strengthening Jewish cultural identity. But what about other possible reasons for observing these laws? If all Scripture is "inspired by God and profitable for teaching" (2 Tim. 3:16), what are we supposed to learn from these laws? Unlike the calendar-related *dogma* commandments, it's hard to find a prophetic dimension to eating kosher. Perhaps, as is popularly taught these days, it has something to do with health? In this chapter, we will first reinforce our new covenant understanding by looking at the original commandments in Leviticus 11; and secondly, explore the question of the biblical diet as a potential key to good health.

The Torah Foundation: Leviticus 11

Leviticus 11 is the foundational, most detailed biblical chapter concerning kosher and unkosher foods for the children of Israel.[135] Without going into detail concerning the various types of foods, there are two things we must notice concerning the language and reasoning behind God's giving of these commandments. First is the repetition of the phrase "ritually unclean *to/for you all*"; it is repeated twelve times in this chapter, starting in verse 4; and the only other time this phrase is used in the Torah is in Deuteronomy 14:7, on the same subject of

---

[134] Many Messianic Jews prefer to keep "biblical kosher" rather than "rabbinical kosher," i.e., not being concerned with the separation of meat and dairy.
[135] The earliest reference to "clean" and "unclean" animals is in the story of Noah in Genesis 6–8. But 6:21 makes it clear that the animals on the ark were not for food; and according to 8:20, the seven pairs of ritually clean animals were for the purpose of sacrifice to God, not human consumption.

kosher foods.[136] In the book of Leviticus, there are a multitude of things declared to be "ritually unclean," especially for the priests and Levites; but this emphasis "to/for you all" is never used, except in these verses concerning food which apply to the whole nation.

When I read Leviticus 11 in Hebrew, the force of the repetition of this phrase is glaring; simply put, it cries out concerning the *relative* (not absolute) nature of the dietary laws. In other words, if God (and Moses) had intended for these laws to have universal application for all mankind (either as a defining boundary of holiness, or for health reasons), then it would have been much more effective *not* to repeat this phrase so often. Read it out loud yourself, in your own language, with a little emphasis on each repetition of this phrase. Remember that in context, this is Moses speaking to the children of Israel. Perhaps Paul had this phrase in mind when he penned the following: "As one who is in the Lord Jesus, I know and am convinced in the Lord Jesus that [no food] is unclean in itself; but to him who thinks anything to be unclean, to him it is unclean" (Rom. 14:14).

Putting Leviticus 11 and Romans 14 together: these foods were declared to be ritually unclean *only for the children of Israel*—for a time and for a certain reason. Under the fullness of the new covenant we understand that this "uncleanness" was relative and temporal; just as it was once only "unclean" to the Israelites, today it is "unclean" only to those who believe it to be so, and not in any absolute way.

The second thing to notice in Leviticus 11 is the concluding, summarizing verses 44 and 45. Moses declares the primary reason behind the giving of the dietary laws—holiness: *I am YHVH, I am holy, and you all are to be a holy people before me, therefore don't eat these things.* Every traditional society had a sense of the "holy" versus the "common" or "profane." Ancient Israel was no different; and in all these cultures the

---

[136] The translation of טמא as "unclean" is not the right fit for modern ears. I prefer "ritually unclean" to avoid any connotations with modern concepts or standards of things like hygiene, cleanliness, or sterility.

holy was associated with a religious "cult"—temples, a class of priests, certain practices/rituals related to the service of gods/spirits, and/or ancestors. The sense is that of entering a kind of space (physical and mental) that is special, spiritual, and wholly set apart from the mundane details of our daily lives. We see all of this in the Torah, especially the book of Leviticus, where most of these purity laws apply only to the priesthood. But here in chapter 11, we are dealing with a commandment for the entire people, one which touches on the most necessary, daily, and mundane aspect of human life—eating and drinking. This is very unique,[137] and is part of the OT foundation for the concept of an entire people, an entire nation that is set apart: a kingdom of priests, a royal priesthood (Ex. 19:6).

Thus, the word "holy" (קָדוֹשׁ) in Hebrew has at least three layers of meaning, all which can be learned from Leviticus 11:44. First, it is a defining attribute of God himself: "for I am holy." God is holy, He is different, He is not part of this world. This is not Hindu monism, or Confucian humanism. He is wholly pure, not contaminated by the sin of this fallen world. Secondly, this same divine holiness is available to us, if we are willing to "consecrate" (also from the same root קָדַשׁ) ourselves. This is human holiness. Lastly, human holiness is here connected to the natural order and the list of "clean" and "unclean" animals. We might call this the "holiness within nature." Under Moses, our personal holiness is connected to what we eat and don't eat. By following God's laws—in this case, what Israel was to eat or not eat—we can become holy, like God Himself, separated from the impurities and abominations of this world. Verse 44 makes the equation very clear: God's holiness = our holiness = what we eat or don't eat.

It should not surprise us, therefore, that the kosher laws (along with circumcision and calendar laws) came to characterize and set apart the Jewish nation for the last 3,400 years. This can also help us understand

---

[137] While other cultures may have dictated certain holy foods to be used in the cultic, religious context, I know of no other with such detailed proscriptions for the entire nation.

Peter's predicament in Acts 10, and the drastic nature of God's message to him and the early Jewish apostles. The Torah of Moses, including these laws, was—forgive the metaphor—being put through a meat grinder, the flesh of the Son of God on the cross, and what was to reemerge on the other side was to forever separate these things from our understanding of the nature of what is holy, what is ritually unclean, and the like.

Clearly God had (and still has!) a purpose for the distinction of the Jewish nation, and at the most basic level, defining which foods we could and could not eat is a most efficient way to accomplish this purpose. By defining Israel in this way, God kept us apart, i.e., "holy." It is my hope that after reading this book, you will have a clear understanding that what defined the boundaries of holiness for God's people under the old covenant has undergone a radical transformation under the new. Under the old, and still under Judaism today, there is no way a pork-eating pagan can be called "holy," no matter how "morally" upstanding he may be. But under the new things have changed, as God declared to Peter through his vision of "unclean" foods: "Get up, Peter, kill and eat! . . . What God has cleansed, no longer consider unholy" (Acts 10:13–15).

The Health Question

If under the new covenant, the dietary laws no longer function for defining the boundaries of holiness for God's people, then what else could they mean for us?[138] A quick look on the internet will give you the answer that many people are finding these days—health! Today, in modern society, there are an amazing variety of ideas about health: from scientific nutritional theories, to traditional diets, to vitamin

---

[138] Clean and unclean distinctions also functioned in qualifying one to participate in the temple service, which does not now exist. We should also note that clean and unclean animal distinctions were noted in regard to the animals in Noah's Ark. There are many different scholars with different views of the reasons for these laws.

supplements, types of purified and electrified water, teas, exercise programs, etc. Increasingly, I hear from believers this way of thinking that connects the Mosaic dietary laws with modern ideas of health and well-being. Such a person will usually quote research about unkosher seafood, like shrimp, as being "bottom-dwellers" and thus eating all kinds of ocean "crap." Or, how pigs are also a kind of garbage disposal animal, whose flesh tends toward bacterial contamination in a way that beef, for example, doesn't.[139] Is there any truth to these things?

To my way of thinking, there are three points which mitigate against this understanding of the kosher laws. The first is biblical, while the second two are facts of our modern world.

1. *The Bible doesn't say so.* We have just reviewed the key OT verses, and there is no hint that God is saying "don't eat these things because they are bad for your health." It is an anachronistic mistake to confuse the biblical, Levitical concept of "ritual uncleanness/impurity" with any modern concept of hygiene or health. As the apostle John's greeting (3 John 2) and Paul's words to Timothy (1 Tim. 5:23) suggest, apostolic new covenant faith is concerned that we live in good health! Our bodies are "temples of the Holy Spirit," and we are to treat them with respect and godly discipline (1 Cor. 6:19). Therefore, if the Levitical dietary laws were about health, we would expect the apostolic NT writers to declare so, and to make these laws part of the "gospel of the kingdom" proclamation that is to go out to the nations. You can't preach a gospel of healing and God's love and at the same time allow your disciples to continue eating food that is slowly killing them! But this exactly what we don't see in the NT! In fact, we see the opposite: Instead of a strengthening of the OT kosher laws to apply to the nations, we see their cancelling; instead of a

---

[139] These "experts" often miss the point that kosher chicken, when not properly handled, can be just as bad a source of bacteria as pork.

"biblical diet" for kingdom health, we see Scriptures like 1 Timo-thy 4:4–5[140] declaring God's sanction on all food.

2. *It is notoriously risky to apply "scientific" findings to biblical truth,* especially in this case of foods and health. Jesus Christ is the same yesterday, today, and forever (Heb. 13:8). The same cannot be said about scientific findings, especially concerning health! When I was growing up in the US in the '70s and '80s, margarine was "in." Animal fats, especially butter, had been deemed by the "experts" to be unhealthy because of their supposed tendency to increase blood cholesterol levels. However, over the last ten years, the situation has been reversed: Butter (a whole, natural fat) is back, and margarine (a trans-fat) is out! Whatever "science" may say today about bottom dwellers or supposed toxins in pork meat, the same experts may be saying something different a few years down the road. In addition, with the globalizing power of the internet, one can go online and find supposedly "expert" studies about almost anything in the universe that contradict each other.

3. *The case of Japan and Okinawa:* Since the advent of modernity and the collection of statistics in developed nations, the Japanese have consistently been either #1 or #2 in terms of life expectan-cy.[141] This is surely one objective way of measuring health on a huge, national scale—right? I lived in Japan for seven years, and I speak the language fluently. I can tell you one thing for sure: For

---

[140] There are some who teach that when Paul used the word "food" in 1 Timothy he meant it Jewishly, i.e., that it could not have included the unkosher foods, which are biblically not fit to be called "food." This doesn't make sense for two reasons: in the immediate context Paul is warning about false, "demonic" doctrines in the end times whereby some will "forbid marriage and will advocate abstaining from *foods*" (1 Tim. 4:3, emphasis added). If the "foods" here can only represent kosher foods, this would imply the preaching of abstention from kosher foods--the eating of *only* unkosher foods. As far as I know, this never happened in church history. Secondly, it is hard to imagine that Timothy—who grew up in a highly Greek-influenced family and society—would "hear" such a restrictive use of the word for "food" here.
[141] Central Intelligence Agency, "Country Comparison: Life Expectancy at Birth," https://www.cia.gov/library/publications/the-world-factbook/rankorder/2102rank.html.

generations, the Japanese have been consuming a *huge* amount of biblically unkosher food—especially from the ocean: sea anemone, squid, shrimp, octopus, all kinds of clams and oysters . . . and the list goes on with things we don't even have names for in English. What's more, much of the time these things were eaten raw! Over the last 120 years, pork has also become a mainstay of the Japanese diet. Ironically, the Japanese with the highest life expectancy come from the southern islands of Okinawa—where pork meat and fat has been central to the diet as long as anyone can remember! What's more, many of the nations presently battling for #2 on the longevity list are also major consumers of *traife*—unkosher foods: Italy, Spain, Switzerland, Singapore. Sure, you can try to attribute Japanese health and longevity to other factors like drinking lots of green tea, good exercise, and environment; or Spanish and Italian good health to the rest of their "Mediterranean diet." Nevertheless, for me the point stands: If eating unkosher foods is indeed a strong, biblical recipe for ill health, then we would expect these nations to not be so high on the list.

Let us conclude with the apostle's instructions in Romans 14:

a. The kingdom of God is not what you eat or drink, but righteousness, peace, and joy (could we add "health"?) in the Holy Spirit (v. 17).

b. There is no food that is to be deemed "unclean in itself" (v. 14). We cannot use biblical texts to sanction or condone one food or another.

c. Concerning these things (food and drink) let each person be "convinced in his own mind" (v. 5), and let's be careful about not judging one another, or being a stumbling block to another. All should pray and get God's conviction and be sensitive to others in corporate settings especially (the whole chapter of Romans 14 proclaims this!).

d. Be careful about what you "teach." If you have faith and personal convictions about these things, keep it between you and God (v. 22)! Don't make a website; don't share with your friends about how changing your diet in accordance with the kosher laws has given you more energy, or cured your acne! If true, according to these verses, it may have been just as much due to your faith, conviction, and discipline than it was to your actual food selections.

APPENDIX 1-2

To Celebrate or Not to Celebrate? Sabbath, Feasts, Calendar, and the Traditions of Men

See to it that no one takes you captive through philosophy and empty deception, according to the tradition of men, according to the elementary principles of the world, rather than according to Christ. For in Him all the fullness of Deity dwells in bodily form, and in Him you have been made complete, and He is the head over all rule and authority. (Col. 2:8–10)

"What about the feasts? Shouldn't we be keeping them instead of the traditional Christians ones, like Christmas and Easter, which are actually based on pagan holidays?"

"They are not just the 'feasts of Israel,' or the Jews, but the Bible says they are the 'Feasts of YHWH', so they are for all who believe in YHWH!'"

"The NT doesn't do away with the seventh-day Sabbath—the anti-Semitic church changed it to Sunday!"

Even more than questions about foods, the other "hottest" topic among those with an interest in Torah is that of the calendar and the Jewish/biblical feasts. For many believers with a faith and desire to connect with Israel and the Jewish/Hebrew roots of their faith, sabbath-keeping and the feasts are a major connecting point. I write this as I am preparing to depart to speak at a church in Malaysia, which has asked me to come to teach about Sukkot (feast of tabernacles) at their first-ever celebration, more or less at the same time as the Jewish calendar.

As we saw in our study of the one new man, especially in Galatians and Colossians, this issue of the observance of the Jewish calendar also was a key element in the first-century, Judaizing Torah teacher's doctrine which Paul so vehemently opposed. In this chapter we will look at the issue, and hopefully come out with a balanced view which honors the essential freedom concerning these matters which the new covenant guarantees us. I will write about Sabbath and feasts as one theological "bundle," as established in the key chapter on the feasts, Leviticus 23.

Before Moses introduces the yearly cycle of the seven "holy convocations," also called *moadim* (appointed times), of the biblical calendar, he writes: "For six days work may be done; but on the seventh day there is a sabbath of complete rest, a holy convocation. You shall not do any work; it is a sabbath to the LORD in all your dwellings" (Lev. 23:3). So before any discussion of the yearly feasts, Leviticus establishes the weekly Sabbath as the first of the "holy convocations." It then goes on to describe all of the seven yearly feasts as being timed with a Sabbath, or containing a kind of special Sabbath day called a *shabbaton*. Therefore, for us in the new covenant, the fundamentals of any doctrine of the feasts should exactly mirror those of our doctrine of the seventh-day Sabbath—the first and most often repeated of the "holy convocations."[142]

---

[142] This is especially important as many teachers today make much of the fact that Leviticus 23 speaks of the feasts as the "*Moadim* of YHVH," as if they are in a special, universal, timeless category unrelated to the controversies in the NT. But this cannot be so easily claimed concerning the Sabbath, since there is so much NT material covering it—from the Gospels through Acts, and to all the Epistles.

Section I. The Foundational New-Covenant Doctrine Concerning Days, Times, Seasons, and Feasts

1. The Sabbath and/or Feasts in Genesis

The first point is something we have already noticed: In the patriarchal narratives which begin from chapter 10, there is no mention of anything calendar-related—not Sabbath nor months, nor feasts.[143] The physical sign of the covenant between God and Abraham was circumcision (Gen. 17:11); the Sabbath is described as the "sign" of the covenant between God and the nation in Exodus 31:13. It is no coincidence then that the new covenant's high estimation of the Abrahamic faith/covenant, in contrast with the later Mosaic *dogma*-Torah, contains teaching which liberates us from any "bondage" to calendrical observances. On the other hand, the Sabbath is mentioned as the sanctified seventh day when God completed His work of creation and "rested." But in Genesis 1 and 2, there is no hint that either mankind would someday follow this divine pattern and rest every seven days—this comes later in Exodus; or that this was the beginning of the institution of a regular, cyclical calendar—monthly or yearly.[144]

2. Yeshua and the Sabbath/Feasts

There are two things to say here, one for and one against the necessity of an ongoing observance of a biblical calendar under the new covenant. First, the timing of Yeshua's crucifixion, resurrection, and the pouring out of the Holy Spirit fifty days later were perfectly timed with the

---

[143] The only calendrical mention in Genesis is in the flood story, which speaks of events that took place in the first, second, seventh, and tenth months of the 600 and 601 years of Noah's lifetime (7:11; 8:4–5, 13–14). Are these the same months later introduced by Moses? Perhaps. Genesis 29:14 also speaks of a "month of days," implying that there was some sense of a lunar, monthly reckoning—but no Sabbaths, names of months, yearly feasts, or any fixed calendar that we know of.

[144] Isaiah 66:23 (Sabbath, new moons) and Zechariah 14:16 (feast of Tabernacles) indicate that there may be biblical, calendrical celebrations in the Millenium. Of course, there are many ideas about how to interpret these verses in light of new-covenant fulfillment.

springtime biblical feasts of Passover, Firstfruits, and Weeks (*Shavuot*). This is exactly in keeping with our understanding of the Lord's teaching in Matthew 5:17–19 (and Hebrews)—that the Torah (and all the old-covenant Scriptures) are first and foremost a prophetic foreshadowing of the Messiah and the Messianic age. We can also look for a future fulfillment of the other major group of feasts in the fall—Trumpets, Atonement, and Tabernacles.[145] There is much to be learned from the prophetic types and "shadows" contained in the biblical calendar—things which shed much light on the timing and work of Messiah described in other Scriptures, like the seven trumpets of Revelation; the "last trumpet" of 1 Corinthians 15:52; the tabernacling of God with us in Revelation 21:3, etc.

On the negative side is Yeshua's challenge and teaching concerning the Sabbath in John 5:1–17. Yeshua honored the seventh-day Sabbath as any normal Jew of His time would have—He didn't open up His father's carpentry shop, or conduct any other business;[146] nor did He set out to travel any great distances. But He did heal people, tell them to "pick up" their pallets and walk away, and allow His disciples to pluck grain—all in violation of the Pharisaic/rabbinic rules of not doing any "work" on the Sabbath. His defense? "My Father is working until now, and I Myself am working" (v. 17). With these words, the Lord does not allow us to understand Genesis 2:1–3 as a statement of either a) that God Himself lives according to a seven-day calendar, whereby something in His universe is transformed for a special seventh-day rest; or b) that the primary meaning of the seventh-day Sabbath is found by our totally ceasing from "work" of any kind. There is a kind of work, and conversely, a kind of rest, that both the Father and the Son are constantly engaged in. This idea receives its fullest explanation in our next verses.

---

[145] Dan Juster argues persuasively in his book *Revelation: The Passover Key* (Clarksville, MD: Messianic Jewish Publications, 1991) that there are still future prophetic fulfillments to the Passover story, especially concerning the plague judgments in the book of Revelation.
[146] Nor did Paul do his tentmaking business.

3. Hebrews 3:7–4:16; 2 Corinthians 6:2

In these key Scriptures the apostle explains the fullest meaning of the Sabbath—and by extension, the feasts as well—under the new covenant. He begins by warning the believers against the tendency to an "evil, unbelieving heart one that falls away from the living God," and challenging us to "encourage one another day after day, as long as it is still called Today" (Heb. 3:12–13). This is the first link to the key prophecy of Psalm 95:7–11 upon which this teaching in Hebrews is based: "*Today*, if you would hear His voice . . ." (v. 7, emphasis added). The Exodus generation of Israelites were guilty of a lack of faith, an unbelieving heart in the power and promise of God; and so He judged them, swearing in His anger to not allow them to "enter into" His "rest." The word for "rest" here, מנוחה *m'nucha,* is the more general term for rest, as opposed to the word in Genesis 2:2 (and God "*rested* on the seventh day") which is simply a verb derived from the same root as the *shabbat* (Sabbath). What's more, in the context of Psalm 95 it is clear that this "rest" is a metaphor for the Promised Land of Israel—or, more accurately, for the promise to that generation of a "rest" (ceasing) from wandering in the wilderness, and being able to "settle down" in the fullness of their inheritance as a new nation in the land promised to their fathers.

Next, in Hebrews 4:3–4, the apostle establishes the connection between this promised "rest" in the land of promise in Psalm 95, the Sabbath rest spoken of in Genesis 2, and the ultimate fulfilling of the whole theme of Sabbath and rest in new-covenant, gospel faith: "For we who have believed enter that rest, just as He has said, 'As I SWORE IN MY WRATH, THEY SHALL NOT ENTER MY REST,' although His works were finished from the foundation of the world. For He has thus said somewhere concerning the seventh day, 'AND GOD RESTED ON THE SEVENTH DAY FROM ALL HIS WORKS.'" Here, Paul is teaching the flip side of the meaning of the Sabbath from what Yeshua taught in John 5—that the seventh-day Sabbath of the creation story means that God's works are already "finished from the foundation of the world." So is God finished working as in Genesis 1–2 and Hebrews 4, or is the Father still working as in John 5? Taken together, it sounds like a contradiction—God is both resting and working at the same time! How are we to understand this?

On the one hand, according to Genesis and the promise in Psalm 95, God finished his work of creating in six days—so He is finished, existing in a place of eternal Sabbath joy and rest; and there remains a promise, an invitation to mankind, to enter into this rest with Him. On the other hand, according to John 5, the Father has been "working" constantly from the time of the creation in Genesis until Jesus' time (and presumably He is still at the same work!)—and the Son is likewise working seven days a week, 365 days a year! Putting this together with the cry of the psalmist hundreds of years after the Exodus generation— "*today*, if you would hear His voice" (Ps. 95:7), the apostle concludes, "So there remains a Sabbath rest for the people of God. For the one who has entered His rest has himself also rested from his works, as God did from His. Therefore let us be diligent to enter that rest, so that no one will fall, through following the same example of disobedience" (Heb. 4:9–11).

How and when are we able to enter this amazing "rest," which allows one to somehow be constantly "working" at the same time? "And working together with Him, we also urge you not to receive the grace of God in vain—for He says, 'AT THE ACCEPTABLE TIME I LISTENED TO YOU, AND ON THE DAY OF SALVATION I HELPED YOU.' Behold, now is 'THE ACCEPTABLE TIME,' behold, now is 'THE DAY OF SALVATION'" (2 Cor. 6:1–2). Under the new covenant—the gospel of grace of faith in Jesus Christ— the "appointed time" (*moed*) for all transaction by faith with God is the eternal *now*! *Today*! Living by faith in Yeshua and "walking" by the Holy Spirit, we are invited into the rest and eternal joy which the Father has prepared for us since the foundations of the world. At the same time, we are invited to "work" by the same Spirit, like Yeshua, doing what we see the Father doing (John 5:19–20). In Him, we are both restfully working, and "workingly" resting. As such, there is no longer a place for any kind of belief in "auspicious" timing—that on Friday evening at sundown, something happens in the chemistry of the universe that allows a special kind of Sabbath blessing (mystical Judaism); or that during the ten "Days of Awe" from Rosh HaShanah (Day of Trumpets/Jewish New Year) until *Yom Kippur* (Day of Atonement) the gates of heaven are open in a special way for repentance and forgiveness in a way that is not normally available during the rest of the year (standard Judaism); or that in the four to six weeks before Easter (Lent) there is a special grace from God for Christians to repent and receive forgiveness.

So before we go on to speak about some of the biblically valid reasons for keeping a biblical feast, we must be rooted and grounded in this first and last gospel doctrine concerning times, seasons, days, Sabbaths, and feasts: All is, and will be, fulfilled in Yeshua—His death, resurrection, ascension, outpouring of the Holy Spirit, His return, and His rule over the universe from His seat on this earth in Jerusalem. Our great High Priest Yeshua has come to make a new and living way to the Father, as the perfect, sacrificial mediator of the promised new covenant. Nothing of the "shadows" from the OT any longer plays a mediating role in our relationship to God; whatever the Sabbath and feasts came to teach, we have their fullness of them in Him, and we can draw near—*all the time*—to His throne of mercy equally at all times, 365 days a year, 24/7. "Therefore, since we have a great high priest who has passed through the heavens, Jesus the Son of God, let us hold fast our confession. For we do not have a high priest who cannot sympathize with our weaknesses, but One who has been tempted in all things as we are, yet without sin. Therefore let us draw near with confidence to the throne of grace, that we may receive mercy and may find grace to help in time of need" (Heb. 4:14–16).

4. The "Genitive" Principle and the Nature of Symbol

One of the most common teachings among today's Torah teachers—and the wrong kind of Hebrew-roots advocates—concerns the supposed turning of the church away from its biblical roots in the Levitical

204 One New Man

calendar, and toward a "pagan" calendar and "pagan" feasts instituted
by Rome and later church traditions. This is often part of a pack-
age of "church-bashing"—a wholly negative critique of most church
traditions as being, at best, unbiblical—or at worst, anti-Semitic and
satanic. Once the supposedly pagan roots of the dates and celebration
of Sunday worship ("sun" day from the Roman sun god), Christmas
(originally based on European celebrations of the winter solstice), and
Easter (named after *Eoestre*, a northern European goddess of fertility
worshipped in a springtime festival) are established, it is an easy step
to attract the unsuspecting student to return to the "pure, biblical"
calendar of YHVH's "appointed times" and "holy convocations." This
way of teaching has had a huge influence, and so we will spend con-
siderable time looking at it.

First, there is a simple fallacy here, one which Dan Juster calls the
"genitive" fallacy: If some day, custom, or celebration was *originally* (had
its genesis in rites that were) pagan or extrabiblical, this way of thinking
says, then it forever continues to have unholy, pagan associations. In
other words, to borrow and invert Paul's phrasing from Romans 11:16:
"If the root is pagan, then so are the branches"; or, "once pagan, always
pagan." In the hands of today's Torah teachers, this fallacy of course cuts
the other way: If some feast or custom is biblical in its origins, then it is
forever holy, good, and perfect. Paul put the axe to the root of this way
of thinking in Romans 14:14, writing about foods: "I know and am
convinced in the Lord Jesus that nothing is unclean in itself; but to him
who thinks anything to be unclean, to him it is unclean." No "thing"
can be thought of anymore as inherently "unclean," or "unholy." It is
just a thing. And the same can be said of a certain time or day of the
year: It must be first and foremost understood as just a symbolic "slice of
eternity," to which can be ascribed many different meanings.

Once when I taught on this subject, I pointed to the squarish,
wooden buttons on a student's Polynesian-looking shirt, and said: "Do
you know the origins of that kind of button? It comes from the garment that Pacific Island priests wore during feasts when they would

drink alcohol mixed with human blood and sacrifice babies to their god, Ish-yayin-dam-to-u!" The student looked down at his shirt, and then looked up at me with shock and dismay. "Should you still wear it?" I asked him and the class. He didn't know how to answer. "It's okay," I told him, "you can continue to wear it . . . and besides, I just made up the whole thing! I have no idea where that style of button comes from!"

On any given day, we are surrounded by objects, practices, customs, musical instruments, melodies, rhythms, words, phrases, foods, bodily movements (dance, yoga), and holidays, etc., that once had their origin in non-Judeo-Christian, nonbiblical cultures—and even things associated with the very pagan religious practices of those peoples.[147] But obviously all of these things have a *symbolic* quality. In one time, place, and setting the thing (or the day of the year or the melody) may have *symbolized* one thing to the people to whom the custom belonged; but now, to a different people, time, place and setting the same may have a totally different meaning—or in the case of square wooden buttons, no particular meaning at all, just a sense of style.

The world is full of myriad examples of this transformation of symbolic meaning from age to age, culture to culture. Just think of the symbol of the cross—what it means to you as a believer, as opposed to what it means to Madonna or the millions of people in Asia who sport one as a symbol of identifying with western culture—but with absolutely no Christian content or faith. Many famous hymns were once bar songs; what the words "Jesus Christ" mean to you and what they mean on the tongue of some people can be totally different. Similarly, there is nothing "magic" in the name, or in the pronunciation thereof.[148]

If we were to live according to the "genitive principle," trying to avoid association with anything that was once pagan, normal life would be impossible as we superstitiously "look over our shoulder" for the

---

[147] This is patently obvious in societies without the Judeo-Christian history or foundation; in the west, it is something from the distant past.

[148] See Acts 19:11–20; and there are those today who teach the importance of pronouncing His name as "Yah-shua."

next thing that might "contaminate" us. This means that whatever was originally intended or celebrated on December 25 in northern Europe 1,500 years ago may have absolutely nothing to do with the contemporary believer's celebration of the birth of the Savior on the same day. When the day is spent with family; in church worship; studying the Scriptures surrounding His birth; contemplating the awesome mystery of the incarnation of God as an embryo in a virgin's womb; and His lonely, humble birth in a Bethlehem manger, there is absolutely nothing "pagan" going on at all—even if presents are exchanged under a yule-tide tree. A tree is a tree is a tree—it all depends what meaning one ascribes to the tree.[149] Paul taught this succinctly in the verses we studied in the chapter on *Kashrut*, 1 Timothy 4:1–5: all *things*, foods, days, seasons, music, etc., can be "sanctified by the word of God (the gospel) and by prayer" (v. 5).

As mentioned, the knife cuts both ways: The genitive-principle style of Torah teaching says that because a holy day, symbol, or food is "from the Bible" than it must be pure, holy, and right for us as believers. In other words, "once holy, always holy." But this is not exactly what God says, not even through the prophets of Israel! Look at a verse like Isaiah 1:13: "Bring your worthless offerings no longer, incense is an abomination to Me. New moon and sabbath, the calling of assemblies—I cannot endure iniquity and the solemn assembly." The meaning and context make it clear: The God of the Bible, the God of Israel, is first and foremost looking at our hearts, our morals, our faith, and our motivations—not which days or customs we practice. One can be scrupulously observing a "biblical" holy day with the wrong heart, the wrong doctrine, and be as far from God as the east is from the west!

---

[149] The biggest challenge is in the first generation when these customs are first "baptized" into the Christian message, while there are when there are still a large number of the people in the culture who make the association with actual worship of pagan gods and the accompanying immorality. This is the situation in 1 Corinthians, and the same today with something like punk music.

In Israel, among Orthodox Jews, we see this "paganizing" of biblical symbols all the time—for example, with the *mezuzah*.[150] Recently, when a tragedy struck a neighbor's home here in Jerusalem, the rumor among the Orthodox in our area was, "her *mezuzot* weren't kosher!" In other words, the *mezuzah* on her doorposts were not rabbinically certified or inspected—therefore, they lacked the power to protect my neighbor's home from bad luck and tragedy. That's right—ascribing divine, almost magical power to a symbol that God commanded simply in order to *remember* His commandments, but using it in this way, is no different from the way all kinds of amulets and talismans are used for good luck in "pagan" cultures throughout the world. This is what the apostle teaches in Romans 2: that the heart of a Jew, with his "holy Torah" practices, can be quite far from God; while a Gentile, in his "paganism," can prove to be more moral and pleasing to God. This is also the message of the parable of the Good Samaritan.

In conclusion: The "roots" or the "origins" of a day or a thing or any other custom have nothing to do with how it may be practiced today, and how it is looked upon by our holy God.

5. Stoichea *"Bondage" and the "Traditions of Men"*

In Chapters 3 and 4 we looked at this subject in the books of Galatians and Colossians. Paul, with his background both in Greco-Roman culture and in Pharisaic Judaism, saw something concerning the cross that no one else was able to see, or at least not to the same depth. He saw that Yeshua's awful death on the cross—as the embodiment of Israel—also meant a kind of death for the *dogma*-Torah commandments which once defined the holy boundaries between Jew and Gentile—God's people and not-God's-people. As he followed the Master's example, he could say of himself that "through the Law, I died to the Law... I have been

---

[150] From Deuteronomy 6:9—the small box containing this written commandment that we Jews place on our doorposts—some just at the front door, others on every doorpost in the home. Orthodox Jews have a custom of touching the *mezuzah* and then kissing the hand when they enter a home.

crucified with Christ" (Gal. 2:19-20). From his position of being seated with Christ, far above all principality and power (Eph. 2:6), he could see something that cannot be seen, or contemplated, by the Orthodox Jew: that "AD"—after His death, resurrection, ascension, and the pouring out of the Holy Spirit into our hearts—we are no longer under law-Torah, but under grace. We are no longer under the Mosaic covenant or any striving for self-righteousness, holiness, or spirituality from "ceremonial," *dogma*-Torah commands—our righteousness is first and foremost imputed to us through faith in the Messiah. Just as with the moral commands, the *dogma*-Torah commands are still there, still part of Holy Scripture, and still function to define the boundaries of Jewish, corporate identity; but we can now say that we are no longer "under" them as commands as we once were—but "over" them, i.e., seated in a place above them. (As we saw, this didn't mean that Paul completely abandoned a Jewish life.) In other words, we can see them now as a kind of culture, but not commandments which define the holy, righteous boundaries of God's people. Now, we can see them for what they are, and also see that to be "under" *dogma*-Torah commands for holiness, righteousness, and/or spirituality is, by nature, the same bondage as to be "under" pagan-dogma customs (Gal. 4:8–11). One set of customs/commands may have its origins in the pagan, Gentile world, while the other set may originate from Moses; but once we are in the dispensation of the fulfillment of God's graceful new covenant, looking to either for holiness/righteousness/spirituality results in the same bondage. But why "bondage"—what kind of bondage? What does it "look like" or "feel like"?

This is where we need to learn from Paul's teaching to the Colossians. At the introduction of the section about the one new man and the abolishing of the *dogma*-Torah (as in Ephesians) the apostle writes: "See to it that no one takes you captive through philosophy and empty deception, according to the tradition of men, according to the elementary principles of the world, rather than according to Christ" (Col. 2:8). As in his other letters, in this verse and the following ones until the end of the chapter, the apostle sets up a stark contrast: life and faith in the full revelation of the divinity of Christ, versus life and faith under bondage to philosophy, empty deception, *stoichea* principles—*according to the tradition of men*. As in Galatians 3–4, there is a clear equivalency established here between both pagan traditions and Jewish biblical ones, like food, drink, festival, new moons, and Sabbaths (v. 16). But how can Paul speak of these biblical, *dogma*-Torah commands as "the traditions of men"? After all, don't they come down to us from Holy Scripture, from God, through Moses?

Of course, there is the divine/Mosaic origin of the commands for Sabbaths, months, and feasts—but how to keep them? When? Who decides? For orthodox (Pharisaic) Jews it is a matter of faith that the rabbis have authoritatively set the times and seasons according to the divine will. However, all that one needs to do today is to get on the internet and do a study of the history of the Jewish determination of the calendar to realize that there has been great controversy, and much development, in how the rabbis have accomplished this. "The history of the Jewish calendar may be divided into three periods—the Biblical, the Talmudic, and the post-Talmudic. The first rested purely on the observation of the sun and the moon, the second on observation and reckoning, the third entirely on reckoning."[151] In biblical times it was originally done by the first, earliest sighting of the new moon—which would then be reported to rabbinic authorities; but this already became complicated during the Babylonian exile when the Jewish community became very spread out. In Talmudic times, after the exposure to the more accurate, yearly solar calendars of Babylon and Rome, the rabbis added astronomical calculations ("reckoning," i.e., calculating) to the method of sighting, including the addition of a "leap" month every two years, so as to keep the spring festivals in the spring, and the fall festivals

---

[151] Joseph Jacobs and Cyrus Adler, "Calendar, History of," *Jewish Encyclopedia*, http://jewishen-cyclopedia.com/articles/3920-calendar-history-of, accessed October 25, 2018.

in the fall![152] Now, since the Middle Ages, the Jewish calendar is established only by calculation.

All of this means that the whole question of the establishing of Sabbaths, months, and feasts has a strong human element to it. It is not just a matter of divine imprimatur! It's the same for the Gregorian seven-day week, and the 365-day year which most of the world follows now: No one can prove that, when the sun comes up and goes down on Sunday, this day is qualitatively different from any other day. It was simply established by men sometime during the Roman Empire and has continued in an unbroken chain down to our day. In the same way, especially given that the biblical calendar was not instituted until the first Passover of Moses' time (Ex. 12:2), no one can prove that starting Friday at sundown we enter a special day which is in fact a multiple of seven from the seventh-day rest when God created the world in the book of Genesis.[153] So the first problem in looking to such observances for holiness, righteousness, or spirituality is that one must submit to the "traditions of men"—in this case, the rabbis of Judaism—in order to tell you when these days actually take place. Historically, and today, there are those who disagree with the rabbinical calculations (Karaites, etc.) as they establish their own tradition of calculation.

The next issue concerns not the "when," but the "how" of the observing of *dogma*-Torah commandments. For example, the major instruction for the Sabbath is to do no "ordinary work" (Lev. 23:3, 25, etc.). Fine. But what does "ordinary work" mean? How is this "work" to be defined? The rabbis settled on an interesting solution: They took the thirty-nine verbs/ categories of work described in the construction of the tabernacle in the second half of the book of Exodus. (These include verbs like "tearing," so

---

[152] Contrast with the Muslim feast of Ramadan, only lunar-based, which moves all over the yearly calendar. Also, some recent scholarship suggests that the original Mosaic calendar may have been some kind of combination of solar and lunar. See Elat Mazir, et al.

[153] In popular and mystical Judaism, there is a belief that starting Friday at sundown, there is an elemental change in the universe that imparts a unique holiness to this twenty-four-hour period called the Sabbath.

a devout Jew will not tear toilet paper off the roll during the Sabbath!). While there may be some merit to this rabbinical interpretation (which is based on the shared word in both Leviticus and Exodus, *malacha* מְלָאכָה) the Scripture nowhere says that this is necessarily the *only* way to define "ordinary work."[154] Obviously, if any community desires to keep a biblical Sabbath rest—as a community—there needs to be a recognized authority entrusted with the establishing of standards, definitions—what is called *Halacha* in rabbinic Judaism.[155] Otherwise, it can mean chaos for the community, with one family driving on the Sabbath which offends another family who doesn't, etc. (the list goes on forever).

The same is true of the feasts. Look at the traditional Jewish celebration of Passover, in which there are a few biblical elements, plus many extrabiblical traditions—created and added by the rabbis—i.e., the "traditions of men." The point here is not that such traditions or calendrical calculations are an "evil," "antibiblical" thing—as many a "fundamentalist" Torah teacher would assert; but rather, as we saw in Chapter 7, they are a necessary aspect in the development of any sustainable community, culture, or civilization. The problem is not that we live under the "traditions of men" in human societies which determine our cultural practices; rather, it lies in looking to these *stoichea*, *dogma* commands or traditions for anything having to do with salvation, holiness, righteousness, or spirituality. It is impossible to live in this world without culture, traditions, standards, and the like; but the new covenant comes along to teach us how to live "in the world" but not "of the world." In the Spirit, at the highest level of truth, we don't live "under" these things, but the opposite! At the highest level of truth and spirituality, we are "in Christ," where "there is neither Jew nor

---

[154] Yeshua likely gives credence to this kind of understanding when He acknowledges the valid authority of the "teachers of the Law and the Pharisees" to determine such matters for the Jewish people in Matthew 23:1–3.

[155] This is one way of understanding Yeshua's teaching in Matthew 23:1–3: He acknowledges some Pharasaic/rabbinic authority in determining the *Halacha* for, at least, the Jewish people of his generation.

Gentile," neither *dogma*-Torah nor pagan custom. Like Paul, we simply must have our priorities straight.

This means that if a modern-day Torah or Hebrew-roots teacher implies the existence of a "pure" biblical practice, uncontaminated by the "traditions of men" he is either naive or lying; it is also very likely that whether he intends to or not, he will place you under his own "tradition" of understanding—and you will end up in a state of confusion and bondage to him or to that group. Further, if any teacher suggests to you that in the Sabbath or in the *moadim* (appointed times) there can be a special quality of meeting with God that is not available to the Christian who doesn't observe it, then he/she is actually in danger of preaching another gospel—which is no gospel at all (Gal. 1:6–9)!

Having clearly established the right doctrinal foundation for any observance of the Sabbath or feasts, we can now move onto some possible reasons why it might be good or advisable to do so. There is more teaching on this subject in the next appendix.

Section II. Biblically Valid Approaches to the Times, Feasts, Seasons

Is it thus wrong to keep a biblical feast like Passover, or *Sukkot*? No, not necessarily—it all hinges on *why* and *how* you are keeping it. What are you hoping to get from it? Did you read a book? Hear a message? What was the "promise" made by the teacher—what did he or she say, either explicitly or by hint, of the benefits that will accrue from observance? If your observance contains the expectation that you will be closer to God, that you will have some kind of special, superior revelation *because of your observance of the feast at the appointed time,*[156] then you are on a slippery slope—one which in Paul's opinion, and my own experience, always leads to a decreased focus on the cross of Yeshua in one's life and preaching, and a reduction of the work of the Holy Spirit in the believer's life, as you fall into a kind of spiritual deception. So how is it

---

[156] Of course, these times are set by the rabbis!

possible, then, to keep a feast in a new-covenantally "kosher" way? After reading this book, I hope you will agree that there are at least five possible ways/reasons.

1. Messianic Jewish Identity and Heritage

The Hebrew calendar of Sabbaths and feasts is part of our culture, identity, and covenantal history which we are instructed by the apostle Paul to somehow maintain (1 Cor. 7:17–22).[157] This is especially easy and "normal" for Israeli Messianic Jews, as the biblical calendar—at least according to the medieval rabbinic reckoning—is our national calendar, making the Sabbath and biblical feasts part of our everyday, national life.[158] Therefore we join with our people in this ancient pattern of life that is part of our covenantal, cultural identity rooted in the Bible. These celebrations are a gracious gift to our people that call us to remember His great deeds in the past, present Messianic fulfillment, and to seek their prophetic meaning for the still future aspects of the kingdom of God. They are also a way of passing our heritage of Israeli-Jewish identity to our children. As Messianic Jews who believe in the "irrevocable gifts and calling" of our nation, we humbly seek to strengthen our national cultural identity and not weaken it (Rom. 9:4, 11:29). We do so with the conviction that the fullness of our identity, in Christ, will serve to bless the nations and help them come to their fullness as well. It is our hope that people in other nations will similarly find ways to "redeem" their cultural patterns, bringing the fullness of the gospel into every aspect of their national life, and thus enriching the beautiful tapestry that is the worldwide body of Messiah (see #4 below).

2. Expedient Study of OT Types and Shadows

---

[157] See more on the "weight" of this command in Appendix 3-2.
[158] In Israel, the seventh-day Sabbath (Friday sundown until Saturday sundown) is our official day off; Sunday is the first day of the week and thus a work/school day for everyone. Almost all Messianic congregations in Israel meet on Friday (a kind of half-day off) or Saturday. The situation is more difficult for Arab-Israeli congregations following church tradition, which requires the public worship meeting to be on Sunday—a work day in the country they live in!

214 One New Man

The old-covenant calendar is full of "shadows" and "types" of the Messiah—His person, His ministry, His death, resurrection, return, and ultimate reign over the universe from Earth (Col. 2:17; Heb. 10:1). There is much to be learned, both about what He did in the past and what He will do in the future, from these "types." All Christians who desire to grow into maturity must commit themselves to regular, systematic study of the entire Scriptures (2 Tim. 3:16). *Thus, it is first and foremost a matter of study, not observance.* I know many Christians who have never observed a Jewish-style Passover Seder, for example, who know far more about the biblical teaching surrounding this holiday than many Orthodox Jews who observe the feast every year in a traditionally Jewish manner.[159] However, for some people—especially those who are more "visual" or "tactile" (touch) learners—a great deal can be gleaned from *the doing* of biblical, and some of the Jewish traditional, practices surrounding the feast. But this could be done at any time of year, whether it be one or two days off from the Jewish calendar (better on a weekend, for example); or six months off the Jewish calendar because of spring being fall, and fall being spring as in the southern hemisphere![160]

Ten years ago, I interned at a church in Korea for three months during the spring. Passover/Easter time came, and about two hundred members went on an outing to a model of second-temple Jerusalem. When we got there, there was a little lamb tied to a tree, whom the children were playing with. They dressed some of us up as priests, and then . . . it came time to slaughter the lamb! This was a real, "live" demonstration! I was shocked! As the token Jewish "priest," I was asked to hold the lamb down while another slit its throat! Till this day, I can still smell the

---

[159] Ironically, the "blood of the lamb" part of the story is greatly de-emphasized in Judaism—probably a reaction against Messianic/Christian claims.

[160] In any case, there is a kind of arbitrary quality to the lunar, Hebrew calendar anyway, as we have to add a "leap month" every few years to calibrate with the more accurate, solar Gregorian calendar. No one can prove that the seventh-day Sabbath we celebrate is indeed in a perfect cycle of seven-day weeks since the creation. After all, until the revelation at Mount Sinai, there is not mention of anything calendrical!

warm blood of that little lamb—and I think of it not just during Pass-over but many times when I contemplate the meaning of the shed blood of our Passover Lamb, Jesus (1 Cor. 5:7). That one experience taught me more about Passover than a thousand Passover Seders!

In summary, these kinds of observances can be powerful aids to our understanding—but the truth to be grasped has nothing to do with the exact timing of our observance, but with the truths that the feast points to!

3. Identification, Intercession, and Evangelism for Israel and the Nations

According to Scripture, the Gentile church is supposed to provoke Israel to jealousy (Rom. 11:11). This has many dimensions to it, but one of them is when the Gentile Christian demonstrates a love for Israel and the Jewish people—and one way to show love is to show an interest, and even an identification with, Jewish culture. An understanding of the feasts, and what Jewish people do and think and pray at these times, can definitely be a part of this. And for those who sense a special bur-den to pray for the salvation of Israel, it can be very helpful to know what happens, what texts are read, and what kinds of prayers are being prayed at the local synagogue during the holy days. This is a great time to pray for Jewish eyes to be opened to see the true atonement that we can only have in Yeshua! In the Messianic Jewish context as well, we seek to emphasize this intercessory dimension: As we live out and enjoy the new covenant fulfillment of things like the Sabbath and feasts, our hearts burn to see more of our people come to faith in Yeshua and experience this fullness; and, as we see so clearly by the Holy Spirit the eschatological meaning the feasts, we often have a strong sense of join-ing with the Spirit in intercession to bring about the onset of end-times events—"The Spirit and the bride say 'Come'" (Rev. 22:17)!

Here's one example: Over the last several years, our ministry Revive Israel has been holding an all-night prayer meeting on *Erev Shavuot*, Pentecost Eve. Our belief is that this is what the disciples did two thousand years ago, and that the prophecy of Joel quoted by Peter ("In the last days . . . I will pour forth of My Spirit on *all* mankind"; Acts 2:17, emphasis added) still awaits some future fulfillment. So we gather to pray all night for God to pour out His Spirit more and more in these last days! We intercede for many things in Israel, the Middle East, and the nations of the world. Now in Israel today, as it was two thousand years ago, *Shavuot* is a major holiday in Israel. We get two or three days off, so we don't have to work the next day, and we can rest after being up all night! We encourage believers from around the world to connect with us through a live webstream—but obviously the number of people who can do this will be limited because of time differences, lack of a holiday rest, etc. Therefore, we also encourage groups to hold their own prayer meeting at a time convenient to them. We believe this kind of prayer is key to releasing many things for the end times.

But this one also comes with a warning: Showing an interest and understanding of Jewish culture is one thing, but keeping it "religiously" is another. If one's goal is to "provoke the Jew to jealousy," then this must be done from a faith-based confidence in one's identity in Yeshua—as a non-Jew. The rabbis actually teach that it is forbidden for a Gentile to keep the Sabbath like a Jew—since this is a special inheritance which only belongs to Israel (see Ex. 31:17, and Chapter 4 of this book). So don't think that you are going to provoke an Orthodox Jew to jealousy by "out-keeping" him with respect to the *dogma*-commands—it may, in fact, have the opposite effect!

3. Creative "Indigenous" Celebration and Witness

I know of some churches in Japan, for example, that celebrate a kind of Passover in the spring, and *Sukkot* (Tabernacles) in the fall. The Japanese have a great knack for creatively mixing cultures, and this is what these brothers and sisters do at these times, combining some biblical elements with some Japanese ones. The leaders believe that this is part of "contextualizing" Christianity in Japan, and creating more indigenous Christian traditions to replace those simply inherited from the Western church. Since all the biblical feasts have a seasonal, agricultural aspect to them, these Japanese Christians borrow some of the biblical symbolism and match it with the Japanese agricultural (especially rice-planting) and harvesting cycles. They celebrate this way usually within a week or two of the Jewish calendar, but usually on a Saturday so as to facilitate more people being able to attend. I know the leaders personally, and they are very careful to not confuse their new tradition with sound biblical, gospel teaching.

The result is a beautiful tapestry—a kind of uniquely Japanese Passover/Sukkot (with rice balls *and* Israeli matzah!) that brings forth the gospel truths therein in a very creative and celebratory way. What's more, they use these times (as in #3 above) to make special intercession for Israel and the Jewish people. In my experience with them, there is none of the quasi-gnostic sense of creating some new, more biblically "correct" (and thus superior to other forms of Christian) tradition.

In conclusion, we can say that every culture has its patterns of times, seasons, feasts, commemorations, and celebrations—these are part of "civilized" human society (Acts 17:26). As human beings—as families, as nations—our lives are enriched by the rootedness of these patterns of life. They are important times of imparting our culture and values to the next generation. For example, think about how much better off the Western world is since adopting the Judeo-Christian, seven-day-week including one or two days of rest, and the celebration of the resurrection every Sunday. (And now, almost the whole world has also adopted this basic calendar.) Also the Christian calendar enriches us with times to recall biblical meanings on some subjects in special ways during the church year. Of course, it is the same with the biblical, Jewish year. It is our prayer that every tribe, tongue, and nation will succeed in creatively "redeeming" their own cultural patterns in light of biblical truth.

4. Sabbath Rest

As we mentioned at the beginning, the seventh-day Sabbath is the foundation, the template, for all the rest of the feasts. God commanded Israel to rest once a week, and He commanded us to celebrate His great works—both in nature and in our history—at various times of the year. Regular rest and celebration is thus an important principle for all of humanity. How much more so in our busy modern world where we can do all manner of "work"—all the time—on a little handheld device connected to the entire world through the internet! So learning to rest, to spend quality time with family and friends, to enjoy the fruits of our labor—rather than living as slaves to the economy—is a vital, biblical concept.

We have forgotten that for most of history, throughout most of the world except the Near East, the idea of a seven-day week with at least one official "day of rest" was not well known or practiced. It is only over the last two thousand years that this calendar has spread to the whole world. Today, most of the world actually has a kind of "Sabbath rest" either on Saturday or Sunday.

But what if the believer wants to dedicate a "day of rest" in a more formal way? Well, this can be a point of valid connection with the Jewish, seventh-day Sabbath, but with the caveat that you keep the day with the understanding that your choice of time and way of rest is no "better" or "holier" or more "biblical" than the believer who chooses Sunday—or any other day of the week, for that matter.

I hope this book has convinced you that under the new covenant, our approach to Sabbaths, days, feasts, etc., has forever been changed. It is good to give the body and mind the rest it needs, as led by the Holy Spirit, but we must always do so with Romans 14 in mind: Let each one be convinced in his own mind, while being very careful what we teach about it, for the kingdom of God is not eating and drinking (or the observance of days), but righteousness, peace, and joy in the Holy Spirit!

APPENDIX 2-1

Matthew 5:17–20: A Difficult Text

When I teach on this subject of the one new man, there are certain Bible verses or interpretations that are always raised in apparent opposition to what I've been teaching in this book. In this appendix, we will focus on one of the most common ones, while touching on a few others.

Matthew 5:17–20

> Do not think that I came to abolish the Law or the Prophets; I did not come to abolish, but to fulfill. For truly I say to you, until heaven and earth pass away, not the smallest letter or stroke shall pass away from the Law, until all is accomplished. Whoever then annuls one of the least of these commandments, and so teaches others, shall be called least in the kingdom of heaven; but whoever keeps and teaches them, he shall be called great in the kingdom of heaven. For I say to you, that unless your righteousness surpasses that of the scribes and Pharisees, you shall not enter the kingdom of heaven.

Here, many claim, Jesus seems to be saying much the opposite of what we have taught in this book. Paul teaches that on the cross, Yeshua abolishes at least some aspects of Torah, but in Matthew Jesus seems to say, "whatever you think, don't think that I came to do that!" These verses from Matthew, near the beginning of the Sermon on the Mount, are by far the most often quoted ones by those who would try to pit Jesus against Paul,[161] and/or claim Yeshua's authority for some kind of ongoing, all-encompassing, new-covenant Torah observance.[162] As we will see, there is actually perfect agreement between what Yeshua teaches here and what is later developed more fully by Paul. The key is to read these verses from Matthew in the overall context of Matthew 5–7 and avoid the pitfall of "prooftexting"—pulling single verses from this or that place in Scripture in order to prove one's pet doctrine.

Before we look in detail at these verses, we must first look at the use of the word "Torah" (Greek *nomos*) in Jewish culture, then and now. The root meaning of the word is "instruction." It can thus refer to revelatory instruction in general, as in Psalm 78:1 (emphasis added): "Listen, O my people, to my *instruction*." Then, of course, it often refers to the five books of Moses and all the teaching contained therein; but it can also to refer to all of the OT, as in John 10:34, 12:34, and 15:25, where Jesus speaks to the Jewish leaders of what is in their "law," but the verses He quotes are from the Psalms and various prophets—not from Moses. Then, in later Jewish use, it can refer to the whole corpus of authoritative rabbinic literature and teaching, under the rubric of the so called "oral Torah." Today in Israel among the Jewish population, we speak of "Torah" in all of these ways![163] (Other verses cited in this manner include Matthew 7:12, 22:40; John 1:17; and Galatians 5:14.)

---

[161] Basically there are two trends, one is to try to interpret Paul in accord with the Torah positive interpretation of Matthew 5:17 (more difficult); the other, in some ways more disturbing, is to claim Yeshua's authority to denigrate a third of the New Testament, namely the writings of Paul—to accuse him of not being a true apostle, i.e., one of the Twelve, a traitor to Torah, etc. Either way, a major watering-down of the authority of the NT takes place.

[162] Ironically, very, very few modern Torah teachers go the full distance and demand circumcision, as Paul mockingly encouraged them to do to themselves, and more, two thousand years ago (Gal. 5:3, 12). In the end, unless one fully embraces orthodox Judaism, one's Torah observance is highly selective.

[163] In modern Hebrew, the word "Torah" can also refer to any kind of teaching or theory, even something totally secular or scientific.

What this means is simply this: For at least the last two thousand-plus years, every Jew who is going to teach "Torah," or say something authoritative about it, has to first define which "Torah" he is talking about. We can't assume that when someone says "Torah" that we are talking about the same thing! If we are going to have clear communication, we simply have to define our terms.

In Matthew 5, Yeshua does exactly that. We must let Him, the authoritative "Torah-giver" himself, define for us the exact parameters of what he means by "Torah" in these verses.

1. Not to abolish, but to fulfill . . .

This means that Yeshua has not come to willy-nilly cancel or do away with the Torah and the Prophets, i.e., the old-covenant scriptural revelation. He has come to fulfill. Imagine the scene: This young rabbi from Nazareth has recently begun his public ministry in the north of Israel (not in the Jerusalem area!), and it has begun with quite a "bang!" He confidently calls to Himself four disciples, then begins to proclaim the gospel of the kingdom, and to demonstrate his miraculous power over all manner of sickness and disease. Quickly, the news about him spreads widely, and in time, "Large crowds followed Him from Galilee and the Decapolis and Jerusalem and Judea and from beyond the Jordan" (Matt. 4:18–25). Now that He has this great following, it has come time for this amazing man to explain himself and this good news that he preaches in more detail—to lay the teaching foundation for what is quickly becoming some kind of new "movement" or community. But just how "new" is it? After all, this is Israel—there is history, there are the scrolls of the Law and the Prophets, the covenants, the promises— and also no shortage of new, even Messianic, movements. In Matthew's rendering, these verses serve as the preface to the Sermon on the Mount that will take up the next three chapters.

It is important to note that the Sermon does not begin with our text, 5:17ff; instead He begins with the Beatitudes (vv. 3–12) and further words of instruction and edification for His disciples (vv. 13–16)

222 Omne New Man

that are not straightforwardly found in the OT.[164] Yeshua's first priority seems *not* to be to emphasize or establish a perfect continuity of
his teaching with the Torah and Prophets, or any similarity to that of
the scribes and Pharisees. Rather, the Master demonstrates His unique
authority as *the* Lawgiver by announcing His good news to the poor and
downtrodden—those who have chosen to follow Him. What amazing
confidence!

And, not a word of it sounds like the *d'var Torah* of the Pharisees:
He is not quoting and interpreting and preaching from the texts, as the
rest of His contemporaries would be doing in the synagogues on the
Sabbath. The good news just seems to flow straight out of Him.

But now, from verse 17, it has come time for Him to put Himself
and His teaching in the context of the history of Jewish revelation,
especially as contained in the Torah of Moses; as if to say, "As wonderful
and as new as it may sound to you, don't think that I am just some
charismatic healer come to teach a totally new 'Torah'; I'm not some
anti-Judaism radical. . . . Everything I'm saying and doing is in some
way continuous with what has come before . . . but it is also new,
because of who I am. Let me explain: I did not come to abolish but
to fulfill. . . ." So it remains for us to see exactly what he means by
"Torah" and by "fulfill," as contrasted with "abolish." Let's allow the
Master to explain Himself.

2. Until all is accomplished . . .

The first thing Yeshua explains is that the "Torah" (i.e., the whole OT)[165]
are first and foremost books of *prophecy and promise*. When He says that
not "the smallest letter or stroke shall pass away from the Law [Torah],
until all is accomplished," this can only be referring to a prophetic

---

[164] Yes, there are some themes from these verses that can be found in the OT, but He is not com-
menting or making reference to any earlier texts as He does from verse 21 forward.

[165] In the Jewish culture, then and now, the word *torah* can refer to: a) the five books of Moses
b) the entire Tenak, or OT; or c) the entire corpus of Pharisaic/rabbinic teaching, much of i
based on the Bible.

understanding of Scripture. Later, in the same gospel, Jesus explains that "all the prophets and the law prophesied until John" (Matt. 11:13). The law of Moses is no less "prophetic" than the books of the prophets or Psalms. But which parts of the Law/Torah is Jesus talking about? Obviously, some material is more easily understood as being prophetic than other material. As noted earlier, we can easily find a prophetic dimension to the calendar commandments (Sabbath, feasts, etc.), but it is not so easy for the dietary or purity laws. No one, then or now, would normally speak of these *dogma*-commandments as those that await a future "accomplishment" or "fulfillment."[166] Paraphrasing from the broader context, Yeshua is simply saying, "As the promised Messiah/King/Deliverer, I've come to fulfill the multitude of prophecies from the OT that speak of me. But I'm also telling you ahead of time, that I won't fulfill all of them this first time around. Heaven and Earth will not pass away until I fulfill every single prophecy, even at my second coming." This is in total agreement with the author of Hebrews: "Now Moses was faithful in all His house as a servant, *for a testimony of those things which were to be spoken later*" (3:5, emphasis added). Unlike rabbinic Judaism, which understands the Torah (OT, Bible) as *primarily* a book of commandments to be kept, the NT says that it is *primarily* a book of prophetic testimonies and prefiguring of what is to come.[167]

3. These *commandments . . .*

The next thing Yeshua teaches is a little more difficult to tease out, but is really the most crucial point for us. It hinges on His use of the relative pronoun in verse 19: *these.*[168] In Ephesians 2:15

---

[166] One might argue that, as in Judaism, the future "accomplishment" points to the day when every Jew actually observes the Sabbath according to the detailed perfection of rabbinic law—and then the Messiah will come. But it seems like a big stretch to me to try and makes these verses fit that understanding.

[167] The rabbis, according to one tradition, actually agree with this, in theory, when they say that "All Scripture speaks of the days of the Messiah."

[168] "These" only appears once in the original Greek; a second "these" or "them" is added in some translations for English smoothness.

(emphasis added), the apostle is careful not to claim that the gospel brings about the abolishing of *all* Torah—only of those specific "commandments contained in *ordinances*"—what we learned as the *dogma*-commandments. Here Yeshua is coming at the issue from the opposite standpoint—not what is being abolished (negative), but what is being established (positive) under His new covenant. Like Paul in Ephesians, His reference to "*these* commandments" immediately begs the question: Which commandments are you talking about? Which commandments, which Torah have you so forcefully come to fulfill/establish and not abolish? What are "*these* commandments" that we must be so careful to keep and teach—even "the least" of them—so that our righteousness might surpass that of the scribes and Pharisees, and that we might enter the kingdom of heaven?

Answering these questions in Matthew is much easier than in Ephesians, as we don't have to go to other epistles or gospels to search for definitions.[169] Immediately following Yeshua's declaration, from verse 21 and for the next two and half chapters, Yeshua teaches "these" Torah commandments—the ones that He has come to fulfill (fill-full!) or establish. This is, by far, the most natural way to read the text and understand what is meant by "these/them" in verse 19: Matthew 5:17–19 serves as an introduction to the rest of the Sermon on the Mount—Yeshua's most complete teaching on "Torah" in all the Gospels. He begins by warning people that the coming of the Messiah and the kingdom of God doesn't mean that we are suddenly free from being moral people.[170] The message is not, "The kingdom is here, let's start the party!" No, as we will shortly see, the message is: "The kingdom of God is here—repent! And understand the depth of God's morals and ethics—how far is the human heart from them, and how radically strict they are."

---

[169] I am aware that in Matthew 23 Yeshua seemingly defines a "tier" of commandments (v. 23); yet I think we must look first to Matthew 5–7 to define what Yeshua means here.

[170] Not as in Islam, which promises the faithful man seventy-two virgins, i.e., a kingdom of Heaven with rewards that are immoral in the present age.

4. You have heard . . .

I have heard and read many teachers who misuse Matthew 5:17 because of an anachronistic, noncontextual reading of Scripture. They imagine Yeshua in their own image, standing in a pulpit with a Bible in hand, waving it around as He shouts, "Don't think that I came to abolish the Torah, these five books of Moses, these 613 commandments. . . . I tell you anyone who teaches such a thing will be in big trouble, even Paul!" They teach as if Yeshua could only be referring to the whole of the written OT, or at least the five books of Moses, and not a specific subset, as He goes on to explain. Rather, we must learn from the actual situation two thousand years ago, and why Yeshua prefaces many of the "commandments" that He teaches on the Mount with: "*you have heard* that the ancients were told . . ." (Matt. 5:21, emphasis added; cf. 27, 33, et al.).

First, Yeshua was not preaching from a written text in hand. There were no portable Bibles back then; instead, the Scriptures were handwritten, hand-copied on heavy parchment scrolls, and kept in the synagogues. It was not the kind of thing you took on a hike up a mountain! This is our first hint that when Yeshua says "torah" He may be referring to something broader than just the written code found in the five books of Moses. Secondly, He was speaking to simple Galilean peasants, many of whom couldn't read and had only learned what they knew of Torah from the teaching in the synagogues. Even for the literate, there were no private, printed books. This means that their understanding of "torah" was more fluid and dynamic than ours (the written page). Also, we know from Judaism that most Jews didn't distinguish between the exact teaching in the written Torah and the traditional teaching of the rabbis/Pharisees (the oral Torah). One such "torah" from the Sermon on the Mount even quotes something that can't be found in the written text of Moses, Matthew 5:43 (emphasis added): "You have heard that it was said, 'YOU SHALL LOVE YOUR NEIGHBOR and *hate your enemy.*'" This strengthens our explanation from #3 above concerning what Yeshua means by "*these* commandments": It is a mistake to jump to the conclusion that when He said that He did "not come to abolish the Torah" that He is automatically talking about what we assume to be "Torah"—namely, the 613 commandments as found in the written text of the five books of Moses.

Further, "you have heard" comes to teach us something else very profound from the lips of Yeshua: When it comes to the kind of moral and ethical lifestyle that our holy, loving God longs to see among the human family (not just "Torah-observant" Jews!), written laws are not "where it's at"! You have to go way beyond the written word to the spirit of the commandment![171] Listen to what He teaches in Matthew 5, the first two "commandments" after the introduction in verses 17–19:

> You have heard that the ancients were told, "You SHALL NOT COMMIT MURDER" and "Whoever commits murder shall be liable to the court." But I say to you that everyone who is angry with his brother shall be guilty before the court. . . . You have heard that it was said, "You SHALL NOT COMMIT ADULTERY"; but I say to you, that everyone who looks on a woman to lust for her has committed adultery with her already in his heart. (Matt. 5:21–22, 27–28)

I know the rabbinic-Pharisaic mind; I live among orthodox Jews, I've studied Judaism in Yeshivas, and I tell you—to our shame—what many an orthodox Jew would ask at this point: "Yeshua, Rabbi-Messiah, can you tell us what you mean by 'being angry'? Can you tell us what exactly is a 'lustful look'? Where exactly are the boundaries?" And I can imagine Yeshua's answer, with tears in His eyes and fire on His tongue: "No . . . I'm not going to tell you. I'm not going to define it for you by some kind of written list of traditional dos and don'ts. I know that's what you want, so that you can deceive yourself into believing that you are morally pleasing to God because you walk high-speed through the

---

[171] Paul puts it this way: "the letter kills, but the Spirit gives life" (2 Cor. 3:6).

city with your head down in order to not even see a woman. But the truest Torah of God is much, much deeper than such a list can teach. It is a matter of the heart, of the inner man, of the spirit. Everyone must learn for himself where exactly are the lines between righteous indignation versus hateful judgment and anger. Every man, made in the image of God and with the help of his conscience and the Holy Spirit, has the capacity to discern the difference between the innocent appreciation of feminine beauty and lust. Let him who has ears to hear—hear!"

This is why, for the next two-and-a-half chapters of Scripture, as Yeshua so authoritatively interprets and "fills-full" the Torah, the tendency is always toward the radical internalizing (and universalizing, i.e., applicable to all men everywhere at all times—not just "Torah Jews") of the commandments. What's more, on more than one occasion, Yeshua actually turns Mosaic commandments completely on their head— teaching that what Moses said was either wrong, temporary, or now passé. (See Matthew 5:27–32 on divorce; 33–37 on vows; 38–42 on personal justice; and 43–48 on loving one's enemy.) It is beyond me how someone can read this and then teach that verses 17–20 are somehow a blanket endorsement of the ongoing validity of all the laws in the five books of Moses!

In conclusion, when it comes to the Torah as a *prophetic* text, Yeshua is very strong on the eternal, enduring nature of the written text. But when it comes to the "moral" Torah law, Yeshua takes a very different tact.

5. Unless your righteousness surpasses that of the scribes and Pharisees, you shall not enter the kingdom of heaven.

Yeshua declares that this issue of keeping and teaching *these* commandments of God properly is a huge one: If our righteous observance of them does not surpass those of the scribes and Pharisees, we may not enter the kingdom of Heaven! If these verses from Matthew 5 mean, as some modern-day "Torah teachers" claim, that *all* of the Torah commandments are still valid under the new covenant, then verses 19 and

20 demand that we must observe things like the calendar, Sabbaths, and *kashruth* in a more exacting and scrupulous way than orthodox Jews! If these things are still somehow part of defining biblical righteousness and/or holiness, then Yeshua is here teaching that we must outperform the orthodox Jews (today's "scribes and Pharisees") in our performance of these commands in order to enter the kingdom of heaven! Does this sound like something Yeshua or the apostles taught elsewhere? Does this sound like the rest of the New Testament?

If such teaching is true, then believe you me, the situation is hopeless. The rabbis have been studying the minutiae of Torah observance—even to the shapes and mystical numerical values of the Hebrew letters—for a long, long time. "Johnny-come-lately" Gentile Christians have little hope of catching up with the quality and, even mystical beauty, of the Pharisaic-rabbinical observance of these things. (Of course, this would mean that all Christians would have to learn at the feet of the rabbis of these minutiae—exactly what Paul so vehemently warned against in Galatians.[172])

6. Where Is Kashrut? Where Is the Sabbath?

Look at what is conspicuously missing from the Sermon on the Mount— not a single reference to any *dogma-stoichea* commandment! No mention of Sabbath, holy days, foods, purity laws, etc. Remember, Paul taught us what aspects of Torah have been abolished as commandments; here Yeshua is teaching and tweaking which aspects of Torah eternally stand

---

[172] I am aware of the modern, scholarly approach to this text based on what is called "redaction criticism:" the view that Matthew was writing to an early, Torah-observant Messianic Jewish community and thus recalls (the more conservative approach) Yeshua's teaching, or puts these words on Yeshua's lips (the more liberal approach) as *only* applicable for Jewish disciples. What to say? Such theories are interesting in the "ivory tower" but extremely problematic when one tries to teach the text to a congregation, or those without education in higher criticism. Not to mention that it renders one of the most important texts in all of the NT (the Sermon on the Mount) useless to non-Jewish disciples—the majority of Christians in the world! As I show here, one does not need to resort to such interpretations in order to make sense of the text in the overall NT context.

as commandments. The absence of the *dogma* commandments is huge and glaring, especially if one is trying to teach their ongoing validity as commands for faith and practice in the kingdom. If this were Yeshua's intention, and the intention of His gospel, then He really messed up! This is His most extensive, comprehensive Torah teaching in three years of ministry. Maybe He forgot to teach about the Sabbath and *kashrut*? Maybe He wanted to, but He got tired under the hot Mediterranean sun and had to cut it short? Or maybe Matthew was an anti-Torah, "self-hating" Jew who left these things out on purpose, even though Yeshua really did teach them? Or maybe it is a conspiracy of the Church Fathers who canonized the book of Matthew, but "filtered" it according to their anti-Torah theology?[173]

All sarcasm aside (not an easy thing for a Jew!), in the world of proto-rabbinic, Pharisaic, second-temple Judaism it would have been a very, very strange thing for a rabbi to give his broadest, most authoritative *d'var Torah* and never mention the Shabbat and the correct interpretation of the laws surrounding its observance! Instead everything Jesus teaches here is 100% applicable, in the most straightforward way, to every human being in every place at every time—exactly like the *dogma*-free gospel of Paul. This is in 100% agreement with the one-new-man gospel of Paul, with the result that the new commandments and holy boundaries" of God's people are no longer to be confused with the *dogma*-commandments of Torah, only the deep morality of Yeshua as taught by the Apostles. In other words, being perfect like our Holy Father is perfect is no longer is to be confused with what we eat or don't, or what calendar we keep (Matt. 5:48; Rom. 14). Instead, the whole of the Law and Prophets can be summed up by the Golden Rule of loving one's neighbor as himself (Matt. 7:12).

Yeshua concludes the Sermon on the Mount with the parable of the two houses—one built on the rock of His words, and the other on

---

Sorry for the sarcasm, but I've actually read or heard Torah teachers suggest all of these possilities—except the first two.

sand: "Therefore everyone who hears these words of Mine, and acts upon them, may be compared to a wise man who built his house upon the rock" (Matt. 7:24). This is a perfect closure to our understanding of Matthew 5:17–19 as an introduction to the pure, authoritative, universal Torah of Messiah and His kingdom. It is both radically new, and also in continuity with the previous revelation under the Mosaic covenant; but this continuity is not a simple, straight-line kind of continuity wherein Yeshua comes to just to make a few simple updates to Torah by way of commentary. Instead Yeshua, by the authority that only He can wield, has given us the Torah that He has come to fulfill, establish, correct, and *upgrade*—not to abolish. Plus, this line of continuity will ultimately wind its way through the crucifixion of the Son of God and His resurrection, which affects the entire cosmos and how we relate to it. The "sand" upon which the other house is built is a beautiful symbol of the *stoichea*-based elements of the created order upon which the *dogma*-commandments of all religions are founded. What Paul saw so clearly is that if you build your house on the sand of a doctrine of uncrucified and unresurrected *dogma*-Torah commands—watch out when the storm comes!

APPENDIX 3-1

Legalism or *Dogma*-Torah Commands? What Did Yeshua Actually Abolish on the Cross?

> *But we know that the Law is good, if one uses it lawfully, realizing the fact that law is not made for a righteous man, but for those who are lawless and rebellious, for the ungodly and sinners, for the unholy and profane.* (1 Tim. 1:8–9)

As mentioned in the introduction, there have been great efforts made over the last few generations to "re-read" Paul, to bring balance to the traditional antinomian (*nomos* being the Greek word in the NT for "law" and thus "Torah") way of understanding Paul. In every Pauline epistle, it seems, we can find at least a verse or two which seemingly disparages Torah, or Torah observance, in some way; but here and there, the apostle also seems to bring balance to such statements by affirming the essential "goodness" or "holiness" of the Torah by way of teaching or his own lifestyle example. In the modern Messianic and wider One Torah movements, much thought and energy has been expended to reestablish either Jewish identity in Messiah, or a justification for Gentile Torah observance. This effort almost always entails the finding of an interpretative way around the plain, or at least traditional, reading of many of the Scriptures written by Paul that we have studied in this book. The best and most popular results are found in three primary categories:[174]

a. All, or at least a majority of, Paul's negative statements about Torah are dedicated in their context to a Gentile audience, with the purpose of laying a *dogma*-Torah-free foundation for Gentile Christian faith and practice. Therefore, according to this view, this teaching was (and is) not directed to, or applicable to Jewish believers for whom *dogma*-Torah observance remains a covenantal obligation—as supposedly demonstrated by the lifestyle of Paul himself. Obviously, this interpretative construct can be foundational for the Messianic Jewish community, but provides no validation for One Torah doctrine and/or "Torah teaching" for Gentiles.[175]

b. Paul is referring not to the written Torah (or part thereof) itself, but rather to the additions made especially by the Pharisees and later rabbis (oral Torah). In my study, this solution is very, very hard to support and thus has been mostly abandoned by serious NT scholars and teachers.

c. The third construct is to interpret Paul's disparaging teachings about Torah as pertaining to the sinful, legalistic, misuse of Torah. This view says that the problem is never with Torah itself, but only with some permutation of human sin and weakness which causes us to not be able to keep the Torah with the right "spirit," but instead always tending toward a kind of "legalistic" approach to it. Or, what has been abolished is the Torah's propensity to magnify sin in this way, as taught by the apostle in Romans 7. An obvious proof text for this view would be Romans 7:14: "we

---

[174] There is a fourth way, too, of basically erasing Paul from Scripture by claiming that he was an anti-Torah heretic, or not genuinely an apostle. There are some in this extreme camp, but they essentially remove themselves from any mainstream dialogue, as they reject the authority of the church fathers and the selection of the NT canon.

[175] A major problem with this view is it tends to resurrect the middle wall of partition between Jew & gentile, based on a fundamentally different theology of Torah for each.

know that the law is spiritual, but I am of flesh, sold into bondage to sin."

Furthermore, according to this view, this "legalistic" approach to Torah, supposedly represented by the Pharisaic/rabbinical approach to it, is what the apostle refers to in Galatians when he writes of the "works of the law," or being "under the law." Therefore, the argument goes, if we are cleansed and made free from sin and live by gospel grace according to the Holy Spirit, we should be able to observe all of Torah in the "right" or "spiritual" way. According to this reading of Paul, the apostle was not "anti-Torah," but "anti-sin," and in particular with regard to some aspects of Torah observance—"antilegalism." Much more than a) or b) above, this construct has had wide influence in both the Messianic Jewish and wider Torah movements. In my survey and experience over the last twenty years of Messianic Jewish and Jewish-roots/One Torah theology, I would say that this "re-reading" of Paul has become, in many circles, a primary hermeneutical/ theological pillar.

In this appendix, we will occupy ourselves with an analysis of this construct.[176] As you hopefully can deduce from what I have written of the one new man, I do not agree with this "re-reading" of Paul; and I will show many reasons why such a reading of Paul—and the New Testament in general—is groundless, inconsistent, untenable, and ultimately unnecessary. Strong words, I know, but I believe it is a grave error that has brought much compromise to the gospel, and confusion to many people.

There are many gifted writers and teachers who have expounded this way of reading Paul, but for time and space's sake, I will "pick on"

---

[176] I use this word "construct," because such an interpretation widely applied becomes foundational for an entire systematic theology and way of reading Scripture, and understanding the issue of continuity (or lack of) from OT to NT; law vs. grace, etc.

234 One New Man

on only one—which is a tribute to the fact that his writings have prob ably influenced more people than any other's. David Stern is my friend a brother in the Lord, and we were once part of the same congregation in Jerusalem. His *Jewish New Testament* (JNT) and accompanying *Jew ish New Testament Commentary* have sold (tens of?) thousands of copies and are widely used in the English-speaking world of Messianic Juda ism and Jewish roots. In addition, his books have been translated into many languages. David was the first to take this interpretative construc to its logical conclusion by retranslating almost all of Paul's seemingly disparaging comments on Torah, and publishing a new translation o the NT. His *Commentary* also provides many thoughtful and insightfu explanations from this perspective. So while we disagree, let it be known that this is an argument among friends!

Let's start off with a few quotations from Stern—both from his NT translation and from the commentary.

1. The key one-new-man verse of this book, Ephesians 2:14–1⁵ (emphasis added): "He has made us both one and has broken down the m'chitzah [divider] which divided us by destroying in his own body the enmity *occasioned by the Torah*, with its com mands set forth in the form of ordinances."[177] Note that accord ing to this translation the enmity which Yeshua has "abolished in His flesh" on the cross is no longer "the Law/Torah of command ments *contained in ordinances*"—as in all major English transla tions—but something which Stern terms "the enmity *occasioned* by the Torah." In other words, not the Torah-*dogma* command. themselves have been abolished, but their tendency to "*occasion* sin (in this case enmity between Jews and Gentiles) by stimulat ing people's sinful propensities" is what has been abolished.[178]

---

[177] D. H. Stern, *Jewish New Testament—A Translation of the New Testament Which Expresses It Jewishness* (Clarksville, MD: Jewish New Testament Publications, 1989), electronic edition.
[178] Ibid.

2. Galatians 3:5–12, and especially the contrast between the "hearing of faith" gospel and the "works of the Law":

> What about God, who supplies you with the Spirit and works miracles among you—does he do it because of your legalistic observance of Torah commands or because you trust in what you heard and are faithful to it? . . . For everyone who depends on legalistic observance of Torah commands lives under a curse. . . . Now it is evident that no one comes to be declared righteous by God through legalism. . . . Furthermore, legalism is not based on trusting and being faithful, but on [a misuse of] the text. (vv. 5, 10–12)[179]

For more examples, see Stern's translation of Romans 4: Where we are used to seeing "Law" (Torah), we see "Legalism"; where we are used to seeing "works of the Law," we see "the legalistic observance of Torah." What follows my analysis of the semantic and interpretative issues.

1. *There is no word, no vocabulary for "legalism," for the first-century Jewish writers of the NT.* Obviously, if one is going to systematically translate *nomos* as "legalism" and not simply "law;" and *ergon nomou* ("works of the law") as "legalistic observance of Torah commands," then one has to prove why the original writer in the Greek language did not use another word, something akin to "legalism" or "legalistic observance." According to Stern, following Cranfield and a few others, the reason why Paul did not write "legalism" (even though that is what he meant) is that no such term existed in the Greek language; or that this important nuance was somehow too difficult to express in that language. And, Stern and others argue, because of what Yeshua said in Matthew 5:17[180] and because of the other positive things that Paul said about Torah, there is no way he could mean

---

[9] Ibid.
[10] See my treatment of Matthew 5:17 in Appendix 2-1.

to disparage the Torah itself, but only its legalistic misuse. I see two huge issues with this line of thinking:

a. The use of *nomimos* in 1 Timothy 1:7–11. In these verses, written by the same Apostle, he makes it clear that under the New Covenant, there is a correct, "lawful" use (*nomimos,* v. 8) of Torah; and thus an incorrect, "unlawful," *misuse* of the Torah, as taught by the "Torah teachers." As in Romans 7:12, 16, or Galatians 3:21, Paul here affirms (v. 8) that the "Torah is good," but with the condition that it be used "lawfully." The next verses describe this "lawful" use of Torah as pertaining not to the "righteous man," but to those (believers? unbelievers?) who struggle with major moral issues in their lives. This is perfectly consistent with the apostle's description elsewhere of one of the primary functions of Torah to define and "magnify sin" (e.g., Rom. 7:7–13). This means, by contrast, that the negative misuse of the Torah by the Torah teachers (about whom Paul is here warning Timothy) has something to do with a use of the Torah that goes beyond its moral teachings, which agrees with everything else we have learned in this book. *Thus, the idea that the apostle Paul was without means or terminology to express the subtleties of a kind of misuse of Torah is simply wrong.* While there may not be an exact match for our "legalism," this passage in 1 Timothy proves that Paul had at his disposal a Greek term to express the general *misuse* of Torah (*nominos* in the negative)—and therefore could have, in the key places in Romans and Galatians, used this term in a qualified way—instead of just writing *nomos* or *ergon nomou.*

b. If the doctrine of "legalism" does in fact play such a large role in Paul's (and thus the NT's) theology of Torah, why the absence of an appropriate Greek or Hebrew term? The argument of Sterr and others is essentially an argument from a first-century "seman tic silence," i.e., the absence of an appropriate Greek or Hebrew (LXX background) term for what is (supposedly) so easil captured and expressed by our modern, English word "legalism." Why is it that for every other major doctrine of the new covenant—salvation, justification, sanctification, redemption, etc.—we have a plethora of Greek and Hebrew terms? Why is it, if they are correct that "legalism" is the right way to read Paul in all these places—making such an interpretative construct hugely important for any systematic understanding of law vs. grace, OT vs. NT—that no word exists? Are we so much smarter, or more "evolved" in our linguistic capability? What makes this supposedly important religious term so easy to communicate in our time, in our language yet so difficult two thousand years ago? No, this first-century "semantic silence" is precisely the basis for an argument *against* Stern's (and many others'!) interpretive agenda: The term didn't exist because the concept didn't exist—or at least did not function in any normative way in religious, theological discussion of the time. And why didn't it exist? This leads us to the next big problem. . . .

2. *What is "legalism"? How do we define it? How does it function in real life?* Here is Stern's best attempt at a definition of what he calls the legalistic "heresy," from his commentary on Galatians 3:12:

> The heresy of legalism, when applied to the Torah, says that anyone who does these things, that is, anyone who mechanically follows the rules for Shabbat, kashrut, etc., will attain life through them, will be saved... No need to trust God, just obey the rules! The problem with this simplistic ladder to Heaven is that legalism conveniently ignores the "rule" that trust [faith] must underlie all rule-following which God finds acceptable. But trust necessarily converts mere rule-following into something altogether different, in fact, into its opposite, genuine faithfulness to God...One could be obeying every single mitzvah (except, by assumption, the mitzvah of trust), but if these things are being done without heartfelt trust in the God who is there, the only God there is, the God who sent his Son Yeshua to

be the atonement for sin (v. 1), then all this outward "obedience" is hateful to God (Isaiah 1:14), and the person doing it, the legalist, "lives under a curse," because he is not "doing everything written in the Scroll of the Torah" (v. 10). He is not "doing" the trust which should motivate all doing.[181]

On the surface, there is much here that most believers would agree with. We know from the new covenant revelation that God's first priority is our faith in Him, not our outward performance, not even of good works. But at the heart of Stern's construct and definition of "legalism" is a contrast and a promise that we need to look at more closely, and ask ourselves the question—is this indeed what the NT is teaching, both here and elsewhere? And, is there any evidence that this is what the "Judaizing" teachers from Jerusalem were teaching in Galatia?

Stern contrasts the one who believes he will be saved by "*mechanically* following the rules for Shabbat, kashrut, etc." with one who keeps the same commandments with "*heartfelt trust* in the God who is there, the only God there is, the God who sent his Son Yeshua to be the atonement for sin." Such faith, he explains, leads to a life of "genuine faithfulness to God." It is no coincidence that in Stern's definition, the commandments he highlights are "Sabbath and *kashrut*," not, for example, "adultery and lying." Remember, the focus and the contention in this debate, concerns *not* the *moral* commandments of Torah or of the NT; but rather, the *dogma*-Torah commandments like Sabbath, circumcision and the dietary laws. Since all agree[7] that there are NT moral commandments much in continuity with the OT, it can be helpful to try and apply this construct of "legalism" to their observance. For example, Paul writes: "*Flee* [sexual] immorality" (1 Cor. 6:18, emphasis added). There is obviously no question here of whether one's "fleeing" should be "mechanical," "heartfelt,"

---

[181] Ibid.

"legalistic," or "from faith." The message is: Do what you need to do, but flee from it!

On the same subject, Yeshua said that it is better to cut out one's eye, or cut off one's right hand, rather than have the whole body sent to hell (Matt. 5:27–30). If your observance of such moral commandments is one day 27 percent from heartfelt faith and 73 percent mechanical; and the next day the percentages are inverted, who cares? (And who is able to accurately measure these things? Only God Himself!) The point is: Don't do it! If you do it, you will not inherit the kingdom of God! Thus, we can see that concerning the *real* commandments under the new covenant, as taught in this book, "legalism" is meaningless as a theological category.

All the confusion comes whenever (however well-meaning) Bible teachers either a) overstate the continuity between OT Law and NT practice; or b) as Stern and others, seek to maintain the functional validity, under the new covenant, of the *dogma*-Torah commandments—as holy commandments. This they may do from the worthy motivation of seeking to maintain (or re-establish) Jewish identity in Christ. Only for these commandments, can we even begin to imagine a logical application of this "mechanical versus heartfelt" duality, which doesn't seem to fit the moral ones. That is, it is possible to imagine the difference between a mindless, faithless, mechanical (read: legalistic) keeping of Sabbath or *kashrut*; versus a more heartfelt, passionate, "faith-full" keeping of the same.

But, immediately (at least for those outside the "ivory tower" of academia) the vexing question becomes: How is it possible to discern between the "mechanical following" of Shabbat, for example, with the "heartfelt trusting in God" observance of Shabbat? And who gets to say so? Is it ever 100% "heartfelt" and 0% "legalistic?" Or vice versa?

I think not. As anyone—pastor or Messianic rabbi (myself included)—who has ever tried to teach this systematic way of understanding Pauline doctrine, one ends up realizing that "legalism" just "doesn't preach." It is simply too subjective a category, and ends up directing our focus not to the content and object of our faith (Yeshua), but rather inward toward a focus on my own "attitude" of faith and the intricacies of my practice. It is a pastoral, teaching quagmire, and Paul knew that from his experience in Judaism.

3. *In the absence of a contemporary term for "legalism," the interpretive construct can only work if (at least) a group of people existed who taught and practiced this "heresy" of legalism.* In order to translate *nomos* as legalism in so many places, despite the "semantic silence," one must at least prove that such legalism existed in the world of the NT; one must prove that this is how Paul's first-century readers/hearers in Galatia, Rome, and elsewhere could have understood the letters, because it was something that was "current" as part of their world-view. This is basic to any biblical hermeneutic. Simply put, you can't preach "legalism" or "antilegalism" if a) there is no word or concept for it; and b) you can't at least point to a legalistic, biblical *someone* as an example. Therefore, Stern and others must posit a legalistic "counterpoint community" who would bring such a usage to life in the minds of Paul's audience. Who is this group? It is the Pharisees, the proto-rabbinic Jewish leaders, of whom Paul was once a "card-carrying" member. Stern writes: "The false doctrine of legalism which Sha'ul (Paul) is fighting is one which he himself once believed, and it must be presumed that he was not alone. While it is unfair, indeed anti-Semitic, to condemn all of first-century non-Messianic Judaism as legalistic, there can be no doubt that the legalistic heresy was a major way of relating to the Torah."[182]

The biggest problem with this line of thinking is the testimony of the apostle himself, especially in Philippians 3:6–9 and in Acts 22:3. In Philippians 3 the apostle sharply contrasts his life before Christ, characterized by a life of righteousness "derived from the Torah,"

---

[182] Ibid.

with his life after, characterized by a righteousness that is from "faith in Christ" (v. 9). Of this previous lifestyle based on a righteousness which is derived from the Torah, he describes himself as "a Hebrew of Hebrews; as to the [Torah], a Pharisee; as to zeal, a persecutor of the church; as to the righteousness which is in the law—found blameless" (vv. 5–6). In Acts 22:3, Paul adds to this self-description of his life before Christ: "educated under Gamaliel, strictly according to the law of our fathers, being zealous for God just as you all are today." Also in 1 Timothy 1:13: "I was formerly a blasphemer and a persecutor and a violent man. Yet I was shown mercy because I acted ignorantly in unbelief."

The point here should be clear: What is missing from all of Paul's pre-Christian self-description as a Pharisee is the struggle with a perverted, legalistic use of the Torah! Further, he describes himself as one who was thoroughly trained in Torah and "zealous for God." So, according to Stern's definitions, Paul's Pharisaic observance was anything but mechanical or legalistic—it was passionate, heartfelt, and zealous! In Philippians, he even says that he was "blameless" in regard to the righteousness which is possible through Torah observance without Messianic faith. But even such righteousness failed to truly satisfy God's righteous requirement (Rom. 8:1-4). Therefore, the apostle knows nothing of a Pharasaic, Sternian "heresy" called "legalism." What about Yeshua?

If one looks hard enough at the religious life of any group of people, one can always find a tendency toward dry, mechanical practice. But is this what the NT is concerned with? Is this, for example, something that Yeshua Himself finds in his critique and rebuke of the scribes and Pharisees? The answer is a resounding *no*! Rather, Yeshua rebukes the scribes and the Pharisees for either a) their wrong faith and/or practice, or b) the evil in their hearts. It is interesting that the Master Himself never comes up with this supposedly all-important word/concept/heresy of "legalism." Instead, ninety percent (I'm guessing) of Yeshua's rebuke of these religious leaders concerns what He calls their "hypocrisy." The problem was not whether their observance of commandments was "mechanical" or "heartfelt," but a more fundamental problem of the heart—one which was all too easy for the Lord to define and rebuke. Since the Lord points to this sin of hypocrisy so often, it is worth taking a closer look, and seeing how it differs from Sternian legalism.

A hypocrite (also from the original Greek meaning) is an actor, a kind of liar with the following characteristics, according to Yeshua: He/she wants praise from men, not from God (Matt. 6:1–6, 16–18; 23:5–7); thinks nothing of breaking God's law in order to observe his "traditions" (Mark 7:6–13); conceals his true motives under a cloak of flattery and pretense (Matt. 22:15-18); does not practice what he preaches (Matt. 23:3); "majors in minors" (Matt. 23:23); hides an evil heart behind a veil of righteousness (Matt. 23:28); persuades others to listen to him rather than God (Matt. 23:15); and is blinded to the truth (Luke 12:54–56). Do you see "legalism" here? Perhaps the closest place is Matthew 23:23—"majoring on the minors": "Woe to you, scribes and Pharisees, hypocrites! For you tithe mint and dill and cummin, and have neglected the weightier provisions of the law: justice and mercy and faithfulness; but these are the things you should have done without neglecting the others." But I hope you can see here that Yeshua is not rebuking them for a mechanical, "faithless" following of the minutiae of Torah and its associated traditions; rather, he is rebuking them for not properly "sifting" or "ordering" the commandments according to the priority of God's heart—as revealed by Moses and the Prophets of Israel. This is exactly what the NT gospel, especially under Paul's teaching, accomplishes very clearly and expertly for us. The heart content of their faith and practice, and their ability to discern God's heart, is all wrong.

What about Paul? What about his own understanding of the "problem of the Pharisees?" "For I testify about them that they have a zea for God, but not in accordance with knowledge. For not knowing about God's righteousness, and seeking to establish their own, they did not subject themselves to the righteousness of God. For Christ is the end of the law for righteousness to everyone who believes" (Rom. 10:2–4). Slightly different from Yeshua's rebuke, Paul chastises his Pharisaic brethren for *wrong* knowledge and thus wrong faith, i.e., not understanding the major change in the dispensation of God's salvation, grace, and Torah that has occurred under the new covenant. In short, they don't believe in Yeshua, who is the end (goal) of the Torah for righteousness for all who believe. Because of His death, resurrection, ascension, and the pouring out of the Holy Spirit, it is now impossible to seek righteousness (salvation, justification, sanctification) by Torah observance—as it may have been possible before. Now, apart from faith in Yeshua, the most "mechanical" or the most "heartfelt" expressions or practice of *dogma*-Torah commands cannot attain God's righteousness, and are viewed from heaven as a hopeless effort in "seeking to establish" one's own righteousness.

4. *Lastly, from what I know of both first-century Judaism and contemporary Judaism, most rabbis would agree with Stern that the primary motivation for obeying God's commandments should be faith and love of God, not mechanical adherence to a legal system.* This means that very few Pharisees, if any, were teaching this supposed "heresy" of legalism. And of Paul himself, Stern writes that he "once believed in this doctrine of legalism," but provides no proof of this from Paul's testimony or first-century Jewish texts. This is because you can't find any proof of belief in this nebulous, nonexistent "doctrine" in Paul's copious writings or in first-century Judaism! Instead, when Paul talks about his past as a member of the "strictest sect" of the Pharisees, he describes himself as being very "zealous" for God and thus Torah (Phil. 3:6; Acts 26:5). Isn't "zeal" *at least somewhat* synonymous with "heartfelt" observance? Before he met Yeshua, Paul's problem wasn't a mechanical attitude toward the performance of *mitzvoth!*

244   One New Man

In summary, it's very hard to imagine a prominent "heresy" for which we have no evidence (unlike gnosticism, for example) of anyone trying to teach it or live it.[183] All of this supports everything we have been saying up until now and explains why neither Yeshua, Paul or any other NT writer rebukes the Jewish leaders for their "legalism."

5. *If Paul, like Stern and others, was preaching nothing against Torah itself, but only against the wrong-headed, legalistic observance of it, why was he so persecuted by the Jewish community?* In reading the NT, both Paul's letters and the book of Acts, one cannot help but be struck by the awful tension that existed between Paul and the leadership of the traditional Jewish community. In almost every diaspora city where he preached, he was eventually "run out of town"—sometimes after suffering great abuse and punishment—by the local Jewish leadership, or by others who were incited by them. In Acts 21–28, we see that the man had become utterly loathsome to the Jews of Jerusalem, like a "public enemy #1." His presence caused riots and efforts to lynch him; even after being arrested and "deported" to Caesarea and eventually Rome, Jewish plots to kill him did not cease.

Why all the fuss? What was the apostle being accused of? "This is the man who preaches to all men everywhere against our people and the Law and this place [the Jerusalem Temple]" (Acts 21:28). Was it all just a big misunderstanding? No, there was something in Paul's preaching which was deeply offensive to the traditional Jewish populace, something deemed to be "against" them, their Torah, and the center of their religion and nation, the Jerusalem temple. Was the problem only the preaching/prophesying of the coming destruction of the temple, as with Yeshua? Was it that Paul, more than any other, was responsible for bringing the gospel to the despised Gentiles?

---

[183] One could argue that there is a stream of teaching in Judaism which says, "Just do it, be mechanical; the important thing is to do the mitzvah."

Yes, it was these things, but there is clearly more to the story, in that something in his message was deemed "anti-Torah", and even "anti-Israel."

As we have learned, Paul's "patriotism" and devotion to his people was greatly misunderstood, precisely because Paul's approach to the Torah established 100%, equal fellowship between Jews and Gentiles— thus posing a great threat to the Jewish authorities' capacity to rule over the nation.[184] Hopefully, you have been persuaded by what I have written in this book that the best way to understand all of this is to see the cutting edge of Paul's gospel as it "exposed" the *dogma*-Torah commandments for what they are, and the role of the *stoichea*, principalities and powers in manipulating these aspects of rabbinic, Pharisaic, "Torah Judaism" to their own wicked ends.

If, as Stern argues, Paul's gospel was in no way "anti-Torah" or "anti-Rabbinically-defined-Israel," but only "antilegalism," then why all the suffering for the apostle? He wrote: "If I still preach circumcision, why am I still persecuted? Then the stumbling block of the cross has been abolished" (Gal. 5:11). According to Stern's (and many others today) version of Paul, this verse might read: "If I still preach a kind of Pharisaic, legalistic, approach to circumcision and Torah observance, why am I still persecuted?"[185] But Paul wasn't preaching legalism or antilegalism, and neither were the Pharisees, as we just learned in point #3 above. If he was only preaching a *dogma*-Torah-positive gospel—one that supposedly empowers the believer (especially the Jewish believer) to keep these commands with greater "heartfelt" integrity (read:

---

[184] This has been repeated in modern times as the mostly secular, Zionist state of Israel came into being: many of the ultraorthodox reject, or are at least ambivalent, concerning fidelity to the national government which of course does not function according to their understanding of Torah. In some cases, there is much vitriol and hatred expressed toward these "Zionists."

[185] He actually translates it as, "If I am still preaching that circumcision is necessary, why am I still being persecuted?" Stern, *Jewish New Testament*.

non-legalistically)—believe me, the Jews of Jerusalem would not have been so upset, even if he was sharing this message with many Gentiles.[186]

The same is true today. I live in downtown Jerusalem among many Orthodox Jews. If my gospel preaching to them was, "Believe in Yeshua the Messiah so that you can have forgiveness of sins, eternal life and more faith, love, and power to keep all the mitzvoth with greater *kavanah* ('heartfelt intention,' a term popular in Hassidism), in a way more pleasing to God," I would regularly have a captive and friendly audience. (That said, the discussion would, most of the time, descend into the subjective realm of: "I have plenty of good *kavanah* without Yeshua, I get it from this or that rabbi's teaching . . . so why do I need Him? Because of the forgiveness of sins? And what about you Messianics? You don't really keep all the *mitzvoth* like you're supposed to. I've seen you driving on the Sabbath; I heard you once ate pork in China, etc.")

Clearly, there was something about how Paul preached the cross and its ramifications for Jew and Gentile which deeply troubled the Jewish community. It had everything to do with the message of the one new man and the abolition—on the cross, in the very flesh of the Son of God—of the *dogma*-Torah commandments that form the heart of rabbinic Jewish identity. Paul saw and preached that in the light and revelation of the new covenant, these commandments no longer have the force they once had to define and mediate the relationship between God and His people; that the Mosaic covenant that included them had become "obsolete and growing old" for this purpose (Heb. 8:13). This message, with its result that in Christ Jesus, there is neither Jew nor Gentile, pierced to the very core of Jewish identity, pride, and racism. This is the reason he became "public enemy #1" in Israel, *not* for preaching a super-heartfelt, Torah-friendly, antilegalism gospel.

---

[186] We can learn from Matthew 23:15 that there were enough scribes and Pharisees interested in preaching Torah to Gentiles—"travel[ing] around on sea and land to make one proselyte"—to earn a rebuke from Yeshua.

Conclusion

We must keep in mind that there is something right and commendable in Stern's (and many others') macro-agenda: to reestablish a firm, biblical foundation for continuing Jewish identity in the body of Christ. But sadly, like some other pioneering thinkers in the modern Messianic movement, Stern imagines that this can only be done by resurrecting a Messianic Jewish community that is "zealous for [Torah]" (Acts 21:20), and therefore "Torah" (as more or less taught in traditional Judaism—minus the legalism!) must still be 100% valid. Thus, a "way around" a more straightforward exegetical understanding of Paul's many disparaging verses concerning *dogma*-Torah commands must be found. In this appendix, we have demonstrated that this particular (and popular) "way around" the antinomian Paul (with all of its "hermeneutical gymnastics" and retranslations[187]) simply doesn't work; and when adapted, makes nonsense of much of the rest of the NT narrative and teaching. Many things seem to make sense in the privacy of one's "ivory tower," but according to the NT the teaching needs to be proved overtime in genuine NT community ("by their fruit you will know them"). My experience, in Messianic congregations in both the US and Israel who adopted Stern's hermeneutic, is that it is a recipe for exactly what Paul so sternly warned us about in places like 1 Timothy—arguments, debates, division—and a focus on the preservation of Jewish (or Torah-based for the Gentile) identity based on a foundation of commands that the NT teaches as having been abolished, cancelled, nailed to the cross, etc. We can only have one center, one source for establishing our most foundational identity as children of God, and it is the Lord Jesus Himself—His cross, resurrection, ascension, and return.

---

[187] This also points to the dangers of relying on Bible translations done by a single person instead of the major translations which are done by a committee of experts. Because of its inconsistencies and failure to prove adequate background for "legalism" Stern's translation probably would not have passed such a committee.

The NT, and especially Paul's teaching, is not so much interested in the "how" (mechanical or heartfelt) of Torah observance, but the "why." Trying to establish a consistent doctrine concerning the "how"—either the external mechanics or internal motivations—of *dogma*-Torah observance is a hopelessly subjective endeavor, that always leads to bondage to the "traditions of men." What's more, this construct, in my opinion, has loosed a wave of confusion on the body of Christ, having become a source of debate, division, and one of the foundations of the One Torah/Torah for Gentiles error. Messianic Jewish theologians who use this construct can argue 'til the cows come home that the continuing validity of *dogma*-Torah commandments, practiced in a nonlegalistic way (or whatever other way), is supposed to be for the Jew only; but as one continues to preach this at the mixed Jew-Gentile Messianic congregation, there will continue to be many Gentiles walking out the door thinking, "If Shabbat and *kashrut* and feasts are still in effect under the new covenant, and they are so wonderful, spiritual, and otherwise beneficial for the Jews, what about me? Hey, there is neither Jew nor Gentile in Messiah, so this glorious Torah and its practices should be for me too! One new man! One Torah for all!"

Even worse, it has opened a whole generation of Messianic and One Torah believers to the possibility of genuine rebuke by the Lord—not for their vaguely legalistic observance, but for the hypocrisy of re-raising and parading the Torah "flag" without the intention to really keep the whole thing—neither mechanically, nor in a heartfelt way. In other words, there are thousands of believers today, both Jew and Gentile, who have been instructed in Torah in such a way that they believe their practice to be more "holy" or "pure" or "biblical" than other nonpracticing Christians; yet their practice itself is inconsistent and hopelessly subjective, a result of having had the plain teaching of a book like Galatians circumvented by an interpretive construct like Sternian legalism.[14] The apostle wrote: "And I testify again to every man who receives circumcision, that he is under obligation to keep the whole Law" (Gal. 5:3). While the particular context of Galatians was speaking to Gentiles who had already been, or were ready, to be circumcised, we can under-stand from the rest of Paul's teaching that the message is: "If you allow yourself to come under the teaching that the *dogma*-Torah command-ments (any of them) are still valid for holiness, righteousness, sanctifica-tion, etc., then know that you are obligated to keep the entire thing as perfectly as you can. There is no 'middle ground' here."

Paul wrote of those who were preaching this message: "For those who are circumcised do not even keep the Law themselves, but they desire to have you circumcised, that they may boast in your flesh" (Gal. 6:13). Bad or "fuzzy" Torah teaching under the new covenant is bad, then and now, for Jew and Gentile. It is a dead-end trap that leads to "boasting in the flesh," a wicked kind of religious hypocrisy, and a judgmental attitude toward other Christians who don't know about, or practice, Torah or Jewish/Hebrew roots like they do—all of this in direct violation of both Yeshua's and Paul's teaching (Matt. 7:1-5; Rom. 14; Col. 2:16–17). May God help us all not to teach Torah in a way that we "not understand either what we are saying or the matters about which we make confident assertions" (1 Tim. 1:7).

I believe that what I present in the first part of the book accomplishes the biblical goal of establishing a place for continuing Jewish identity in Christ for Jewish believers, while at the same time taking very seriously that when Paul disparaged Torah, he meant it like he wrote it, and one doesn't need all the hermeneutical "gymnastics"—or a PhD—in order to make sense of the message. Yes, these *dogma* "commands" still function in defining the boundaries of Jewish identity, especially as the ethnic/national culture of our people as it is rooted in our covenantal identity in the nation of Israel; but because the new covenant has freed us from looking to these things as a source of personal sanctification or spirituality, we are permanently freed from any subjective concern about how heartfelt or mechanical our observance might be. We are seated with Him above these things, and so we preserve and enjoy the essential freedom for which He purchased us by His blood.

APPENDIX 3-2

Levels of Commandment and Instructions in NT Greek

"Are there 'commandments' in the NT? If so, how do they differ from those under the old covenant? Or under Judaism?"

As we have seen in this book, much of what the apostle Paul wrote concerning the one new man—in its context—hinged on the correct understanding of the Law (Torah) under the new covenant. What's more, we saw that what was at stake was nothing less than the identity of God Himself— if it comes out wrong, then God is forever "parochialized" as the God of the Jews and our Torah culture only (Rom. 3:27–31). Without the new covenant, mankind cannot sift between "culture and command," and we are forever destined to a kind of servitude to *stoichea*-based culture that blinds us to the one, universal God and our full brotherhood with those from other people groups, societies, and cultures.

In a way, what God did through *dogma*-Torah and Israel is to allow one people to take this principle to its logical end: By lending divine authority to the *dogma* commands of Moses, He allowed the sin of ethnic pride to bear its fullest fruit in our people (Gal. 3:21–4:11)—this is one of the "benefits" of being chosen!

But, as we discovered, it is not that the NT does away with all Torah, understood as the eternal, universal laws of God—what the apostle calls the Torah of the Messiah (Gal. 6:2). We also learned of the apostle's own continuing Jewish identity and practice, and that in 1 Corinthians 7 the apostle had some strong instructions for his congregations concerning the maintaining of Jewish—and non-Jewish—identity. But can we call these "instructions" commandments? Exactly what weight do they carry? These are the questions I will deal with in this appendix.

The first thing to note is that in the Torah there are several Hebrew words for the instructions of God: *mitzvoth* (commandments) is the most common and broad, followed by *huqim* (statutes), and *mishpatim* (judgments).[188] But, from the words and their usage themselves, it is no simple matter to make any systematic categories, or priorities—as in the classical Christian formulation of "moral, civil, and ceremonial." The words are often used interchangeably. Further, the lists of commands, with the exception of the Ten Commandments, don't easily lend themselves to any kind of neat sections or categories. Leviticus 19 is a perfect example: The second of the greatest commandments, according to Yeshua, is found in verse 18, "You shall love your neighbor as yourself" (Matt. 22:39). Before it, from verses 9–17 are many moral instructions of the highest order—how we treat the poor, the handicapped, and hired workers. But then in the following verses, until the end of the chapter, there are all kinds of commandments (statutes) that are mixed together: Verse 19 speaks of not sowing two kinds of seed in one field, and not wearing a garment that is made of mixed materials; verses 23–25 are agricultural laws related to the timing of planting and harvest; verse 26 contains both a prohibition against eating blood, as well as a warning against practicing divination and witchcraft; verse 27 commands against shaving the beard and the corners of our hair, as well as the prohibition against tattooing the body, etc. A simple reading of this chapter can help us to understand why in Judaism the 613 commandments of Torah are viewed as a whole, and why "picking and choosing" is forbidden.[189]

---

[188] They are listed together in several verses like Genesis 26:5; Leviticus 26:3, 18:4–5; Deuteronomy 4:40; Ezekiel 36:27, etc.

[189] This is also why Paul writes to the Galatians that if they allow themselves to become circumcised under the misguided Messianic Judaism of the Jerusalem teachers, then they must "follow the whole [Torah]" (Gal. 5:3).

When we come to the Greek NT we find a similar situation: there are many words which are translated: "command," "instruct," "precept," "order," "charge," "direct." Yet, if we look closely at the contexts we can easily discover the "weight" of each type of instruction. Actually, in one NT chapter which we have already studied, 1 Corinthians 7, we can discover almost all of the different words—as the apostle is very clear to distinguish between the different levels of authority and command. In general I find two categories—divine command and apostolic instruction—and several levels within each category.[190]

Category A: Universal, Divine Commandments

Level 1. "what matters is the keeping of the commandments of God" (1 Cor. 7:19).

The Greek word for "commandments" in the above verse is *entolay*. It is the same word used more than fifty times in the LXX for the Hebrew *mitzvoth*, and thus the closest equivalent to the use of the term in the OT and in Judaism. It is the same word used when Yeshua says, "If you love me, you will keep my commandments" (John 14:15); "A new commandment I give to you, that you love one another, even as I have loved you" (John 13:34); and of the saints in Revelation "who keep the commandments of God and hold to the testimony of Jesus" (Rev. 12:17; cf. 14:12); other key verses are Matthew 5:19, Ephesians 2:15, and Romans 7:8–13. In this last example, Romans 7, the apostle uses the word repeatedly as a synonym for all of Torah.

This is the first and highest level of "commandment" under the new covenant. These are the universal, moral commandments as taught by Yeshua and the Apostles—equally applicable to every

---

[190] One of my mentors, Asher Intrater, calls this a "ladder" of commandments with respect to the faith of Jewish believers. See Appendix 6 of his book, *Who Ate Lunch with Abraham?*

believer—everywhere, all the time. These are, according to the new covenant, the moral boundaries which define the holiness of the people of God—the moral dimension of what it means to be "in Christ." These are the commandments of which the apostle writes that those who willfully continue to disobey them will "not inherit the kingdom of God" (1 Cor. 6:9-11; Gal. 5:21; Eph. 5:5). The violation of these commands are the sins which "lead to death," the ones concerning which we must be quick to rebuke one another, and in the event of an unrepentant attitude can lead to "excommunication" from the people of God (Matt. 18:15–20; 1 Cor. 5; 1 John 5:16–17). Under the new covenant, these are the only commands on the level of the OT *mitzvoth*, the violation of which led to either capital punishment (stoning) or being "cut off from the people" (Gen. 17:14; Lev. 23:29, et al.).

Level 2. "But to the married I give instructions, not I, but the Lord, that the wife should not leave her husband" (1 Cor. 7:10).

The second Greek word for "command" or "instruct" in 1 Corinthians 7 is *paragellia*. This word was not used in the LXX, but was used in contemporary Greek for military or governmental orders, and ordering unclean spirits, etc. It is never used as a synonym for the totality of Torah, like *entolay*. In the present example, the apostle makes it clear that this is a divine decree, not just his personal opinion as an apostle—as in other places: It is God's will, even His command, that married Christian couples should not divorce; and if they do separate, they should not remarry. But the fact that he doesn't use the word *entolay* or its derivatives is instructive: The case of marriage and divorce involves a relationship, in which there is always the possibility of extenuating circumstances like abuse, adultery, etc., and is thus somewhat contingent on another person's behavior.[191] And so I believe this universal divine decree does not carry the same weight as the other moral

---

[191] Of course Yeshua allows divorce in the case of adultery.

commandments which every individual is responsible to keep. Thus, divorce is never found in the above lists of commands/sins for which the penalty is losing salvation (not inheriting the kingdom of God), or being cut off from the people of God.

Paragellia is also used by Luke in Acts 15:5 (emphasis added): "But some of the sect of the Pharisees who had believed stood up, saying, 'It is necessary to circumcise them and *to direct* them to observe the Law of Moses.'" Here too, it is doubtful that these Pharasaic, Messianic Jews believed that the Gentiles being circumcised and keeping all of the Torah was a prerequisite for personal salvation.

> *Level 3. "But this I say by way of concession, not of command . . ." (1 Cor. 7:6)*

The third Greek word used by the apostle in this chapter is *epitagay*. It is also used of divine command, but most often refers to something other than the moral commands of God for people. Instead it is often used for the "commanding" of God by sending the gospel, or sending out an apostle, or in the "command" to preach the gospel and to teach God's people (Rom. 16:26; 1 Cor. 7:25; 2 Cor. 8:8; 1 Tim. 1:1; Titus 1:3, 2:15).

Category B: Apostolic Instruction

When Paul's apostolic instructions do not have direct, divine authority, the apostle is very clear to make sure this is well-communicated. This distinction is essential to our faith, practice, and teaching—and one which is often violated in the discussions of Torah, identity, and the importance of ongoing Jewish covenant. There are, I believe, several levels.

> *Level 1. "Only, as the Lord has assigned to each one, as God has called each, in this manner let him walk. And thus I direct in all the churches." (1 Cor. 7:17)*

Of course, we have looked at these verses very closely in the main part of this book. The Greek word here for "direct" is *diatasso*. This word is used throughout the NT for all kinds of orders, even commands—but mostly of a one-time nature, not universally applicable (Matt. 11:1; Luke 8:55, 17:9–10; Acts 18:2, 23:31; "gave order," 1 Cor. 16:1, cf. Acts 24:23). If Paul had only said, "thus I direct (Greek *diatasso*) in all the churches—if you are circumcised, stay that way," etc., then I would not put this one at such a high level. But he introduces this by saying, "as the Lord has assigned to each one, as God has called each"—thus adding some divine "weight" to his instruction.

As we discovered in this book, the issues of identity, culture, and calling are very important ones—our divinely ordained "portion" in this life. But, it must be in this second category for the following reason, hinted at by the fact that Paul writes "as God has assigned to *each one.*" Not every single Jew will find and express his Jewish identity in the same exact way, and the same can be said of members of all national/ethnic groups. Yes, *dogma*-Torah commands like Sabbath and food laws can give a general framework, but within these there can be a great variety of interpretations, traditions and culture—all of which can change dramatically over time and place.[192] This is in keeping with the NT emphasis on personal freedom (Rom. 14, etc.). If this kind of "direction" or "instruction" were in the first category of "divine commands," as in non-Messianic Judaism, then it leads to the bondage of being "under the law" and lends tremendous authority to the traditions of men as they decree the rules for "correct" or "incorrect" observance of such commands.

Level 2. "But to the rest I say, not the Lord, that if any brother has a wife who is an unbeliever, and she consents to live with him, let him not send her away." (1 Cor. 7:12)

---

[192] In Judaism, there are all kinds of different traditions about how to observe certain aspects of the kosher laws, the holidays, etc.

This next example is not based on any Greek word, but simply by the Apostle's careful qualifying of this instruction to those Christians married to an unbelieving spouse who is still willing to live with the believer: "I say, not the Lord." This is biblical, apostolic wisdom justified by the reasons in the following verses. But the message to the believers is clear: "Take this as the trustworthy opinion of an apostle, your spiritual father. This is how I see it, but there's room for debate and different views. We will not judge one who disagrees . . . all things are lawful, but not necessarily helpful."

APPENDIX 3-3

Why We Don't Believe in a Pretribulation Rapture

> *For the Lord Himself will descend from heaven with a shout, with the voice of the archangel, and with the trumpet of God; and the dead in Christ shall rise first. Then we who are alive and remain shall be caught up together with them in the clouds to meet the Lord in the air, and thus we shall always be with the Lord.* (1 Thess. 4:16–17)

These verses from 1 Thessalonians have caused much controversy over the last 150 years—the same time period that we have been studying. Many Bible-believing, Bible-loving Christians with a premillennial view of the restoration of the kingdom of God on Earth—with its capital in Jerusalem—have also been taught that there is another great Pauline mystery being taught here concerning the so-called "rapture of the church." Namely, that the true believers will not go through the final period of God's judgments (wrath) on the earth called "the great tribulation," but will instead be "raptured" to heaven until the ultimate, physical return of Jesus to the earth. Most who subscribe to this view believe, based on prophecies in the books of Daniel and Revelation, that this will happen three-and-a-half years, or seven years, before Jesus returns. This teaching has become a major pillar in the dispensational worldview, as discussed in the last few chapters of this book—and a big part of popular Christian culture in the USA from books/movies like *Left Behind.*

As one can hopefully infer from reading this book, our perspective is quite different. We see the prophetic dynamics of the one new man (Ephesians) and the fullness formula (Rom. 9–11) leading right up to the second coming. This means that the church—understood as Jew and Gentile, Israel, and the nations together in Messiah—will have a great role to play during the last days on the earth. We believe that we will be here in the midst of the great tribulation, but that Yeshua has promised to equip and strengthen us, seeing us through to our ultimate victory together with Him at His return. What's more, it will also be a time of incredible harvest. This harvest will not happen just supernaturally; it will be the same dynamic as always—God working through His people to preach the "gospel of the kingdom" to every nation (Matt. 24:14).

Below are four major reasons why we strongly believe that the "pretrib rapture" theory/doctrine is "dead" wrong, and why it has a dangerous influence on its adherents—one which fails to prepare them for the reality of what will actually take place during the end times.

1. Pretrib Rapture: A New Doctrine Not Seen in Church History before Modern Times

The idea that the believing church will be raptured to heaven in a secret, "pre-second coming," before the actual second coming, is a very serious doctrine with very serious consequences. Both Jesus and the Apostles taught many things about the end of days, the days before His return and the establishing of His kingdom on Earth. If part of His plan were that at the start of, or in the middle of, the great tribulation at the end of the age, the believers would be caught up to heaven while end-times events continue to unfold down here on Earth, we would expect to see this taught clearly in the Scriptures; and we would expect it to have become a major pillar of the doctrine of the earliest church. Instead, we see the opposite: It is not taught by Jesus or the Apostles, and it is

impossible to h.
centuries following.
Rather, the overw?. of the teaching in the apostolic age or in the
literature of the church fau. stimony of both Scripture and the
tolic eschatology a) was clearly e first two centuries is that apos-
a literal second coming and literal Mennial; b) clearly believed in
believed that the church would be hem on Earth; and c) clearly
coming. Earth until the second

2. The Eternal Separation of Israel and the Church:

The doctrine of this mysterious "pretrib rapture" first came n the scene
only about 150 years ago with the advent of Dispensationasm. The
two great figures at the founding of this Dispensational "school" of
theology were C. I. Scofield and John Nelson Darby. As already noted
in Chapter 19, there is much that we can find in agreement and be
thankful for with respect to dispensationalism; however, its view of the
eschatological (and eternal!) destinies of Israel and the church is not
one of them. For both Darby and Scofield, an eternal distinction exists
between two groups of God's people: the heavenly body of Christ—the
church; and the earthly Israel—the Jewish people. As a result, classic
dispensationalism came up with a clearly delineated, dualistic view of
prophetic Scripture: Some prophecies apply to Israel and others apply
to the so-called "church"; God's plan for Israel is earthly, and His plan
for the church is heavenly and spiritual. In extreme cases, this dualism
goes so far as to posit that the church is the bride of Christ, while Israel
is the bride of Jehovah-Father God.

---

[193] The two possible references in early church literature are from the Shepherd of Hermes and
Victorinus. But even hard-line dispensationalists admit that the references therein to avoiding
wrath and persecution at the end of days are vague, and it is hard to establish a clear doctrinal
witness from them.

A quick read of this book should dis... ...ons of such a dualistic,
eternal separation between Israel an... ...h.[194] As we have seen, the
very mystery of the one new m... ...e fullness formula surrounds
how God is bringing Jew and ... together as one body in Messiah
in this age; or how the Ge... ...come part of the commonwealth of
Israel; or how the Genti... ...grafted into the essentially "Israeli" olive
tree; or how the Jews ... ...e saved, i.e., becoming part of the *ecclesia*,
or church.

And what ... ...ut the Jewish, first-century apostles? Were they part
of Plan A o... ...lan B—Israel or the church? What about the present day
Messianic ...wish remnant?[195] As we saw, God is not a God of Plan A and
Plan B; ... is not "schizophrenic" in relation to Jew and Gentile, or Israel
and th... church. He does not have two different peoples or two different
brides. In Christ, He has promised to bring all "things in heaven and
things on the earth" together under one head (Eph. 1:10). Therefore, we
must be careful of any of the theological conclusions that are based on this
classic dispensational foundation—such as the pretribulation rapture of
the church, leaving Israel (the Jewish people in the land) alone to endure
the greatest period of wrath/tribulation in the history of the world.[196]

3. Historical Background for the Rise of "We Are Not Destined for Wrath," Pretrib Rapture Doctrine

Much pretrib rapture doctrine focuses on the (wrong!) interpretation
of 1 Thessalonians 5:9: "For God has not destined us for wrath, but

---

[194] Not to mention that the strict use of the terminology "Israel and the church" is not exactly biblical. That is, they are not taught as dualistic opposites nor a complementary pair; rather, the overwhelming use in the OT is "Israel and the nations;" in the NT, "Jew and Gentile."

[195] When dispensationalists talk about "Israel," they almost always mean "unsaved Israel." For them, Israel's glory is always future; as such dispensational theology doesn't know what to do with the Messianic Jewish remnant, who are, in the most foundational way, both "Israel" and the "church."

[196] Not surprisingly, classic dispensationalism grew most at the end of the nineteenth and early twentieth centuries, a time when the church was very much on the defensive from modernism, science and moral relativism. The "pretrib rapture" theory seems to reflect this defensive, "bunker-mentality" spirit of many believers during this time.

for obtaining salvation through our Lord Jesus Christ." In fact, dispensational theology seems almost obsessed with the issue of believers not having to endure the terrible great tribulation of the last days, the likes of which Yeshua said "has not occurred since the beginning of the world until now, nor ever will" (Matt. 24:21).

Dispensationalism arose at a time when it seemed like a great shaking, even "falling away," was taking place in the church (2 Thess. 2:3). Modernism, liberalism, and the "social gospel" were overcoming many a church and denomination around the turn of the century (early 1900s), and it seemed like there was only a small remnant who still believed in the veracity of the Bible taken in a more or less literal way. This remnant felt more and more marginalized by mainstream denominations and by western society—whose morals and standards were changing very quickly.[197] Marginalized, yes; but persecuted, no.

Dispensational theology arose in nations (US and England primarily) where many Christians felt a deep sense of "light vs. dark" conflict with the wider culture, but they were not in fact actually persecuted in any serious way by their increasingly free, liberal societies. Finally, dispensationalism grew during a time of the incredible flourishing of knowledge, science, and technology—and this influenced how people interpreted the Bible. In particular, dispensationalists began to force many Scriptures—especially prophecy—into hyperrational categories of (supposedly) literal, systematic understanding. In short, the rationalistic, scientific spirit of the age dictated that biblical prophecy should fit together as its own kind of "science," whereby timelines and detailed charts could be made in order to determine the exact times and seasons of prophetic fulfillment.[198] So

---

[197] In many ways, the recent ruling by the US Supreme Court to legalized gay marriage is a final fruit in this long process of the "de-Christianizing" of Western, "post-Christian" society.

[198] This marked the beginning of the time of many false (obviously) calculations of the return of Christ; and gave birth to end-times cults like the Jehovah's Witnesses.

264 One New Man

these four things came together to produce this new doctrine of the pretrib rapture:

a. the lack of serious persecution of Christians in Europe and America—and so by experience the conclusion: "We, the faithful remnant, are not destined for tribulation and wrath, but salvation."[199]

b. the Israel (earthly Plan A) vs. church (heavenly Plan B) dualism: "We, the church, have a heavenly destiny different from earthly Israel, especially at the end of the age."

c. the increasing sense of "sons of light vs. sons of darkness" dualism: "We are so different, so separate from 'the world,' that it only makes sense that we have no share in its destiny of judgment and tribulation."

d. an overly rational, systematic understanding of prophecy premised on the Israel vs. church dualism: "Since the church is not destined for wrath but obtaining salvation, it must be that the focus of fulfillment of the worst end-times prophecies of judgment and cataclysms pertain to earthly Israel, not the church."

Then where is the church? A-ha and voila—behold, the doctrine of a secret coming of Christ to rapture His church before the great tribulation!

4. Biblical Evidence against the Pretrib Rapture Doctrine

The earliest church was premillennial; they believed in the imminent return of the Lord to rule and reign over the earth for one thousand years. There is much teaching in the NT about the Lord's second coming, but nowhere is it even hinted that there would be second *comings*,

---

[199] Twenty years ago, I remember the incredulous looks on the faces of house-church Chinese Christians when I told them about this pretrib rapture theory that had captured the imaginations of so many western Christians. Their reaction: "The believers don't go through persecution/tribulation? Then what have we been through the last twenty years!?"

as in the dispensational scheme—one a secret, heavenly coming to rapture the church to heaven; and then, after a significant amount of time, a final, full-blown return to the earth in glory. It is only when certain Scriptures are twisted out of context that one can begin to even imagine such a scheme.

A look at the most detailed verses teaching the rapture in the context of 1 Thessalonians makes it perfectly clear. From verse 13 of chapter 4, Paul turns to a teaching on the end times, the resurrection, and the second coming—with a focus on the very order of events, and a particular concern for those who have already died in Christ. He writes, "we who are alive, and remain until the coming of the Lord, will not precede those who have fallen asleep" (v. 15). Could it be any clearer? "We who are alive and *remain* until the coming of the Lord" is in contrast to those who have already "fallen asleep," i.e., died in Christ—*not* in contrast to those who have already been raptured!

Secondly, verses 15 and 16 teach that this rapture will *by no means precede* the resurrection of the dead in Christ. The resurrection of the dead will come first, and the resurrection takes place at the end, at His second coming, after the great tribulation. If the rapture "by no means precedes" the resurrection, then it must be after the tribulation as well. Only *then* will we be caught up in the air to meet the Lord (v. 17). In summary, Paul is clearly teaching the believers in Thessalonica that in the last generation before Jesus' coming, there will be a church—made up of Jew and Gentile alike—who will be alive, i.e., here on Earth, when He comes! And the fact that he writes "*we* who are alive" means he includes himself in this End Times' church, and thus cannot be speaking about another group of people that will come to faith only during the last days of the great tribulation while Paul and the rest of the "saints" of his day have been raptured to heaven.

There are six more NT passages that speak clearly about the timing of the second coming, the resurrection from the dead, and the rapture. Like 1 Thessalonians 4, they all teach of a rapture which occurs at the end of the Great Tribulation and that occurs more or less simultaneously with the second coming of Jesus in glory.[200]

1. Matthew 24:29–31: "But immediately after the tribulation of those days. . . ." In the Mount of Olives prophecy, Yeshua speaks clearly of His coming in glory, and of sending angels to gather His elect from the four winds—i.e., from the whole earth. This "ingathering" of His people is described as occurring after the tribulation. So whom is He gathering?[201]

2. Matthew 24:38: "until the day. . . ." Yeshua compares His coming to the flood of Noah. People were eating and drinking until the very day that Noah entered the ark and all was destroyed. There was no gap between the day of His coming and the destruction of all things by water. The world became increasingly wicked right up to the time of the flood—and Noah and his family were there until the very end. At Yeshua's coming, one in a field will be taken and another left; two women grinding, one taken and one left; the believers will be taken up to heaven to immediately receive our resurrection bodies.

3. Mark 13:24: "after that tribulation. . . ." Mark repeats the teaching on the Mount of Olives with all the details in Matthew describing the tribulation, the second coming, and the rapture. He also repeats that the rapture is "after" the tribulation.

4. Luke 17:27, 29: "until the day. . . on the day. . . ." Luke repeats Yeshua's teaching comparing His coming to Noah's flood, and

---

[200] Much of the following section is based on Asher Intrater, "Teaching: Rapture after Tribulation," Revive Israel Ministries, August 16, 2009, http://reviveisrael.org/archive/language/english/2009/08-16-rapture-after-tribulation.html.

[201] Once the dispensational view is embraced as "gospel" truth, then verses like this are interpreted to speak of a remnant which miraculously comes to faith during the tribulation, even though all the true Christians were raptured away and not there to preach or disciple! Further, in the parable of the wheat and tares, it is the tares who are first gathered for burning (judgment) at the great harvest of the Lord, and only then is the wheat gathered. So again, obviously, the wheat (the righteous, the saints, the church) is there until the very end (Matt. 13:24-30).

adds the comparison to the destruction of Sodom. As with Noah, so with Lot—total destruction came immediately. All people—both the "righteous" and "unrighteous"—were there until the end; there was no time gap. On the same day, at the same time that Lot and family were "raptured" away by the angels, the fiery judgment came upon Sodom and Gomorrah.

5. *1 Corinthians 15:52: "at the last trumpet [shofar]. . . ."* At the *last* trumpet, the dead will be raised and we will be changed. Revelation describes seven trumpets during the tribulation period. (The seven trumpets are connected with the feast of Trumpets [Lev. 23:24], the last trumpet with the Day of Atonement [Lev. 25:9].) The rapture occurs at the last trumpet, after the seven trumpets, after the tribulation, immediately after the resurrection of the dead.

Conclusion

"What's all this splitting of hairs concerning end-times prophecies?" some might protest. Or, "Let's not worry about these future things. . . . I'm a *pan-millenialist*—it will all *pan-out* in the end!"[202] Why is it all so important?

Think of it this way: What if you were training an army, which by its very definition is preparing for the eventuality of war, and in the middle of the training period you took the soldiers aside and said the following: "I have just heard from our commander in chief, and he has promised that when the worst of the actual battles come, he's given our battalion special favor: We will dial a secret code, and super-secret-stealth helicopters will come and take us all up and out of harm's way. He will send another army to do the fighting—we won't be on the battleground during the worst of the war!" How do you think this would affect the spirit of the training from the following day forward? Would the men

---

[202] I think I first heard this from Cindy Jacobs, or Peter Wagner, quoting Cindy's father.

drill with the same focus and motivation? Would they be alert, looking to keenly obey every order of their superiors? Obviously not.

Or, what if you were training a sports team for the playoffs, and you similarly told them: "When we get into the final rounds of play, someone else will take your place on the court; you won't have to play." Talk about a "spirit-breaker"!

This is the problem with the doctrine of the pretribulation rapture: It makes for a church with a "bunker" mentality—a church that will bury its head in the sand (or the clouds?) as we get further into the end-times events, wondering if the present tribulation is truly the last one, and looking for God to "beam them up" and out of the tribulations. It leaves the church with entirely the wrong "spirit" concerning the end times, and totally unprepared for its actual role to stand with Israel— the central, earthly focus of the Antichrist's vitriol—and not abandon her! Paul also taught that a great "apostasy" or "falling away" from the church would happen during these very last days before His coming. (2 Thess. 2:1-3) One wonders: could it be that a large number of these "apostasizing" believers will be those who were taught that they would be raptured away when times of tribulation come? Imagine such a person's sense of confusion and disappointment with God and church when they find themselves totally unprepared to go through this most difficult time in human history!!

When Yeshua speaks of these events, it is of a different spirit entirely: "But keep on the alert at all times, praying that you may have strength to escape all these things that are about to take place, and to stand before the Son of Man" (Luke 21:36). Or, "pray that your flight will not take place in winter, or on a Sabbath. For then there will be a great tribulation, such as has not occurred since the beginning of the world until now, nor ever will. Unless those days had been cut short, no life would have been saved; but for the sake of the elect those days will be cut short" (Matt. 24:20–22).

First, Yeshua is clearly speaking to His disciples that they will be here on this earth, especially in Israel/Jerusalem during the tribulation.

Second, at least for the saints in the Jerusalem area at His return, there *is* a flight to avoid the worst of the tribulation, but there is no suggestion that this is a secret rapture into the heavens. Thirdly, He wants us to be prayerful, awake, and alert; His promise is to *deliver us from out of the tribulation*, just as He has delivered His people throughout history, by means of the miraculous intervention of God in the midst of our earthly circumstances! Of course, at the end of the great tribulation, this will be accomplished by nothing less than the second coming of Jesus in glory, along with a multitude of angels and resurrected saints in order to fight against the Antichrist and his armies. The last, great cry/prayer of God's people (the spirit and the bride) on Earth before His return is, "Come Lord Jesus. . . . *Maranatha* . . . Blessed is He who comes in the name of the Lord!" (Rev. 22:17-20; 1 Cor. 16:22; Matt. 23:39), not, "Lord, rapture us up to heaven and out of this world so that we can avoid your wrath and the suffering that will come upon the earth!" It is "Lord, come!" *not* "Lord, take us out of here!"

How does this all connect to the one new man? Yeshua's prophecy in Matthew 24:22 is tantalizing in this respect: He says that the days of this great tribulation will be cut short, for the "sake of the elect." How short? He doesn't say! I believe this points to two fundamental truths about the nature of God and biblical prophecy (especially apocalyptic/end-times prophecy) that we have studied in this book.

First, God takes no pleasure in judgment; His will is for "all men to be saved and to come to the knowledge of the truth" (1 Tim. 2:4). The God of the Bible is not a sadist! While the obvious purpose of God's wrath and judgment is to punish sin, it is always His deepest desire that men would repent and turn to Him as a result. As we can learn from the book of Jonah, this is *the primary* reason that God issues specific prophecies of judgment—to warn sinners to turn from their ways. If there is sincere repentance, as there was in Nineveh, God is happy to "change His mind" and show mercy, even on those "dirty," Gentile, pagan sinners (Jonah's perspective). Yes, in the end of days, there will be great tribulation, but Yeshua instructs us that God longs to cut short the days of the great tribulation on behalf of His beloved ones, His elect. But Yeshua didn't tell us how short, or why God might cut those days short.

Could it be that much of the answer to this mystery depends on us? On how unified and reconciled is the body of Christ? How "spotless" will His bride be? In the body, will there be unity between Jew and Gentile, Japanese and Chinese—loving, serving, and interceding for one another? Will we be standing in faith, interceding, crying out for the salvation of the world and the return of the Lord?[203] Or, will we be like Jonah, with a "God, you take care of it yourself; don't involve me, I'm getting out of here" attitude? Will we be hiding in a theological bunker (or whale's belly!) expecting God to take us out of the world while the Jews in Israel suffer? In short, could it be that it depends on how much genuine, overcoming faith Jesus will find among us on the earth when he returns (Luke 18:8; James 1:12; Rev. 2:17, 26; 3:21)?

I believe so! God is not a sadist, and we are not masochists. Nonetheless, we are willing to endure whatever suffering, even martyrdom, that will come our way because of His name, so we are not perversely looking forward to the great tribulation. He taught us to pray that it be cut short, that our escape from Jerusalem might not fall on the Sabbath, etc. How effective will those prayers be? That depends on us!

---

[203] I believe that God will pour specific end-times revelation and instruction only insofar as the body is reconciled and unified and in proper alignment with Him and with one another.

BIBLIOGRAPHY

Dawn, Marva J. *Powers, Weakness, and the Tabernacling of God.* Grand Rapids: Eerdmans, 2001.

Intrater, Asher. *Who Ate Lunch with Abraham?* Frederick, MD: Intermedia Publishing Group, 2011.

Juster, Dan. *Jewish Roots,* 2nd Edition. Shippensburg, PA: Destiny Image Publishers, 2013.

Juster, Dan and Intrater, Keith. *Israel the Church and the Last Days.* Shippensburg, PA: Destiny Image Publishers, 2005.

Martyn, J. Louis, *Galatians: A New Translation with Introduction and Commentary.* The Anchor Yale Bible. New Haven, CT and London: Yale University Press, 1997.

Soulen, R. Kendall. *The God of Israel and Christian Theology.* Minneapolis: Fortress Press, 1996.

Williams, Jarvis. *One New Man: The Cross and Racial Reconciliation in Pauline Theology.* Nashville: B&H Academic, 2010.